FEW CANADIANS HAVE EVER HEARD OF KANANASKIS,
but it has a primary place in any honest history of this country. It was
there in 1940, in a camp designed for prisoners-of-war, that left-wing
Canadians were interned without trial for two years. One of them was
the late writer William Repka. His wife, Kay Repka, has finished the
book he cared most about—the story of sixteen of those internees,
three of their gallant wives, and of the infamy which results when a
country suspends justice in the name of "prevention."

An interesting sidelight: the present Attorney-General of Manitoba,
Roland Penner, is a son of one of the internees. When the father was
released, Winnipeg promptly elected him to city council at the head of
the polls.

—*June Callwood*

Dangerous Patriots

DANGEROUS PATRIOTS

CANADA'S◆UNKNOWN◆PRISONERS◆OF◆WAR

WILLIAM REPKA
AND
KATHLEEN M. REPKA

New Star Books • Vancouver

First printing November 1982
5 4 3 2 1

Canadian Cataloguing in Publication Data

Repka, William.
  Dangerous patriots

  ISBN 0-919573-06-1 (bound).—ISBN
0-919573-07-X (pbk.)

  1. World War, 1939-1945 - Prisoners and
prisons, Canadian. 2. Political prisoners -
Canada. 3. Concentration camps - Canada.
I. Repka, Kathleen M. (Kathleen Mary), 1918-
II. Title.
D805.C2R46   940.54'72'71   C82-091325-1

The publisher is grateful for assistance
provided by the Canada Council.
Printed and bound in Canada.

New Star Books Ltd.
2504 York Avenue
Vancouver, B.C.
Canada V6K 1E3

To Joe and Debbie
Paul and Carol
Joanna and David

In memory of William Repka

CANADA

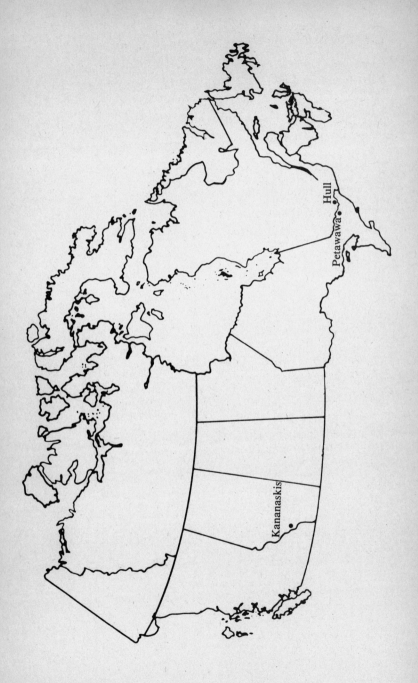

Hull

Petawawa

Kananaskis

Contents

Foreword

1982 marks the fortieth anniversary of an injustice that violated the spirit of Canadian democracy during its war against fascism. For most Canadians, the mention of wartime internment brings to mind the removal from the west coast and the internment in the interior of Canadians of Japanese origin, and perhaps the internment of some fascist-inclined German Canadians. However, in the earlier part of the war, before Japan's entry made the Japanese Canadians an object of suspicion and attack, some hundred others, most of them Canadian citizens, were interned for up to two years in camps at Kananaskis, Alberta, Petawawa, Ontario, and Hull, Quebec. Many others, who were arrested and held for internment, had their cases dismissed or received suspended sentences. Still others received and served jail sentences for up to two years. Some of them, upon release from jail, were immediately rearrested and interned. Some were charged with such things as distributing leaflets, but in the case of those interned, no charges were laid. Exact numbers are hard to obtain, but in all, some 250 people were involved, including a number of women who were imprisoned, though not in the camps. Of those actually in internment camps, over a third were of Ukrainian or other Slavic origin, while another large number were Jewish.

In the fall of 1942, now forty years ago, the last of those who were interned in wartime concentration camps in Canada were released. William Repka was one of them. He always intended to write the story of their internment, which the authorities kept as secret as possible. He started to collect the reminiscences of some of the men who were interned. At the same time he endeavored to find official information to provide a framework of fact for the personal accounts, but at that time all information relating to this episode was

9

classified and inaccessible to the public. Sharing as I do his conviction that this story should be made known to all Canadians, I have undertaken to complete the work, which was interrupted by his final illness.

The book contains accounts by sixteen of the men who were interned and three wives. Each shares his or her own experiences of the events surrounding arrest and internment, and the campaign for their release. Most of the material was in the form of taped interviews; a few accounts were written and mailed in from distant parts of the country. All were based on memory, with some checking of letters and other documents for dates when this was possible. As these events took place over forty years ago, there are instances where different people have given differing accounts of the same incident. As the people are scattered across the country from Vancouver to New Brunswick, and as some are no longer living, it has not been possible to reconcile all such discrepancies. In any case, perhaps there is value in having different perceptions of the same event.

Joe Wallace is mentioned in a number of the recollections and all pay tribute to him and his poems, which brought comfort and support to the men in their ordeal. He is represented in this book by a number of his poems, written while interned.

Unfortunately no photographs of the camps were taken at the time of the internments. So far as can be discovered, none were allowed. Photographs of the internees are included in the book above captions indicating the place of arrest and the dates when their internment began and ended.

I share the hope that motivated Bill Repka to undertake this book, that it may bring to a large section of the people of Canada knowledge of an event in their history which received no press coverage at the time it happened and which has been officially kept secret for four decades. The victims were never publicly, officially vindicated or in any way compensated for the loss of two years of their lives. Their internment was a denial of the civil liberties which we in Canada take for granted. It is still relevant to all of us today as long as governments remain free to assume blanket powers to by-pass or override the regular course of justice in the administration of the law. As long as the emergency powers of the government and the extra-legal powers of the RCMP are not clearly defined, our civil liberties are also in doubt. I hope this book may play a part in making people aware of these dangers and of the ongoing need to defend the democratic rights we value in this country.

To all those who contributed to the book I express my deepest gratitude. (There were some who found they were unable to contribute because it was too painful to recall that period of their lives.) Special thanks to Mitch Sago and Ben Swankey, who have been consistently helpful and supportive of my work. I hope that they and all the other internees will be satisfied with the result, and that their children and grandchildren may understand them better as a result of this work. Thanks also to Joseph Zuken for his introduction and the legal and historical background it contains. His contribution is of special interest because it was he who acted as legal counsel for some of those interned and who fought to have confiscated property returned to the internees.

Thanks also to the staff of New Star Books: to Lanny Beckman for his encouragement and suggestions, and to Lynda Yanz and David Kidd for very thorough and competent editorial work. Their understanding of and sensitivity to the nature of this book and its contributors have made working with them a pleasure. Grateful acknowledgement is made to Progress Books, Toronto, for permission to reprint the poems of Joe Wallace, from *Joe Wallace Poems*, which first appeared in *Night Is Ended*, Contemporary Publishers, Winnipeg, 1942.

Kathleen M. Repka
September 1982

Introduction

We are not enemy aliens. We're Canadian anti-fascists.
—Joe Wallace, poet,
Communist, internee

This book is unique and shocking: unique because for the first time it tells the personal history of a disparate group of Canadian radicals and trade union leaders who were interned in Canada during the first two years of World War II; shocking because, under the enormous powers of the Defence of Canada Regulations passed by an Order in Council under the War Measures Act, confirmed anti-fascists were labelled "enemy aliens" and "enemies of the State," interned without trial and deprived of basic human rights which were available even in wartime to persons charged with crimes of rape or murder.

Let us put these startling events in the context of the times. Before the war began, the Soviet Union campaigned in the League of Nations for a collective security pact to halt Nazi aggression. Britain, France and other members of the League refused. Their policy of appeasement gave one concession after another to Hitler, hoping that he would turn his military machine against the Soviet Union. In 1936, when Franco launched his attack on the Spanish republic, supported by military aid from both Italy and Germany, the western democracies declared a policy of non-intervention. Only Mexico and the Soviet Union broke through the blockade to send aid to the republic. In 1938, British Prime Minister Chamberlain supposedly brought "peace in our time" with the signing of the Munich Pact. This allowed Hitler to take over Czechoslovakia unopposed. Mackenzie

12

King, among others, congratulated Chamberlain on his statesmanship.

As hopes of collective security to stop Hitler faded, the Soviet Union, in August 1939, chose to sign a non-aggression pact with Germany, an act of desperation to gain time to build up its own military strength for the expected Nazi invasion.

On September 1, 1939, Hitler invaded Poland and two days later the British government declared war. Canada followed on September 10. In the expectation that the British and Canadian governments would now fight Nazi Germany in earnest, the Communist Party of Canada called for support of the war effort. The period that followed became known as the "phony war," for the western powers sat back and made no attempt to fight. It seemed that their basic policy had not changed even with the declaration of war. In response the Communist Party put forward a policy of "Keep Canada out of the War."

On January 11, 1940, the federal government amended the Defence of Canada Regulations to give itself the power to arrest and detain people without having to lay charges or hold trials. In June, an Order in Council was passed declaring the Communist Party and a number of other organizations illegal, and banning the publication of their newspapers.

I am convinced that the Canadian government would have taken its arbitrary action against the Communists and other radicals even if the Communist Party had not opposed the war in its initial stages. The government felt it had a score to settle with Canada's radicals and militant labor leaders for their effective work in the turbulent days of the Great Depression. In those days when thousands of people were caught up in the struggle for jobs, a living wage and a place to live, many came to believe that a socialist or communist system would be better than the capitalist system which seemed to have broken down. They admired the Soviet experiment and many joined the Communist Party of Canada, especially people of Russian or Ukrainian origin. The war provided the opportunity and the Defence of Canada Regulations the weapon for the government to deal a blow to these activists.

However, this book is being published not to recall the history of the war and the policies of the various governments and political parties, but rather to emphasize the broader issues involved. This was stated well by the wives of the internees in their pamphlet, "They Fought for Labor—Now Interned" (March 1941):

> They (the authorities) begin by attacking the "left." But once fundamental civil rights are destroyed, no section of the population is safe from these attacks...
> Democracy cannot be revoked or invoked at will, extended to some and denied to others. Democracy belongs to the people who won the right to it by struggle.

The RCMP functioned as the political police and provided the minister of justice with a list of organizations and newspapers. Included in the list was the Canadian Labor Defence League, the defence arm of the left-wing labor movement. As a recent law graduate, I had the opportunity to be defence counsel for a number of people charged in Winnipeg under the Defence of Canada Regulations and for some of the internees. What I learned from that experience was certainly not taught in law school.

Section 21 of the Regulations stated:

> The Minister of Justice, if satisfied that, with a view to preventing any particular person from acting in any manner prejudicial to the public safety or the safety of the State, it is necessary so to do, may, notwithstanding anything in these regulations, make an order...directing that he be detained in such place, and under such conditions, as the Minister of Justice may from time to time determine; and any person shall while detained by virtue of an order made under this paragraph, be deemed to be in legal custody.

I was in the courthouse for Alderman Jake Penner's appeal against the order for his internment. The Court of Appeal dismissed the case because the minister of justice had made his decision on the advice of the RCMP that Ald. Penner had been arrested under the Defence of Canada Regulations and was "deemed to be in legal custody."

Jake Penner remained interned without any evidence produced against him. It was only after his release, many months later, that Jake Penner could test the court of public opinion when he was re-elected to City Council at the head of the polls and he went on to become the dean and the conscience of Winnipeg's City Council.

The same procedure of trial by file prevailed in the cases of the other internees. The so-called appeal provisions to an Advisory Committee were a farcical travesty of justice. No witnesses were produced by the prosecution. The internee had to prove his innocence. Even if the Advisory Committee made a favorable recommendation, the minister of justice was not bound to accept the recommendation. We tested the procedures in a few cases before an Advisory Committee and had to denounce the proceedings as contrary to every concept of natural justice. It was only after the character of the war changed and public opinion was building for the release of the anti-fascist internees that other Advisory Committees were established to free them.

On the other hand, those charged with specific offences under the Regulations had their day in court. The evidence against them was slight but the times were against them. No jury trial was permitted. Some were freed by an appeal court or had their sentence suspended, but they were immediately arrested again in the courthouse by the RCMP for internment. In other cases the magistrate was so zealous to convict that he imposed "hard labor" with a jail sentence. When one of the prisoners was brought into court under a writ of *habeas corpus*, he was ordered released because the Regulations did not permit the imposition of "hard labor." Incidentally, the order of release never took effect; the man was rearrested and interned.

In addition to the deprivation of basic rights, Ukrainian working-class halls were confiscated by the Custodian of Enemy Property. Those in Winnipeg were disposed of to organizations which had expressed strong fascist sympathies.

Upon their release, after two years of confinement as enemies of Canada, the internees became involved in the war effort. Many enlisted in the Canadian armed services. As a final irony, some lost their lives in the war.

It can and did happen here. Under the most questionable circumstances, the War Measures Act was again invoked during the so-called October Crisis of 1970. And only a few short months ago the federal Liberal cabinet passed an Order in Council known as the Emergency Planning Order. In the event of war, it directs the solicitor general to once again establish "civilian internment camps." The scope of this bill goes beyond even the War Measures Act, as it also directs the government to run the whole social and economic structure of the nation. Nor is the new Constitution with its Charter of Rights a guarantee of rights and liberties. The War Measures Act and this new order override it. The only real guarantee rests with the people.

In concluding, I should like to pay tribute to Bill Repka for his recognition that these events are a significant part of our history and for his work in having them recorded, and to Kathleen Repka for bringing the work to completion.

Joseph Zuken
August 1982

Preface

This is the story of a motley collection of men from all across Canada who were arrested and, without being allowed to see family, lawyers or friends, were whisked away to jail or prisoner of war camps in Kananaskis, Petawawa and later Hull. The men ranged in occupation from lumberjacks, farm hands, miners and factory workers, to university professors, a doctor and other professionals. They were taken from their beds, their homes, their places of work and off the street. Many were detained for over two years.

Many were strangers to one another but very quickly discovered that Canada's political police had indeed been selective. Almost all of them had one thing in common. Throughout their lives, from the youngest in their mid-twenties to those who had lived more than six decades, they had demonstrated their opposition to fascism and Naziism. They were well known as anti-fascists; many were Communists. Some had risked their lives to stop the advance of fascism in Spain. Many were involved in actual physical fights with the Brown Shirts, Hitler's supporters in Canada, who paraded and held rallies in places like Winnipeg's Market Square.

When we sing "we stand on guard" for our lovely land, we should also be aware that in the years 1940-42 a great injustice was perpetrated against many more than the hundred or so who were interned. The democratic rights of loyal anti-fascist Canadians were outrageously violated during the anti-fascist war. To date, these events have been a carefully preserved secret, and the overwhelming majority of Canadians are unaware of what happened. It is important that these stories be told. Freedom belongs to those who are prepared to fight for it. The struggle for it never ends. It must be constantly won again.

Although all have interesting stories to tell, a book this size can only begin to record their reminiscences. I hope that this collection will help to pave the way for other books, articles and documentaries which, together, will tell the whole story. Those who are still alive continue to be part of the struggle to make our country a better place to live in.

William Repka
July 1979

I
KANANASKIS

William Repka

Lethbridge, Alta.
September 1940 -
September 1942

It was harvest time in the Alberta sugar beet fields and every hour away from work, especially with the war on, meant less cash for the long winter ahead. But on September 8, 1940, the beet workers were not in the fields. They were waiting at the bus station. The men were in overalls or rough trousers, heavy field boots and sun-bleached shirts. The women came in their East European *frustkas*, faded shawls that covered their heads.

The group had come to see their union organizer, who had been arrested under Section 21 of the Defence of Canada Regulations, put on a bus to Calgary; from there he was to be taken to an internment camp at an undisclosed destination. Some came out of curiosity, but most came to express solidarity with a co-worker who had fought for the recognition of the Beet Workers Union of Canada in its struggle to improve the harsh life of Canadian farmworkers.

Handcuffed, I was paraded in front of this toil-worn group. In the very few seconds it took to walk from the police car to the bus, I could only catch glimpses of the clenched fists and tears of frustration. There was nothing they could do—the Hungarians, Slovaks, Czecho-Slovaks, Ukrainians so recently brought to Canada to work in the beet fields.

The gathering of beet workers at the Lethbridge bus depot was not just an expression of union solidarity. The RCMP could have prevented the gathering and spirited me away to the internment camp or some other stopover in a car, but that would have failed to accomplish the major purpose of the operation. We had just won a substantial wage increase for all the beet workers by threatening a strike. The authorities wanted to spread the word about what would happen to those who dared to struggle for better pay and working conditions on the southern Alberta beet fields and make clear that this kind of reckless activity couldn't go on. They wanted a dramatic illustration of the fact that under the Defence of Canada Regulations a "labor agitator" could be interned without trial or any other recourse to democratic rights.

The bus left as soon as the tall mountie and I were seated. As we pulled out I caught a painful last glimpse of my unhappy friends. There is an advantage to being handcuffed. I could wave with two hands, like a boxer, to the sombre crowd. As I slumped down in my seat I had bleak thoughts about my immediate future. What did the Canadian establishment have in store for me? I had read quite a bit about Hitler's fascist concentration camps and the fate that befell many of his anti-fascist victims, even before the mass extermination of the Jews. Many were tortured to wring out confessions about their friends and co-workers. Some were shot "attempting to escape." We were in Canada, but I could not even phone my family or a lawyer. Were we establishing a Canadian fascism to fight an anti-fascist war?

This had all started when I attended a conference of the League against War and Fascism in Edmonton in 1939. A delegation from the Lethbridge Beet Workers Union approached me. They told me that the beet workers in southern Alberta needed someone who could speak Ukrainian and some of the Slav languages. After some discussion with my family and friends, I agreed to go. I was soon elected union secretary and spokesperson.

As the union had no money, I hitch-hiked to Lethbridge from Edmonton. The sugar beet acreage at that time was spread out among several irrigated areas around Lethbridge, near Picture Butte, Taber and Magrath, and employed some 3,000 workers. Thinning, hoeing and then digging up, cutting off the tops and loading the full-grown beets is hard physical work. It was not uncommon for children to go out in the fields to help parents make their livelihood. The pay for the back-breaking work was low and often the housing and other conditions were abominable.

Most of the workers were from Eastern Europe. We were lucky to have John Beluch as president of the union; he spoke seven languages. Through his efforts and those of many workers scattered all over the area, we were able to hold a number of local conferences, and we made some spectacular organizational gains by the spring of 1940. An elected committee went to the Beet Growers Association with a series of demands for the coming season, including the demand for a substantial wage increase. In close touch with the sugar company, the farm owners replied that it was war time, and in that context the demands were unreasonable.

I sent letters to all the unions I could reach, outlining the conditions under which our members worked; I asked the unions to send resolutions of support for our demands to the Beet Growers Association and to the sugar company. We had a lot of support, but the opposition was always there. One day I was called into the Lethbridge police station and asked why I was stirring up all this trouble. I told them my job was to improve the lot of members of my union and that everybody knew they were underpaid and their cause was just. We finally did win a substantial wage increase which, it was rumored, would cost the industry a million dollars or more.

Very soon after, at a victory conference, I was elected delegate to the coming convention of the Canadian Congress of Labor (CCL) to be held in Ottawa in September of that year. I wasn't sure I could afford to go. Because of the scattered membership of my union and the difficulty of collecting dues at the height of the season, I was very short of money. Although I had the impressive title of executive secretary of the union, there had never been wages for the title or the work. I had barely enough for an attic room in a miner's home and a meal ticket in a local eatery. We were living on enthusiasm in those days. A trip to Ottawa as a delegate to the CCL convention, however, and staying at a hotel, was a different matter. As there was not much to do in the union office at this time of the year, I decided to go harvesting to raise some extra money. I didn't know that I'd never make it to the CCL convention and it wouldn't be lack of money that would keep me away.

A farmer near Milk River asked if I could run a combine. Bill Humeniuk and his wife were childless, but they had a little dog—a bright, lively, friendly little terrier. On the morning of September 7, just before we were to start combining, I was playing with the little dog and his tooth caught on my trouser and tore it the full length of my leg. Bill offered to take me into town and buy me a new pair of pants. When we arrived in Milk River, Bill dropped into his bank. While I was waiting in the cab of his half-ton truck, an RCMP officer came over and asked if I was Bill Repka. When I told him yes he said I was to come with him. I asked why and he quite matter-of-factly said I was going to be interned. He was polite but very firm. I think his name was Carter.

At this point Bill returned. Flabbergasted, he began to protest, but the officer wouldn't argue. He simply told Bill that I was to be interned. That was that. At that moment a farmer stopped to talk to the policeman and gave me an opportunity to tell Bill to rush home, go through my things, and take out any addresses or letters which might implicate others. I told Bill there was nothing he could do under the circumstances and that arguing was quite useless. When we left for the police car, Bill took off.

So there I sat in the RCMP car—torn pants and all—and in some shock, I must say. We drove to Bill's place to pick up my bag and then set out for Coutts, right on the border between Alberta and Montana. I was kept in the Coutts jail until the afternoon, when the officer drove me to Lethbridge. It is a frightful feeling to be shown a prison cell, to be pushed in and then to hear the steel door close and the key turned. I was being told that I was a menace to society—that at 25 years of age I was not safe to have around.

On that trip to Lethbridge the officer kept telling me that there were all kinds of police work for a bright young man and that a person need not wear a uniform to be on the police force. Up to that point I had been preoccupied with thoughts about the implications of my arrest. But when I heard that, I felt acutely insulted; he was trying to recruit an informer! "Do I look like a stool pigeon to you?" I said in some heat. My anger and intense emotion put him on the defensive and he mumbled something about "just doing his job." After that there was not much conversation till we reached Lethbridge and he turned me over to the police there.

It happened that John Beluch, our union president, arrived at the police station just after I did. John was from Hungary and by this point in the war all "aliens" had to report regularly on their activities. When John walked in to report, he saw me behind bars. Wide-eyed, he looked around to see if anyone was watching, then quickly came over to the cell block. He was very shaken by my story and before anyone at the station noticed him he hurried out the front door. Years later he told me about organizing the group at the bus station and protesting to the authorities.

In the Lethbridge jail, two RCMP officers, pretending to be sharp investigators from Regina, tried to get information from me about people I knew, names, addresses. They were particularly interested in knowing who were the leaders of the union and which of them were Communists. I told them it was an insult to be asked such questions; I was associated with a large group of working people who earned their living in the most difficult way possible, and they wanted me to condemn them? Shame on them! The officers put on a great show of anger. They implied that terrible things would happen to me if I didn't talk. They were just like little boys playing cops and robbers. All the same, I did feel very vulnerable, one never knew what the RCMP would do.

By some odd quirk of the human mind, at this dangerous moment I remembered the story of the old Swiss watchmaker who built clocks that went "tick, tock, tick, tock." However, one clock he built would only go "tick, tick, tick, tick." This infuriated the craftsman and he said to the errant clock, "I'll make you 'tock.'" It's strange what you think of at times like that.

I think the police were surprised when they took me to my lodgings in Lethbridge to poke around for names of leaders and their activities. When one is caught up in the labor movement, with every moment taken up organizing, material things matter very little. I showed them up to my attic room, for which I was paying $5 a month. In it there was a stand with hangers for a few, very few, clothes. An orange crate was my "dresser." A small alarm clock, a round looking-glass, shaving equipment, and some pencils and papers completed my worldly goods. (Friends had kindly removed a whole library of labor and Marxist books.) When the police saw my place, I think some of their illusions about how labor leaders lived were shattered.

I was soon back behind bars again. In spite of my protests, 24 hours had gone by and I had had nothing to eat. "But Bill," one of them said, "you haven't given us anything!"

After finally getting fed, I lay down on the cot in the cell. The day had gone surprisingly quickly, but for the rest of the night I wasn't going to get much of a chance to think about what was happening to me. Two big policemen brought in a noisy Ukrainian who had been drinking. The man was enormous, 6 feet 3 inches, shoulders like a bull and massive hands. He came down the corridor, struggling and shouting. "Let me go, I haven't done anything."

The two hefty policemen unlocked the door of the cell and unceremoniously shoved him in. He continued to rattle the bars and scream. "You dirty bastards, you've locked up an innocent man." Then in one of his quiet moments he said to himself, "*Shlag be ich trafev*" (damn them). At that point I spoke to him in Ukrainian and said it wouldn't help to keep screaming. He was startled for a moment. Then he whispered, "*Sche troshke*," (just a little more) and proceeded to bellow at the top of his voice. When the beer wore off he quietened down and I was able to sleep. When he was released to go to work next morning, he was quite apologetic for disturbing my sleep.

About 9 a.m. my next cell mate arrived. His fists were clenched and his eyes were bright. He was a small, slight man, perhaps 50 years old. The police brought him into a cell and locked the door. The man sat down and said in a voice that combined tears and elation, "I got him, I finally got him." It was a while before he noticed that I was nearby in another cell. As soon as he saw me, he started to talk. He had to tell somebody the story.

"It was my foreman on the extra railway gang. He has been trying to get rid of me for months. He has a relative that he wants in my place but I have the seniority so he couldn't fire me. But he is a big man, and he kept chewing at me, telling me how useless I am and how terrible my work is. He used every chance to pick on me and make my life miserable.

"We have a big sledge hammer at work. He managed to break it and then told me to fix it. It was broken at the head so I fixed it with the old handle, which made it slightly shorter. He flew into a rage because I hadn't put on a new handle. When I told him there were no new handles around he screamed at me for not waiting for one.

"This kind of thing had been happening all along. If I did something, why did I do it? If I didn't do it, I was still wrong. But this time was the worst. He was going to talk to the manager about how useless I was and that I had no business on his gang. He poked his big finger into my chest and looking me straight in the eye said, 'This time I'm going to get you fired.'

"That's when something in me snapped. There was a can of gasoline on the workbench. I grabbed it and threw it over him, took out my cigarette lighter, and lit him. He burst into flames. He ran out of the shed screaming and rolled in the grass. I just stood there and watched. People came running and put the fire out with coats. The ambulance came and then the police. I told the police what I'd done."

He seemed relieved to have told me. I sat through it all in disbelief. I said I was sorry but he said, "Don't be sorry. He had it coming to him." Soon two policemen came and took him away, to a hospital I think. I never did hear how the case ended.

Next a woman was brought down the corridor by a policewoman and pushed into the general cage. She was a vivacious, blue-eyed blonde who was feeling sorry for herself but at the same time was quite self-righteous, and so wanted to tell me what had happened to her.

As a very young girl she had been urged by her parents to marry a much older farmer in Saskatchewan. He had a farm and money and needed a pretty wife. When things didn't work out she left him and the children, and ran away. She had little education and there was no work, so she began taking on men. She talked about being in business for herself in a very matter-of-fact way. She had come to Lethbridge, and because she was pretty and smart, she was soon doing very well, thank you. But she soon ran into the established prostitution industry in Lethbridge. After being given a few hints that she should get out of town, she was arrested. She expected to get six months in Fort Saskatchewan Jail.

"But now I am a criminal and will have a record." She was suddenly crying like a little girl, overwhelmed by her problems. "But how else can I live? I never learned to type or sew so I could earn a living. I would love to find some other work but there is nothing else I can do. I was very good for many men, made so many of them happy. And now I am a criminal!"

She sobbed for a while but soon she was her bright self again. There was no one about, so she said, "There won't be any men where I am going. And no women where you will be. We might as well have some fun." I hadn't expected that. And then there were all those bars.

"Never mind," she said cheerfully, "put your arms through the bars like this." She reached through aggressively and capably. I found all that tenderness through the jail bars most unsatisfactory, embarrassing in fact. "Never mind," she said. "This will make both of us feel better." There is something very powerful about any kind of affection under those circumstances, and I will always think kindly and gratefully of that young lady.

Later she reached into her purse and offered me some condoms, saying she wouldn't have any use for them for more than six months. I told her I wouldn't be needing them either, since I had no way of knowing if I would ever get out.

"My goodness," she said, "What are you in for? Murder?"

It was not easy to tell her about unions and the League against War and Fascism. I didn't go into much detail, but she understood enough to say that she was on the side of the unions too.

She took a long look at the condoms. "I hate to flush them down the toilet. Somebody might find a use for them. I'll put them in the water closet; if someone comes, tell them they are there."

Soon the matron came and took her away. As she was leaving she said, "You are a good friend, Bill."

The hardest feelings to deal with when you are alone and behind bars are loneliness and isolation. I had been happy working with very many people, speaking at meetings, eating in people's homes and surrounded by warmth and appreciation wherever I went. It is a marvelous feeling to be accepted and respected by a large group of people. To be suddenly cut off, with no access to family or friends, to find myself treated like a criminal, handcuffed and interrogated like some pariah, was very hard to take. Sometimes I was frightened, sometimes furious, and I felt quite helpless all the time.

Finally a tall beanpole of a mountie came to take me to Calgary. The conversation on the bus trip to Calgary was not unpleasant. The youthful policeman even took my handcuffs off while I went to the washroom. Here an amazing thing happened. A man came up to me and without saying a word, but with deep compassion in his eyes, passed me a large package of cigarettes. It was a nice gesture, perhaps from a person who knew how I felt. He was saying, "It's not the end of the world."

When we arrived, a police car took me to the central post office and I was taken a few floors up to the RCMP lock-up in the building. In the corridor was a desk for the guard. It was set up on a bit of a platform so he could see into the large room that was enclosed by iron bars. Inside the enclosure were a number of cells with bunks. I was booked in and led into the enclosure.

There were a lot of interesting people, including a man who told me he was caught stealing. He pointed out someone in for assault and battery. There were also some people from Winnipeg whom I recognized from pictures I had seen in labor and progressive papers. They were there for hearings that were being held in Calgary at that time. It was encouraging to find that I was not the only one being interned. I was immediately warned that there was a stoolie in our cage.

Before long a very pleasant older man with graying hair offered me a cigarette and asked, "What is a nice young man like you doing here?" He wanted to know where I was from and what I was in for. The man got very little from me except generalities. I told him he should be very careful because the jail was full of spies. When he left he looked at my cigarette stub as if it had been wasted.

Finally I got into my cell and onto the steel bed. I was

alone with my thoughts and my memories of stories of union leaders in Hitler's jails. As if to emphasize my helplessness, I could hear marching nearby, obviously a platoon of police. I couldn't hear the commands, but it sounded as if they were forward marching, and left turning, and right turning, and halting, in heavy unison. This not only made sleep impossible, but also disturbed my thoughts. I could almost see them goose-stepping around the drill hall.

Late in the night, when it seemed all the other prisoners were asleep, two policemen started a quiet but interesting conversation.

"This young union leader [I was sure he was referring to me] will not be allowed to see a lawyer or his friends. He is going to be interned. What kind of justice is that?" asked the younger policeman.

The old guard snorted, "Justice? You should know better than that. Let me tell you a story. My great uncle was a policeman in southern Alberta at the time the Lethbridge jail was being built. I still remember one of the stories he told. It was when there was still mostly ranch country around there, hundreds of square miles with no fences. There were lots of quarrels over who owned the new-born calves and foals not yet branded. The newspapers were full of stories of rustling, and threats of death to rustlers who were caught. However, the ranchers continued to lose livestock, and the newspapers and the law became a laughing stock.

"The pressure to find a culprit mounted. Finally a half-dozen Indians were arrested on the streets of Lethbridge and brought to the jail. One of the group, a young man from northeast of Edmonton, was charged with being the head of the gang of cattle rustlers. The young man protested that he had no horse, did not know where the ranches were, and so had no way of rustling cattle. The newspaper printed a large picture of him as a suspected cattle rustler. Ranchers came into the court, some of them drunk for the occasion, and of course they recognized the Indian at once as the cattle thief and leader of the gang.

"The judge, who was so drunk he had to be helped up to his bench, sentenced the man to be hanged. Indians and others who protested were accused of impeding justice and were intimidated with threats. One honest rancher pointed out that the young man could not possibly have been the rustler, but he was quickly shut up by the judge and the prosecuting attorney. The whole affair was played up for all the ranchers and citizens and all potential rustlers to show that rustlers could be hanged.

"As there was no gallows at the new Lethbridge jail, one had to be built in a hurry. The trap door, built in haste, didn't work. Rather than allowing the victim to fall free, it opened slowly and he slid down it. When the rope was cut, the prisoner was still alive. They finished him off with a claw bar. Afterwards, an announcement was made to the assembled cattlemen and curious citizens that the cattle thief was dead; justice had been done.

"So you see," said the older guard. "Justice? Fair play? That Indian was no more guilty of cattle rustling than I am, but the cattle ranchers needed a body, someone to be found guilty and hanged. Justice had nothing to do with it. The same goes for that poor young bugger in there you call a labor leader. He hasn't done anything that dozens of others aren't doing right now. But if your job depended on establishing a case against him, and the authorities demanded it, what would you do? The laws are framed to protect those who have property. As a young policeman you had better learn that lesson very well. Justice? Don't make me laugh."

The old guard's lesson came somewhat as a surprise. I had naively felt I was helping to make Canada a better place to live in by helping to bring up the wages and working conditions of the poorest section of the population. As a long-time anti-fascist, I couldn't understand why I was being treated as a criminal in my own country.

Next afternoon a group of us, accompanied by soldiers with rifles and bayonets, boarded a bus which took us to the train. We stopped at a railway station (I think it was Seebe) in the foothills of the Rockies. We were transferred to trucks and driven off into the countryside.

It was late evening when we arrived at the big outer gate of Kananaskis Internment Camp. My first glimpse of the camp was the glare of huge, high-powered lights all concentrated on us. The groups of men standing around with rifles were not reassuring. We could see the barbed wire fences around the place, at least twelve feet high. There was no doubt that it was a concentration camp. We were booked in and taken to the quartermaster's stores for camp clothing.

Next morning I was taken to the parade ground. The number of my little disc was 590, so I took my place between 591 and 589. I was very quickly part of the routine of the camp.

Pat Lenihan

Calgary, Alta.
June 1940 - September 1942

After the war was declared in 1939, the Canadian Labor Defence League (CLDL) called a meeting in the Labor Temple on a Sunday night to explain the fascist-type measures that were being adopted by the Canadian government. As alderman in Calgary, elected in 1938 for a two-year term, I was asked to speak at the meeting. There was an overflow crowd as usual. I denounced the war, saying it wasn't our war, it was an imperialist power struggle and we should have no part in it. I denounced the tactics of a government that would start arresting people because they expressed their opinions about the war.

In all my speeches since 1931 I had predicted an imperialist war and had opposed it. We Communists consistently fought the two main dangers facing the world, the rise of fascism and another world war. We figured that the object of that war would be to wipe out the Soviet Union. In fact, during the first part of the war, you couldn't really call it a war. The two sides never fired at each other. Some newspapers actually reported that the Germans and French were kicking footballs between the battle lines. Negotiations were still going on with

Germany in an effort to turn the war against the Soviet
Union. Wherever our speakers pointed out these things, they
were arrested and sent to jail.

Unfortunately there was a Calgary *Herald* reporter at the
CLDL meeting that Sunday night and he took notes of my
speech. Next day there was a report in the *Herald* that was a
muddle of everything I said. The account was slanted; I'm
sure it was deliberate.

A couple of days after the meeting two RCMP officers
came to my home and told me that I was under arrest. It was
close to Christmas 1939. Fred White, one of the labor
aldermen, provided my bail money of $5,000. I came up
before a magistrate on a charge of causing disaffection to His
Majesty's forces. The other charge was sedition.

The CLDL hired a lawyer, Barney Collison, who advised
me to ask for a jury trial. At the trial the reporter from the
Herald had to get on the witness stand. Barney Collison
really cornered him. Collison questioned him about how he'd
recorded my speech. I had spoken for an hour and a half and
Collison wanted to know if the reporter had used shorthand.
In fact, the reporter had only taken rough notes. Collison
was able to make a point of that in front of the jury.

The jury took about three hours to come back with a
verdict of "Not Guilty." Of course I was against the war, but
that was not the charge. They could not prove that I had
made statements that were seditious or caused disaffection to
His Majesty's troops. I was released and went back to my
activities. I kept attending City Council and doing all kinds
of organizing work.

The Communist Party had had legal status since the King
government repealed Section 98 of the Criminal Code in
1936. The Party held mass conventions every year in Toronto
and was openly active until the time the war broke out and
the War Measures Act was put into effect. At that point the
Party had to go underground. I didn't go underground
because I was a public figure and had to attend Council
meetings and function as a representative of the people.
Given the number of arrests that were taking place around
the country, I knew that it wouldn't be too long before I was
arrested. In fact, I was one of the first to be arrested in
Western Canada after the War Measures Act was declared.

I was arrested just before my daughter was born on June

21, 1940. It was a few days after the fall of Paris and after
Mussolini entered the war. They took me to the RCMP
barracks on top of the old Post Office. My wife Anne
insisted on seeing me. They refused to let her but she came
back a second time and said she was going to stay and have
her baby right there in the building if she wasn't allowed in.
They talked it over and permitted us a short visit, as they did
the next day. There was a screen between us so I couldn't kiss
her or touch her hand.

She had discovered that a friend of ours, Kovack, from
Edmonton was there as well. He was very prominent in the
Party in Edmonton. He recruited more members, sold more
papers and collected more money than anyone else. Every
time I was in Edmonton he was always at the bus station or at
the train to meet Anne and me and would invite us to stay the
night with him. He kept a little boarding house. He was a real
friend as far as we were concerned, but when Anne saw him
in the barracks he was in RCMP uniform.

When you are active in the working-class movement
you've got to be aware of these things. It's like the exposure
of RCMP activities today. I'm 75 years old now and it's no
news to me. This type of thing has been going on for a
hundred years and now it's on a greater scale than ever.

After my wife was taken to the hospital and gave birth to
our daughter June they let me out of the cell. They told me
that I would be able to see my wife and then I was to be
interned in Kananaskis. The military escort took me over to
the hospital and up to my wife's room. I was allowed about
fifteen minutes with Anne. I didn't tell her about
Kananaskis. I figured it might upset her. I told her that one
of these days I'd be out again. I said goodbye and the next
thing I knew I was wheeled up to Kananaskis and put into the
camp.

It was a civilian camp. They had another big camp for
German soldiers. There must have been 500 German fascists
and sympathizers who were picked up here in Canada, along
with a handful of Italians. The prisoners at the camp were
from all over the west. I was the only anti-fascist. You should
have seen the greeting I got when I arrived. I was known as
the Communist alderman from Calgary. They'd walk past
me and say "Communist scum." I was the most lonesome
man in the world. I didn't think I'd last 24 hours.

Still there were no charges against me. By this time I'd attended two kangaroo courts. There were three judges, but no lawyer. They wanted to know when and how I'd come to Canada. They told me that I was a Communist and that I was this and that. There was no place for a statement from me; the hearings were just occasions for answering questions. They had documents that related how I had said this in such a place and at such a time. It was ridiculous.

I spent about a year in Kananaskis. In that year about 50 or more anti-fascists were brought in from Winnipeg, Vancouver and Alberta. Right from the start, as soon as we had a group of twenty, we demanded the right to have our own spokesman. We wanted nothing to do with the Nazis. I was our first spokesman. One of our main demands was that we wanted a camp of our own where we had no association with the Nazis. The only thing we had in our hearts for them was hatred.

The Nazis were totally convinced about fascism. Whenever they felt like discussing things with us we'd tie them up in knots completely. They were blinded by their beliefs. They'd say, "Roosevelt! Oh that Jew!" We would ask them how they came to that conclusion and their favorite answer was that "the Fuehrer said so." It could be broad daylight, twelve noon, but if the Fuehrer told them it was dark outside, well then it was dark.

It wasn't true that the Communists did not change their thinking about the war until the Soviet Union was attacked. The view changed as conditions changed. When Hitler overran France and the French ruling class deserted their country, the French people fought on in the underground resistance. This was the beginning of the change in the character of the war—from an imperialist war to becoming a people's war against fascism. In Poland too, the Polish government fled to London and the Communists started organizing the guerrilla movement.

A Canadian warship, the *Prince George* I think it was, captured a German merchant marine ship and brought it into Vancouver. There must have been a crew of 50 on it. They were brought into the civilian camp where we were. Of the 50, about ten of the seamen were anti-Hitler, anti-fascist. When they'd walk by us they'd clench their fist; that was the Communist salute in Germany. One of them made two

Indian heads for me as a souvenir.

While we were in Kananaskis we got jobs working in the soldiers' and sergeants' messes, washing dishes and cleaning up. We cherished this because it gave us a chance to get out. We also got to know lots of the soldiers. All of them were veterans. They knew me from Calgary, from strikes and meetings. Some of them had participated in the unemployed strikes through the servicemen's organization. They didn't hate us. In fact, they treated us as humanely as possible under military law. I must say the same for the officers. They gave us everything they could in that situation.

We learned to make the most of our conditions. Officially we weren't allowed current newspapers or radio, but it didn't take too long before we had way and means of having the *Albertan* smuggled in.

Before I was interned, when it began to look as if I might be arrested, I packed two large boxes full of fine books I'd collected over the years. Some of them had been autographed by authors like Dr. Bethune and Ernest Hemingway. My wife and a man called McIntyre took the boxes to the store of a sympathizer in Calgary. Anne told the man who owned the store never to give them to anybody without her being there. He had an idea what the boxes contained.

After about two years, when people were expecting us to be released, Anne went to the store to collect the stuff. The man thought Anne had already received the material. He claimed that McIntyre had come with a note signed by Anne, to release the boxes to him. Later we got proof that he was an agent working for the RCMP.

Anne Lenihan

Pat was paid $40 a month as alderman in Calgary. That was $5 more than relief. When he was interned, they put me on relief. They had to support me and the children. There was no problem about getting relief; in fact, the mayor asked me to come and see him if they discriminated against me. The relief allowance at that point was $16 a month for rent and $15 for food. We also got medicines and shoe repairs. In the beginning we stayed with my parents for about a week so we wouldn't go hungry, but they were in no position to support us. My dad was getting the old-age pension and mother received some money for losing a son in the war. My only brother had been an officer in the Air Force and was killed.

Inspectors used to come and examine your place to see if you had any luxuries and to see if you were living within the limits of the relief payments. Somebody told them I used to go away and stay with my parents for a week or so. One inspector questioned me about that. I asked him to show me how to live on $31 a month and then I would stay away from my parents' place. He didn't say another word. He just said, "Don't pay any attention. Do whatever you like."

There's one thing I can say. I was not discriminated against or persecuted. There was a very strong sentiment here when Pat was interned. Pat was liked as a leader and people didn't think he should be interned. There was some kind of a hearing here when he was in Kananaskis. They had a lot of character witnesses. You should have seen the people who came—the labor aldermen, two Social Credit aldermen, and Fred White, a leader of the CCF. Fred was an alderman and then later an MLA. There were five or six aldermen from the Council who came to the review board. They didn't agree with Pat's principles but they knew he was honest and sincere.

Peter Krawchuk

Winnipeg, Man.
September 1940 -
January 1942

In June 1940 the government decided to ban a long list of organizations, making them illegal. Among those banned was the Ukrainian Labor Farmer Temple Association (ULFTA). Even after the ban we continued to issue our papers, the daily *Narodna Hazetta* (People's Gazette) and weekly *Farmerske Zhyttia* (Farmer's Life).

But people were arrested. We knew that Alderman Jacob Penner was arrested on the street in Winnipeg, and John Navis was arrested in a car en route to Winnipeg Beach. They were put in Headingly Jail and then sent to Kananaskis. John Boychuk was also arrested, but he was released because his name was misspelled and they thought they had arrested the wrong man. Early in July, Tony Bilecki, John Dubno, Matthew Shatulsky, Peter Prokop and others from our organization were arrested.

I didn't think I was on their list; I was young and had not played a very important role by that time. So I took on the job of getting the paper, which had already been prepared, to the printer. When I arrived at our print shop, the printers told me the police had just left a few minutes earlier and were looking for me. I left immediately and went to my brother-in-law's house for a few days; they hid me in a box underneath the house. Then I went on to another brother-in-law's in St. Boniface where I hid in the cellar any time anyone came to the door.

I continued to work while I was in hiding. The Workers Benevolent Association (WBA), a Ukrainian insurance society, had not been banned, though the books were taken away for checking. Through the summer a few of us would meet in the park to consult with the person who worked in the WBA office. Early in September I prepared the first illegal paper, *Za Voilu* (For Freedom). A woman took the manuscript and a typewriter under her coat and carried them to another house where I would type it during the night.

One day it was decided that Steve Macievich and I should consult a lawyer. The lawyer was not in his office and his secretary told us he would return from court in a couple of hours. We decided that a movie theatre would be the safest place to pass the time. We went to the Capitol Theatre on Portage Avenue. I remember the show was *Foreign Correspondent* with Joel McCrea.

After about half an hour a man sat beside me. He looked at me once or twice and then said, "Peter, what's your last name?" I asked him why he wanted to know and he pulled a folder from his pocket marked "Royal Canadian Mounted Police—William Grinley." I'll never forget that name.

He told me to come with him, that he had some questions for me. He pointed to Steve, who was sitting a few rows back, and told me to tell my friend to come too.

"He's no friend of mine," I said.

We argued for a minute but the policeman wouldn't be convinced and made Steve come with us. When he ushered us out I heard Steve whisper, *"Propalo, petre, propalo."* (All is lost.) In the end they didn't hold Steve.

They took my name and address. This is all I gave them, that and my identification card. I still have that card. I had registered in Gimli, while I was staying with my father-in-law helping him on the farm.

"Oh, you're a farmer," said the policeman. "You are a farmer like I am a priest!"

They wanted to know who my friends were. I named some of those who had already been interned. John Navis. John

Dubno. Tony Bilecki. They weren't happy with that but didn't push the matter further.

I was kept in jail for a few hours before being allowed to make a phone call. My wife was staying with a friend, so I called my brother Nick. In fact, Steve had already called my wife. I told Nick I was being sent to camp and would be at the CPR station in a couple of hours. I asked him to bring my wife and my other brother John.

My two brothers, my wife and a friend, Mary Navis, were at the station when I arrived. The policeman who escorted me had the decency to go to the other corner and talk with two other policemen while I talked to my wife. We left for camp that night. It was September 8, 1940.

The policeman I rode with was a smart cookie. He asked lots of questions, asked if I knew Annie Buller and others. Did I know Mitch Sago? he asked. And by the way, what nationality was he?

"I don't know," I answered. "Probably Japanese. Sounds like a Japanese name."

He was always pumping me for information. Actually he wasn't a bad policeman. He told me he had orders to handcuff me but that he hated to do it. He said it was his job and I shouldn't think badly of him. I guess there was some humanity in him. He didn't make the trip difficult. At some of the stations a captain or lieutenant would come and talk about the army; he did all the talking. I kept quiet. I was under escort, and besides, I didn't speak English very well.

In Calgary they took me to the top of the Post Office building. They put me into a cell, behind the bars, and I sat on the cement floor. I was sitting there in the dark when I heard a voice say,

"What are you in for?"

"I belong to the labor movement," I said.

"Look, I'll tell you something," my cell mate said. "I used to belong to the labor movement. I was in the trek from Vancouver to Regina. Sure, I was fighting along with the boys. I still support it. But it didn't improve my situation so I took my life into my own hands. You know what I do? I'm a safe cracker. That's the way I make a living. O.K., they got me and I'll spend a few years in the can, but then I'll be out again. I'm for the working class, but I have my own way."

The next day I was taken in a half-ton truck to Seebe, a

small railway siding some fifteen miles east of Banff, and from Seebe Station seven miles south to Kananaskis. Here in the wilderness the Canadian government had set up an internment camp. It was originally meant for German prisoners of war. For us it was a concentration camp.

As I approached the big gate of the camp, the first people I saw were Tony Bilecki and John Stefanitsky. They were nailing tar paper on the roof of the soldier's hut just outside the wire. They shouted down to me, *"Shcho ty ne mih schovatysia. Ty durenn. Tebe tut potribno?"* (What happened to you? Couldn't you hide? You fool. Do you think we need you here?)

I had thought they would be so glad to see me. I was worried that they considered me a bit of a traitor since I hadn't been arrested. And here they were scolding me for getting caught!

Thus I entered the great gate at Kananaskis. That was the end of my freedom for a year-and-a-half.

Kananaskis is an Indian name. The camp itself was surrounded on the south and west by very high hills, on the north there was the Kananaskis River and on the east a flat plain all the way to Seebe station. The camp was divided in two, the administrative section and the compound. The compound was surrounded by two rows of barbed wire with a guard tower every 200 yards or so. There were soldiers with rifles and machine guns in each tower. Not far from the two rows of barbed wire there was another wire inside the compound. If you passed it the guard had a right to shoot at you.

The guards changed every two hours. I know because Bill Rigby and I worked in the guard rooms inside the compound. One of these rooms was for the soldiers that were amongst us, inside the barbed wire without arms or ammunition. Then there were also rooms for the armed guards. The soldiers that guarded us were of the Home Guard, most of them World War I veterans. There were about 300 guards in all.

There were 795 persons in camp. Over 600 were Germans, 40 were Italians, and 39 anti-fascists. The anti-fascists were of different nationalities but most were Ukrainian. Most of the Germans were from Canada but some had been picked up from civilian ships. Among these seamen I found one

Communist and one socialist who were very friendly to us.

Some of us were Communists, although not all by any means. The camp commandant red-baited us all the time. He was rude and reactionary. He hated Communists and used to tell the Germans to make sure they wiped up the floor with the Communists. To make us more vulnerable he split us up. He put each one of us in a hut with eleven fascists. We demanded our own hut but didn't get it till May 1, 1941.

The camp was built as a triangle. The prisoners' barracks started from the north and came south in rows. In the western part of the compound there was a kitchen, ablution huts and latrines. In the southern part (the tip of the triangle) there was an office for the camp prisoners' spokesman and a guard room. In the southeastern corner there was the isolation hut called the "cooler," which was a jail inside the wire for those who broke camp regulations.

In the southwestern part of the compound there was the hospital and a big recreation hall where they showed old movies. In the middle of the camp there was a big square, the parade ground, which was surrounded by single logs. The Nazis called the parade ground the "Hitler Platz." In the evening and on Sunday the younger Germans played football there. The prisoners had a canteen to buy tobacco, chocolate bars, matches, scribblers and writing material, soap and toothpaste, toothbrushes, safety razors and other necessities.

In every hut there were twelve beds. In the middle of the building was a table made of rough wood with benches, and in the corner there was a box stove or a big barrel stove. The barracks were built of pine wood, but between the boards there were often cracks where the wind blew in a gale, bringing in snow, sand and just plain cold. There were shelves, a water pail with one cup for drinking, and a urine pail. The roof was covered with tar paper, and the windows were covered with barbed wire strands over the glass. The doors were closed with a hook on the outside, not a lock.

Almost all movement outside of the hut was controlled. If it was necessary to go to the latrine in the night, you had to knock on the door for the guard and wake everybody up, not only in your own hut but in the huts around you. If you had to go to the administrative office to see the commandant, or to get something from the quartermaster, you had to go first to the guard room, and then, under escort, you could go through the gate. You could get clothes, shoes and supplies from the quartermaster. When you got back you were searched.

The RCMP brought new prisoners first to the guard house, to the soldiers on the outside, and then they brought them inside the compound. I was taken to Major Jordain. He was the assistant to the commandant, the second-in-command. I got instructions on how to behave, whom to salute—when and how, and what my "rights" were. Then, after being "baptized," you went back to the guard room. There they assigned you a bed in the barracks and you were free, so to say, to mix with the others. Every prisoner who arrived was immediately surrounded by friends. Naturally everyone wanted to know how things were back home because everything could not be written in letters. Any news at all was welcome.

Our days in camp started with a gong at 6:30 a.m. After the gong, everybody rushed to the ablution huts. The seven o'clock gong meant we were to go to the dining room, line up for food and sit down at our table. If we were late we didn't get a meal. The third gong, at 8:00, called us to the parade ground where we all stood in rows according to our numbers. The sergeant major called us to attention, then the commandant would arrive and the check began. They went down the line from one to another. You showed your number disc, and when he called your number you had to shout "Sir." Those who were sick in the huts or in the hospital were checked there.

After parade, everybody was detailed for work. Different crews went to various jobs. Prisoners worked till 11:30 and then gathered again in the parade ground for another check before lunch. At 1:15 there was another check before being assigned to the afternoon work crews. The last check was at 5 p.m.; supper was at 5:30.

Every prisoner had some sort of duty. Only those over 60 were not required to do physical work. Some went as far as ten or fifteen miles out in the bush and cut mine props and logs for timbering coal mines. We were paid twenty cents for a day's work. We didn't get paid in money. We received yellow paper tokens which had buying power in the camps only.

At 8 p.m. a gong told us to go to our hut. Soon a guard

would come and close the door and put the hook on the lock. The evenings and Sundays were "free time." Between 8 and 9 p.m. we could sit, read or play cards. Many prisoners worked on souvenirs of wood or other materials. But every so often the sergeant major and another soldier would come to the door. We'd all have to stand at attention beside our beds.

Every prisoner had to wash his own clothes. There were some prisoners in the camp who were expert at this. They took a person's clothes and washed them for five cents. There were others who did other services. I remember Mike Binowsky used to cut hair for five cents.

Every month prisoners could write four letters of 24 lines and four postcards of seven lines. A letter in English, German or Italian would go through censorship and would then be sent to its address. Letters in other languages went to Ottawa to be censored. The return address was only your name and Internment Camp K, P or H, depending on whether you were in Kananaskis, Petawawa or Hull. Our letters were heavily censored. I still have letters with a heavy black smear over the words. In some cases the words were just cut out.

We tried to keep up on what was happening outside the camp. The camp received two daily papers, the Calgary *Albertan* and the Edmonton *Journal*. The whole of Camp Kananaskis was allowed only ten copies and these always arrived days late. Each hut of twelve men had one paper for about an hour, after which the paper had to be handed on to another hut. The paper was censored. All war news was cut out.

The Nazis in the camp always tried to use us for their dirty work. When they couldn't get us to clean up for them they tried to get the Italians. The Nazis in Kananaskis had no use for the Italians because the Italians didn't want to fight for Hitler, particularly in Greece where they were beaten, and in Albania and Africa.

There were some very nasty Nazis in camp; many of them were real fanatics. I remember one German who tamed a crow to eat from his hand and jump on his shoulder. He kept trying to teach the crow to say "Heil Hitler," but all the crow would say was "caw, caw, caw." This went on next to our hut and we split our sides laughing at his efforts.

One of the more notorious Nazis in camp was a priest who originally came from the Ukraine where he owned a factory with 600 workers. After the revolution he ran away to Poland and later came to Canada. He had already been arrested once for Nazi activity long before being sent to the camp.

One day as I was walking with John Navis we passed the priest, who was writing something. John asked him what he was doing.

"I'm writing a book," he said. "I am writing now in German but soon, when the war is over, I will go back to Russia and I will publish it in Russian." He was already over 60 but he actually thought he would still get to the Soviet Union to publish his book!

It is ironical that when my wife sent five volumes of the works of Taras Shevchenko, the Ukrainian national poet, the camp authorities called this German Nazi priest to give his O.K. He could decide whether or not the volumes would be allowed in.

Some of the Nazis in camp were released early, especially those with money or government connections. But not all the Germans in camp were Nazis, and some became disillusioned with Naziism. I remember one young German from Vancouver who was in our hut. He was beaten very, very badly and ended up in the hospital because he took an anti-Nazi position. Our group made representations to the administration to have him taken to a different hut where he wouldn't be in so much danger.

In November 1940 some of us were called for examinations. I received the following letter from the office of the justice department in Ottawa. It was dated November 1, 1940.

Dear Sir:

I have been directed by the committee appointed by the Minister of Justice to deal with your objection to your detention to advise you that your detention has been deemed necessary in the interest of the State because representations have been made that you

a) studied under the Ukrainian Labor Farmer Temple Association;

b) associated with the Youth Section of the Ukrainian Labor Farmer Temple Association;

c) are a Communist propagandist and organizer;
and in view of the above it would appear that you are
disloyal to Canada.

Unless you make representations with regard to the
date of hearing you will be heard by the committee at
Kananaskis on or after the 12th day of November and I
would suggest that you be ready to present your case
that day.

> Yours truly,
> W.R. Jackett
> for the Advisory Committee
> on Orders of Restriction
> and Detention

Some who weren't members of the Communist Party were
charged as being Communists. I remember when Anthony
Biliuk was asked if he was a member of the Communist Party
he jumped up and said, "Me? A Communist? What do you
mean? I have a house." He was the only one of us who had a
house. At that time no one who was a Communist could
afford a house.

Nick Kaschak could hardly speak English and when he was
asked whether he was a member of the Communist Party, he
said, "Communist? What Communist Party? Horrible
Judge, reply once more please." He had meant to say,
"*Honorable* Judge, *repeat* once more," but he had got his
words wrong. When he came back from the hearing he was
afraid he would never get out of camp, but two weeks later he
was released and sent home. By playing dumb he got out of
the internment camp.

There was also a young fellow by the name of Max from
La Pas, Manitoba. Max was not a Communist but he was a
member of the ULFTA. He was one of the few anti-fascists
who'd had a public trial before coming to the camp. Max
hired a lawyer to defend him. At the trial the judge asked him
what he thought of Soviet Russia.

"Judge," Max said, "you want to know what I think of
Soviet Russia? You give me $300. I will go there and when I
come back I will tell you. I wasn't there so I don't know what
I think."

When the crown prosecutor put another question to him,
Max's lawyer jumped up and said, "I object." At that point

Max grabbed his lawyer by his jacket (Max was a big man) and said, "Why do you object? I hired you to defend me, not to object."

When Max entered the court room he had three charges against him, but when he left he had five. He was sentenced to one year in Brandon and then they brought him to Kananaskis. At first he didn't know we were there. He thought everyone in camp was a German prisoner of war. As a Jew he knew that his life would be tough. When he met us he joined our group.

As a group we became quite close while we were at the camp. We were very well organized. We were quite a mixed bag in terms of national origins—24 Ukrainians, six Anglo-Saxons, two Germans, two Poles, two Jews, two Finns and one Hungarian. Our group had its own executive. When we got goodies from our friends on the outside the committee divided it up among all of us.

When we received parcels from home they were examined first in the guard room. But our friends were quite smart. They used to wrap the parcels in the *Canadian Tribune* and that was one way we got some real news. Actually, some of the guards were very friendly and when the better guards were on duty some quite good reading material got through.

One of the guards had fought against fascism in Spain. He was a friend of Calgary alderman Pat Lenihan prior to his arrest. Pat was a Communist and labor alderman in Calgary and here was a personal friend of Pat's guarding him at the camp. As you can imagine, this man helped us a lot. If he was on duty you could be sure that your parcels would come through the way they should.

Bill Rigby and I organized quite a large library. Mine was mostly Ukrainian books but Bill put together a very good English library. Often we would get together and Bill Rigby would give lectures about the labor movement and international events. Jacob Penner and John Navis would reminisce about the 1919 General Strike in Winnipeg. Later we organized a school in German taught by Jacob Penner. Michailo Sawiak organized an English school and when Sawiak got sick Bill Repka carried on. Bill Rigby and I used to smuggle in the uncensored copies of the *Albertan* and Edmonton *Journal* from the guard room whenever we could. The conditions were lousy but in spite of it all we managed to continue to study.

We had celebrations on November 7, 1940, May Day 1941, and on the anniversary of the mass arrests. On July 6, 1941, we had a joint dinner with singing and speeches. The Ukrainians of our group had organized a choir and John Weir wrote a song, "Dark Our Days in Kananaskis." Ben Swankey and Bill Repka made up the music for it. I'll never forget that celebration; it was also my 30th birthday.

Hitler's attack on the Soviet Union on June 21, 1941, was a turning point in the camp. It radically worsened relations between us and the Germans. They had never been friendly but they always implied that we were their allies—junior allies. We were tolerant and tried not to create incidents or fights but we always took the stand that Communists and fascists had different ideologies and would never be in agreement. But after the attack on the Soviet Union we repeated our demands for political prisoner status within the camp. When this was refused we appealed to the government. We demanded that we should be immediately separated from the Nazis and that until we were separated we should have protection from the Germans.

On July 21 we were notified that we should be ready to move out at 4:00 the next morning. At 9:00 the first transport pulled out with prisoners being sent to Fredericton, New Brunswick. These were all Germans; they were singing their fascist songs as they drove off. We were in the second contingent which was headed for Petawawa, Ontario. We were transferred by train, 50 prisoners to a railway car. We had to sit on benches and could only get up if we had to go to the washroom. We were watched every minute by soldiers with rifles and tommy guns.

Our friends in Calgary found out that we were being transferred and sent a telegram to people in Winnipeg saying that the train would be passing through the CPR station. A demonstration was organized but when the police found out, they made sure that the train was speeded up as it passed through the station. Some of us were barely able to catch glimpses of friends through the windows.

On July 24, after three days on the train, we arrived at Petawawa.

Tony Bilecki

Winnipeg, Man.
July 1940 - September 1942

It was a bright summer night, July 6, 1940. Dawn was beginning to break through as I delivered milk to my last few customers. I was about to go to the restaurant for a cup of coffee and to record the morning's deliveries in my book. Around 5 a.m., as I was driving along Selkirk Avenue in the north end of Winnipeg, two police cars stopped my wagon. The cop asked me if I was Anthony Bilecki. When I answered yes, they informed me that I was under arrest and had to go with them. I told them that I wouldn't go until I finished delivering the milk and took the wagon back to the People's Co-op. I jumped on the wagon and started driving.

Seeing my determination not to abandon the milk wagon and my responsibilities, two policemen boarded the wagon and travelled with me to the co-op on Dufferin Avenue and McGregor Street. Many people on their way to work witnessed this parade, one police car in front of my wagon, the other behind, and two burly RCMP men standing with me in the wagon while I held the reins of my horse.

As soon as we came to the co-op, I unloaded my wagon and gave all the money I had collected to the man in charge. I

50

didn't have time to mark all the names of the customers in my book. Then the police took me in their car to the RCMP barracks. They said they were under instructions from Ottawa to arrest me on the basis of the War Measures Act. There was suspicion I was being disloyal to Canada and thus could be dangerous to Canadian interests in wartime. At the RCMP barracks I came into a large room where I recognized several friends who used to work with me. The RCMP then began interrogating us.

Before I proceed further I should give some background. I came from the mining town of Drumheller, Alberta, where my father was a coal miner. After he lost his job in 1929, my family moved to Montreal where I attended school and worked at occasional jobs until 1936. In 1936 a special higher educational school in Ukrainian language, history and journalism was opened in Winnipeg by the Ukrainian Labor Farmer Temple Association. As I belonged to the youth section of the ULFTA, I submitted my name and was accepted for the school, which was held in Parkdale* near Winnipeg.

When the course finished I was asked to remain to work as a journalist for the *Ukrainske Robitnychi Visti* (Ukrainian Labor News); the paper was later renamed *Narodna Hazetta* (People's Gazette)—the first Ukrainian daily newspaper in Canada. I remained at the paper as an editorial worker until 1938 when I began working as an organizer of the Communist Party of Canada in Ward 3, Winnipeg. I worked at that until 1940 when the Canadian government declared the Communist Party and other organizations illegal. The ban included the ULFTA and the paper I had worked for. When that happened I asked for a job at the People's Co-operative. The only job available was milkman and I accepted it. I had to work. I had a son and wife to provide for.

It was on that job that I was arrested.

The interrogation in the RCMP barracks lasted the whole day. After that we were taken to Headingly Jail just a few miles west of Winnipeg. It is difficult to explan how an innocent person feels when thrown into jail among criminals.

*Orphanage and Old People's Home owned and operated by the Workers Benevolent Association of Canada during the 1930s.

All your movements are controlled. You get up, you go for meals, you exercise, all by the whistle and to commands. But it wasn't too bad. We weren't there for very long.

After two days we were told we would be leaving. That is when we received a real shock. We were chained. Just imagine! I had never had handcuffs on my hands, let alone a long, heavy chain. They chained us in twos and marched us to a special van which took us to the back doors of Winnipeg's CPR station. Then they loaded us in old colonial cars to go west. Only later did we learn that we were going to Kananaskis, an area in the Rocky Mountains west of Calgary.

The train ride was uneventful. Once the train was underway they unchained us, but we had to be seated at all times. We could not go to the bathroom without permission. We could not even get up to stretch our legs without their approval. When we passed through larger towns we had to pull the blinds down—I don't know why. Night was the worst. We had no beds. The seats in the train faced each other. Two persons sat facing two others, with no room to stretch.

In the morning we arrived at the small station called Seebe, in the foothills of the Rocky Mountains. They loaded us on army trucks, this time without chains, and took us to Kananaskis Camp. The trucks were completely open which meant that the cold wind went right through you. Some of us got miserable head colds and chest coughs.

We came to a huge army camp. It was a new camp, not yet finished. Nevertheless, it housed several hundred Germans, some of them sailors from merchant ships. There were also a number of Italians. When our trucks rolled in the Germans gathered around and greeted us with their fascist salute. They thought we were a new shipment of compatriots. We did not reply at the time. We were dismayed and shocked. Why had they brought us to a camp intended for German prisoners of war? We were not enemy aliens. We were Canadians. It was unbelievable that we would be brought to such a place when Canada was at war with Germany.

We were marched through the hall on the soldiers' side of the camp, past the commandant of the camp and the German camp *fuehrer*. I don't know whether this *fuehrer* was elected by prisoner-internees or appointed by the military commandant. After briefing us on camp protocol, the camp commandant turned to the *fuehrer* of the camp and said, "Here are your new prisoners of war. They are Communists. It is up to you to show them what German supremacy means." We could hardly believe our ears.

Each of us was assigned to a separate hut, eleven Germans or Italians and one of us to each hut. We protested; we wanted to be together. But the commandant said there was no separate room for us, and in any event, he wasn't taking suggestions from the likes of us. He was very blunt. "You have no rights," he said. "You do what I tell you."

What could anyone say? Here we were: unjustly arrested and interned in hostile surroundings, among people who were hostile to us. We had to be always on guard to make sure that nothing happened to any of us. Can you imagine 36 of us in a sea of German and Italian prisoners of war?

The authorities kept us under surveillance always. We were given special tasks where they could keep an eye on us. Any time we would begin to talk to the prisoners of war, the soldiers would stop our talking. Perhaps they were afraid that we would spread communist ideology among the prisoners.

Nevertheless, that did not stop us. We did a lot of talking. First of all we made it clear to everyone that we were one group. There were different nationalities among us—English, Polish, Ukrainian, Jewish—but we were a group of Canadian anti-fascists. Because of the danger we faced, we immediately organized ourselves. We told the Germans that if they had any complaints they were to come to our spokesman and we would deal with problems. They were not to touch any one of us for any reason whatsoever. That's the way we protected the few Jewish internees that were among us. We made clear to the authorities that they were not to force us to do things that were against our principles. Our dignified behavior and collective actions strengthened everyone's respect for us and gained us quite a bit of authority.

On one occasion the prisoners of war in the camp planned a concert. We were asked to participate, and accepted the invitation. We gathered together in the recreation hall to practice our choral numbers. There were a few good singers, but all of us took part. We practised a few Ukrainian songs and some Canadian workers' songs. When the evening of the concert arrived, we went to the hall and the entire hall rose to greet us with the fascist salute. In reply we gave them our working-class salute, with the clenched fist raised over our heads. It was a response they hadn't expected. However, the beautiful renditions of Ukrainian and Canadian songs more or less thawed the ice. In the end they actually applauded us.

I was in camp over my birthday. I'll never forget it. My wife sent me a birthday cake. After a preliminary examination of the cake by the camp authorities where they put spikes through it to make sure there were no hidden messages, I finally got the cake. I divided that cake into 36 pieces and each one of our group received a piece. The German prisoners saw me cutting the cake in the recreation hall and they couldn't believe it. They didn't share collectively like we did.

The authorities always locked the doors of our barracks at 8 p.m. and lights went out at 10:00. That night, after they locked us up, I took my piece of cake, the one I'd kept as my part, and divided it into twelve so that each man in the hut could have a taste. After some discussion among the others in German, the elder of our hut came up to me. "Well," he said, "I did not know—I just could not understand or imagine what you Communists stood for. This gesture of yours, dividing your cake among your friends and then sharing it here with us—you have not only made me your friend, but you have made us respect your principles and ideas. If anyone does anything wrong to you, just call me. If you complain, I will always take your side." I was as moved as they were.

Although ideologically we were enemies, dignified and proper behavior often saved us. I was forced to live with eleven strange men who were at first hostile. I had to be decent to them, and I must say that they were always decent to me. After lock-up in our huts and during recreational periods, we had discussions on many questions. They often asked my advice and interpretation of the news.

There is another incident that I'll never forget. For Christmas my wife sent me about two pounds of mixed nuts. The parcel came quite some time before Christmas but just to be mean the commandant waited till Christmas Eve to notify me that the parcel had arrived. He asked me to come to the provost's hut to claim it. When I got there they requested that I sit down and start cracking all the nuts open. Nuts, it seems, could hide secret messages. They assigned one man to watch me while the others looked on. It was my first Christmas away from home and family and here I was forced to sit in the guard hut cracking nuts. It was a strange thing, but once I resigned myself to my task I found that it made me feel even closer to my family.

I started to relax and take my time. I ate some nuts right there. I offered some to the guards. I did it deliberately, slowly, just to show the commandant he wasn't going to break my morale. It was clear I wasn't the only one angry at the commandant for ordering such a task. The guards didn't appreciate being given the useless task of watching me crack all those nuts. When I finally came back to my hut with the nuts and told my hut-mates what had happened they were all really angry, but we also had a good laugh about it. Of course we all shared the nuts.

At camp we were all obliged to do physical work. I chose clearing the forest. There was a whole section of burnt-out forest that we had to clean up. It was a dirty job. You came back to the camp covered with soot. But that job gave us an opportunity to be in the fresh air and outside the camp. Many of us welcomed that.

Later I changed jobs. Healthy individuals were needed to work in the sawmill. I think it was a private individual who operated it and he asked for prisoner labor. The authorities sent two truckloads of us to work there. The good thing about that work was it gave us an opportunity at lunch time to speak with other workers and learn the latest news.

For all the work we did outside the camp compound we received the magnificent sum of twenty cents a day. Just imagine, twenty cents for a day's labor! True, it was not hard work. We were not rushing around, except in the sawmill where we had to keep pace with the machines. But it was work. Instead of allowing us to put all our energy into the war effort to defeat fascism, the authorities were wasting taxpayers' money keeping us interned and doing unnecessary jobs.

The days went by monotonously. Winter came and went and finally the spring sun began to shine. It lifted our spirits and we began to enjoy our beautiful Rocky Mountains, the beauty spot of Canada.

After Germany attacked the Soviet Union, things became more tense between us and the German prisoners. Some of them made threatening gestures and called us names. We were afraid they might launch an attack on us.

After a while, rumors began to spread around the camp that it was going to be closed and that we would be moved. The day came when we were told to pack up. We were herded on trucks and then on old colonial rail cars.

Just imagine our feelings. Winnipeg! Our home! On the way east we managed to smuggle out a few written messages revealing that we were Canadian anti-fascist internees. The guards pulled the blinds down when we went through towns. Even so, we knew when we were in Winnipeg. As the train was going through the Point Douglas and Elmwood districts of Winnipeg we sang "O Canada" just to let people know we were there. Later we learned that some people had heard we were coming through and had come to the station, but they were refused permission to see us.

John Weir

Winnipeg, Man.
October 1940 - September 1942

Two years may not be such a long time, but the two years I spent in the internment camps were two years too many.

My parents came from the foothills of the Carpathian Mountains in the western region of the Ukraine, which was then under the foreign rule of the Austro-Hungarian monarchy. They emigrated to Canada before I was born. I was born in 1906 on a homestead in Broad Valley, in the inter-lake district of Manitoba. Early in 1907 my father, who had been a lumber worker most of his life, moved to the Fraser Valley of British Columbia. My first job at the age of twelve was as a cook's helper in a lumber camp. After that I went back to school and finished two grades of high school in Abbotsford and then went to Vancouver to attend business college. I worked in a store in Straiton, B.C., and then the family moved to Ontario. I worked on the construction of the Welland Canal and later on a railway extra gang. In 1923 I went to California. I lived there for a while and then moved to Detroit to work in the Briggs auto plant. By the end of 1924 I was back in Toronto.

My views were moulded by my father and the society I

grew up in. My father was fourteen when he joined a young workers' socialist study circle. Although he did not have more than two years village schooling, he read a great deal, and in British Columbia he was elected to the local executive of his trade union. He participated in socialist activities all his life. He knew several languages and wrote articles for many papers. In 1920 he took me along when a group went to Vancouver for the May Day meeting.

When we moved to Toronto I started attending meetings and lectures at the Labor Temple and the Ukrainian cultural centre. I joined the Young Communist League which had just been set up. By this time I was also writing articles. My apprenticeship was with the "wall newspaper," a bulletin board type of publication for which I wrote and drew cartoons. I continued to be involved in various groups and in early 1927 I became a member of the Communist Party. In March I moved to Winnipeg to work on the magazine *The World of Youth*. That's when I first got involved in municipal election work and politics. My interest in Canadian history stems from this time and has been growing ever since.

We learned a lot about capitalist democracy during those years. There was the internment of foreign-born workers during World War I, the outlawing of socialist groups and publications, the brutal smashing of the Winnipeg General Strike and the adoption of Section 98 of the Criminal Code which legalized arbitrary powers of the government, suppression of public meetings, and hounding of trade union organizers. Then came the Estevan strike.

On September 29, 1931, the news came over the radio that three miners had been killed and many others injured during a parade. The Canadian Labor Defence League asked me to go there and offer any help we could give them. In fact, the RCMP had fired on a peaceful parade, and scores of people were injured. When I came to Bienfait, I walked into a boarding house where neighbors were extracting a bullet from a youngster who had been wounded. The local doctors refused to treat the wounded, some of whom were arrested. I read the funeral oration at the burial of the three men. The Estevan strike was the beginning of my "university" education, which continued in Alberta during miners' strikes, unemployed struggles, and farmers' campaigns, working with angry and dedicated people.

In 1934 I returned to Toronto and worked on *The Worker* and *The Daily Clarion*. I became a member of the Newspaper Guild and for some months was business agent of the Artists Union. During this period I also became involved in civic politics and was elected for two terms to the Toronto Board of Education.

We constantly fought against fascism and war. Over a thousand Canadians went as volunteers to defend Spanish democracy from fascist invasion. We hoped for an alliance with the Soviet Union that would prevent war or put an end to fascist aggression, but the western capitalist states pursued other aims. They hoped to push the fascist powers to war against the USSR so they could move in when it was over and pick up the pieces. They miscalculated. Hitler turned first to subdue Western Europe and World War II began. The Communist International and our Party recognized that it was an imperialist war. I spoke against the war and when a public meeting in a farming area adopted a resolution against the war I published a report of it in the Winnipeg *Midwest Clarion*.

I was in my apartment in March 1940 when the police arrived and took me to the station. I was released on bail before the preliminary hearing. At the hearing two stool pigeons were brought in, one from Toronto to testify that I was a member of the Communist Party and its central committee, and another from Saskatoon to affirm that he had sold issues of the paper with the anti-war news story I'd written. Since I did not deny my political affiliation or responsibility for the article in question, the hearing was soon over and trial set for the fall.

Throughout that period people were being picked up and interned. I went undercover in order to be able to defend our position and myself in court. The day prior to my trial I was given a message to drop in on my lawyer before going to the courthouse. As I walked into the building I noticed a man in civvies on the ground floor looking out the window. My lawyer told me to go ahead and he would meet me in the courtroom. As I left the building, the man I'd seen in the lobby followed me. Just at the corner he came up to me and asked for my registration card. He escorted me to RCMP headquarters.

My friend and co-worker Bill Tuomi had been similarly apprehended and soon the two of us, "braceleted" together, were on a train headed west with two mounties to keep us company. Some passengers recognized us; one woman began to weep. After several hours the handcuffs were removed. One of the officers even tried to be friendly, telling us what a beautiful place the internment camp was. I told him that if they put barbed wire around heaven that would make it hell.

After a night in the Calgary jail we were taken to Kananaskis. Anxious to avoid condemnation for resorting to concentration camps, the government placed us in prisoner of war camps and we were dubbed POWs. The German fascist members and sympathizers, and later the crew of a sunken German ship, made up the bulk of the internees at Kananaskis. In accordance with international rules, the inmates had a committee of top Nazis that dealt with the commandant. Later we Canadian anti-fascists won the right to have our own spokesman but at first we were scattered in huts together with the Germans and we weren't recognized as a separate group.

It was very instructive to come in contact with Nazis first-hand. There were sessions in which they discussed in what part of Canada they would carve out their estates after the war. While there was little if any chance to escape, it had been made clear to the Germans that those who attempted to do so would be decorated by the *Fuehrer*, so attempts were made. When men tried to escape, the guards rushed into the compound and we were all confined to our huts.

The guards were concerned about our safety. In general they were working men who had gone through the experience of World War I and the Depression of the 1930s. They had put on the uniform again to fight fascism, not to imprison anti-fascists. They often brought us news from the outside. This meant a lot to us, since we had no visitors, no radio, and only old newspapers. The newspapers were censored, so the sort of news we were interested in was usually cut out. Letters were also heavily censored. The record would be incomplete without credit being given to our war vet guards.

We tried to keep up our political education any way we could. The library was very poor. Political literature was of course prohibited although I was fortunate in getting a large volume of the *Selected Works of Mark Twain*, a complete edition of O. Henry's works and W.S. Gilbert's plays. We even began putting out an underground, handwritten "newspaper."

We had study circles and argued about our main aim while in the camp: should it be to carry on propaganda among the other inmates or to struggle for separation from the fascists and thus help the movement on the outside for our release?

The latter was chosen. Since our repeated requests for segregation were ignored by those in charge, we used a little "direct action." When a large new barracks hut was built, we moved in. We were not evicted. Thus about half of us were partially "liberated" from Nazi occupation.

Of course we did not neglect opportunities to talk with the other prisoners. There were several German anti-fascists among them, well schooled in underground behavior. We exchanged bits of information with them, with the utmost caution. I remember there was a Danish seaman who was part of the crew of the German ship. He spoke English very well and would often drop by for a talk. We mostly talked about politics and the war. In the end he became a convinced anti-fascist. When he wrote a letter to the authorities offering to join the Canadian armed forces to fight Hitler, the letter had to go through the hands of the camp committee. He soon received a reply. An SS squad came to his barracks, ordered all the others out and proceeded to beat him mercilessly. The next thing we knew he was in the camp hospital.

We were afraid for his life but we couldn't get through to the camp commandant. At the review next morning I stepped out of line and walked up to him and told him what happened. He looked past me as if I wasn't there. Later when our spokesman, Fergus McKean, talked to him about it, he just said, "What do we care if Germans kill one another?" He would have responded just the same if it had been one of us. He really didn't care.

Once we had a separate barracks we could do lots of things we hadn't been able to before. We had concerts after lights out and talked about different interesting experiences. We found in our group one whose grandfather had been in the surveying team that was sent to the Red River after the western territories had been annexed to the Confederation of Canada. Another's grandfather had fought with Riel against the occupation of the Metis lands by the new rulers from

Eastern Canada. I started writing songs and Bill Repka and Ben Swankey led us in singsongs. Pat Lenihan treated us to delightful, satirical Irish songs. There was one memorable occasion when we celebrated May Day 1941. After dinner we stayed behind and took over the mess hall, locked the door and conducted a real concert meeting with speeches, singing of the Internationale and other songs. Some of the Ukrainian comrades had formed a choir and they sang.

There were some farcical episodes as well. Once one of us received a bag of walnuts. The officer passed the walnuts and we hurried to shut ourselves in our hut and open them. We knew there might be a message in them. We cracked the nuts and sure enough there was a message. Hungry for news, we painstakingly put the pieces of paper together. What we read though, was a very cordial letter from a friend telling us that we were not forgotten and wishing us all sorts of good things. Bless his or her heart, it was touching, but what we wanted was news.

Ben Swankey

Calgary, Alta.
July 1940 -
September 1942

I was arrested in Calgary in April 1940. The police raided my room and found some anti-war stickers. I thought I had those stickers well hidden but they seemed to know exactly where to find them, which always made me think that they had inside information. They had found similar stickers pasted on Calgary streets in the period just preceding my arrest. I was charged with pasting them up. At the trial they had no difficulty proving that I had possession of such stickers, but since I was charged with distributing and pasting them up they had to let me go for lack of evidence.

Two incidents about that trial stand out in my mind. The first concerned a bottle of glue that was found in my room. The police claimed that this was the glue used to paste up the stickers. Now this wasn't true. The glue that had been used for the stickers was homemade and altogether different from the bottle that I happened to have in my room. I told my lawyer I'd bought the glue in a store and we agreed to ask for a police lab test to prove that the paste on the stickers found on the street was different from the glue in the bottle in my room. The interesting thing was that when the police lab people gave their report on the witness stand, they claimed that the two kinds of glue were identical. This was entirely false. So far as I can tell this was framed-up evidence.

The second event concerns one of the star witnesses for the prosecution. He was none other than Roy Koijch, who appeared on the witness stand in the uniform of a sergeant of the RCMP. Now Roy Koijch had been a treasurer of my Party club in Edmonton, the Queen's Avenue Club of the Communist Party. He was there spying on Communists, a common practice of the RCMP. They were spying not only on Communists, but on labor organizations of all kinds. Their role was not only gathering information; they also carried on disruptive activities within these organizations.

In any case, my lawyer prevented Roy Koijch from testifying because, while he could have testified about my membership in the Communist Party, he knew nothing about my alleged activities pasting up anti-war slogans. My lawyer successfully convinced the judge that Roy had no evidence that was worth hearing. He was dismissed from the witness stand, much to the chagrin of the prosecution.

In the end I was found not guilty and discharged. But as I was leaving the courthouse—actually on the steps of the courthouse—I was rearrested, and this time it was under Section 21 of the War Measures Act. Under this act the government had the power to arrest a person and confine him wherever they wanted, for as long as they wanted, all without a charge or a trial.

I was held in the Calgary City Jail for a month, mixed in with pimps, drunks, lawbreakers of all descriptions. Eventually I was sent to the Kananaskis Internment Camp, which was in the mountains south of Canmore in Alberta, not very far from Banff. There I was met by Pat Lenihan, Calgary Communist alderman, and a large number of people from Winnipeg, 30 or 40 of them, mostly of Ukrainian descent, who had been arrested a short time before in Winnipeg.

Not all those arrested were Communists. Some were simply citizens with left-wing views of one kind or another who had been labelled as dangerous Reds by RCMP informers. One of them, Anthony Woytyshyn, had left the communist movement years before and become an avowed and public anti-communist. In Kananaskis he aligned himself with the German Nazis. Apparently the RCMP files were a little out of date.

I became just a number—number 279. I still have my identification tag with the plastic string that I had to wear around my neck all the time. Like the others who were interned there—as prisoners of war if you please—I was dressed in jeans and a jean jacket, with a big red circle on the back to be used as a target in case of escape.

Along with the Germans and Italians in the camp, we were officially labelled as "enemy aliens," a term we greatly resented. Many of us were born in Canada. Others had become naturalized Canadians. Still others had applied for citizenship, but had been refused on the recommendation of the RCMP because of labor activities or left-wing views. All of us were proud to be Canadians, even if at times we strongly disagreed with government policy. To be called enemy aliens was insulting, to put it mildly. We understood, of course, that the government used this term for its own political purposes.

In camp we all had to work. I loved the outdoors, so I joined the road-building gang. We were putting a road through the surrounding mountains. I was given the job of supplying the work gang with water, fresh cold mountain water, which I got from a creek about a quarter mile down the mountain. The guards used to let me go alone. I really welcomed the fifteen to 30 minutes of freedom.

Some of the guards we had in the camp were quite sympathetic. Many had been members of the single unemployed ex-serviceman's organization in Edmonton, where they were familiar with Communists like Alex Miller, who was also interned with us and who had been one of the leaders of that organization.

I recall that one of the guards used to bring me the daily newspapers, which were banned for prisoners. I would read them while I was at the creek getting water and then memorize what I had read. In the evenings I would pass on the news to my fellow internees in the hut. The guards who were sympathetic to us also took letters out for us and mailed them to our friends and families. One guard, who was a particular friend of mine, used to give me a certain percentage of his wages every two weeks for tobacco, chocolate bars and so on.

Jake Penner, the Communist alderman from Winnipeg, was interned with us. He was already quite old then. Jake was a model of self-discipline and an example to all of us in the camp. He shaved regularly, he kept his clothes clean, and his bed was made at all times. He was calm, composed and unruffled. It was a policy of his to maintain complete self-control and engage in constructive activity. When you are in prison, this kind of conduct is essential in maintaining your sanity.

When Hitler launched his blitzkrieg against the Soviet Union on June 22, 1941, it decisively affected the whole character of the war, and like everyone involved in the war, we had to reassess our attitude.

The British ruling class, for example, without abandoning its basic anti-Soviet views, took the realistic position that an alliance with the Soviet Union was necessary to defeat Hitler. In Kananaskis, we Communists had some heated debates over what our position should be. Naturally, we wanted to see Nazi Germany defeated, and we wanted to see socialism in the Soviet Union saved. We were faced with the question: should we now support the war effort in Canada, and in fact, demand that it be intensified?

For some, like myself, the need for a change in approach was not easy to accept. How could we support a government that had interned us and banned our party? How could we trust this government to really join with the Soviet Union to defeat Hitler?

We debated this question back and forth.

I remember one argument put forward by Bill Repka that helped to change my mind. "Look," Bill said, "when your house starts on fire, you run to ask all the neighbors to help put it out. You don't ask them what their politics are, as long as they are pouring water on the fire." That made sense to me.

We finally arrived at the unanimous decision that we would support the war effort.

A strange thing happened the day the Soviet Union was invaded. On that Sunday, one of the crew members of a German ship that had been captured off the coast of Mexico, all of whom had so far appeared to be ardent Nazis, came over and quietly told us that he was a Communist. He said that the attack by Hitler on the Soviet Union was the beginning of the end for Naziism. How right that estimation turned out to be! We were happy, and surprised, that even in a Canadian POW camp, a German Communist was still active. He took his life in his own hands exposing himself to us. The Nazis had a Gestapo operating in the camp and any dissidence was severely dealt with.

Even inside the camp, the German Nazis engaged in sabotage of the Canadian war effort. One of their methods was to destroy camp supplies. It was common knowledge that whenever they secured kegs of nails from the storehouse for building operations, they would bury them in the camp grounds and claim that they were all used up.

The Nazis made a number of attempts to escape. It was easy enough to get away. You could walk away from a forestry or road-work gang and not be missed for several hours. But the problem was where to go. Kananaskis was deep in the mountains. To reach Calgary you had to go through a large Indian reservation in the foothills. The Indians had been enlisted by the military and RCMP to help catch any internees that tried to escape. As far as I know, none of them ever made it. Those that were caught were sent to another camp.

Soon after the Nazi attack on the Soviet Union we were transferred from Kananaskis to another internment camp, in Petawawa, Ontario, not far from the training centre of the same name. The guards on the train were not the ones we had in Kananaskis; they were a new group from the east, all young and members of some special force in the army. It quickly became obvious that they had been given orders not to talk to us. They didn't even know that we were Canadians and anti-fascists; they just thought we were "enemy aliens."

We decided to educate them. Whenever we had a chance we would try to engage them in conversations about who we were and why we were interned. We talked about the war and about our wish to be released in order to join the army.

Some ten years ago or more I visited Kananaskis. The camp was greatly changed. One of the guard towers was still up but the barbed wire was gone, as were all the huts. In July 1981 I visited it again. This time it was completely unrecognizable. It has become the site of the Environmental Science Centre, run by the University of Calgary. That's all to the good; I'm glad it's being put to constructive use.

Former prisoners John Weir and William Repka examine barbed wire found at Kananaskis internment camp site in 1973.

William Repka

I arrived at Kananaskis at night and was placed in a barracks with eleven Germans. They all thought this fair-haired young man was a member of the master race. They gave me a hearty welcome until they discovered that I wasn't German at all, that I was a leader of a union and was completely opposed to their ideology and outlook on the world. Over the time I spent with them we had many discussions. They were disappointed that I was Ukrainian and a Communist, although they did seem to take solace in the fact that the Canadian government was having enough trouble that it needed to intern its own people.

The Germans in my hut didn't make things too hard for me. They thought that the Moscow-Berlin Pact meant Canadian socialists and German National Socialism had much in common. They'd tell me that socialism in Germany had its own particular form. They had taken over the country and were now building up armies to protect themselves from their enemies. This was their approach to me, although they knew better. They knew about Hitler's pledge of *"Drang Nach Osten"* (Drive to the East) and his plans for world conquest.

Because I was young I was given a job in forestry. Each morning prisoners were taken out in open five-ton trucks to a spot in the woods where we chopped or sawed down trees and cut poles four to six inches in diameter for mine props. The government sold them to the mines in the Crowsnest Pass. We stayed in the bush all day while the guards stood by with rifles. I had a partner who was, I think, shell-shocked. He was very inarticulate; he had no English at all and my German couldn't get through to him. We worked together as best we could.

We cleared a large area around Kananaskis and I have

often wondered what that area has been used for. I went to see the place a few years ago and found most of the huts were gone. One of them was still standing, with the word "Freedom" painted on it in huge letters. The place is now part of the University of Calgary grounds and has some very big buildings on it.

At work we had two daily coffee breaks and soup and sandwiches for lunch. I remember Philip Lysets introduced me to roasted apples. We would put the apples right into the coals of the brush we burned. They were delicious after the hard work in that cold air.

While I was working I spent a lot of time thinking about my situation. You can't get away from feeling hurt and alienated when you are locked up in your own country. I was born in Canada, but coming out of school in the Depression meant I was locked into a permanent state of poverty. For youngsters leaving school in the thirties there were very few alternatives. You could go into business and begin to rip off your own people or work with other poor people to climb out of that poverty. These thoughts were constantly on my mind as I worked in the various parts of the camp.

After I'd been in camp for quite a while I was transferred to another forestry group where I was witness to a near murder. Kurt was a small German Nazi who used to come out with us. He was Canadian but was intensely nationalist about his origins. He was about 40, with a wizened, lined face, pointed nose and restless, angry eyes.

Kurt used to make a point of taking off on Hans, a big Austrian with a pleasant square face. Hans was a quiet, self-effacing person. At every opportunity Kurt kept saying that Hans was stupid and clumsy. Every time something went wrong it was those stupid Austrians who were at fault. The little Nazi continually got his digs in about the master race and how soon they would be running everything with German efficiency, culture and knowledge. He was even more infuriated by the Austrian's claim that *Der Fuehrer* himself was of Austrian parentage. For Kurt that was impossible. The stupid Austrians didn't know a thing, and Hans, according to Kurt, was the image of all Austrians.

This went on and on, day in and day out, with poor Hans trying to avoid the barbs of his tormentor. But one day, at coffee break, Kurt stuck his finger into the coffee mug that

Hans was carrying. It was supposed to be a joke but it was in very poor taste. In great embarrassment, Hans poured his coffee on the ground and went to stand in line for another cup. Kurt laughed at him.

"That's right. Get another cup. And keep it away from my finger."

After the coffee break, just as the prisoners were moving away from the lunch wagon towards the woods, we heard a scream. Everyone rushed back to see what the trouble was. The scream had come from Kurt.

The coffee incident had been the final humiliation for Hans and when the group had broken up Hans caught Kurt behind the tent and pinned him to the ground. He took out a sharp pocket knife, pinched some of the protesting German's skin under one ear and put the keen edge of the knife to it.

"Stay away," Hans shouted to us. "Stay away or I'll kill him. I'm going to show this *schweinerai* what it means to torment people."

Hans proceeded to cut a scratch around Kurt's throat. Carefully, slowly, he moved the knife across the German's throat, not deep but right from ear to ear.

"This is only a scratch," said Hans. "I could just as easily cut your throat. This is to show you what can happen if you torment people enough."

Kurt was white with fright and pain. When Hans finally got off Kurt, the guards immediately grabbed the two men and hustled them off to camp. They pushed the rest of us into trucks and everyone was taken back to camp.

As a result of the incident, feelings between the Austrians and Germans reached a fever pitch, with some hot-heads taking sides. Finally there was a hurried call for a meeting of the Nazi camp council. The council issued a private ultimatum that anyone raising the issue again would be severely and physically dealt with. They also put up a public notice stating that the "misunderstanding at the forestry detail was just the result of an argument between friends."

Our spokesman in the camp was Alderman Jake Penner of Winnipeg. Some time after his arrest Jake was ordered to be brought to court on a write of *habeas corpus* for a hearing on the validity on the internment order. When he failed to appear, the judge asked where Jake was; he was informed by the RCMP that Jake was in the internment camp at Kananaskis. They had, it seemed, "lifted" *habeas corpus*. The judge was indignant: "I want him here. That is what this is all about."

Finally Jake was brought to court, the judge having upheld *habeas corpus*. The judge then upheld the order for internment and ordered Jake back to the camp.

After Jake Penner's arrest, the Winnipeg City Council moved that he be expelled from council for failure to attend. His son Norman, then nineteen years old, read a long deposition on behalf of his father, recounting his service to the people of North Winnipeg, whom he represented. Thereupon the motion was shelved. A few months later the Manitoba legislature passed a law, the Public Office Disqualifications Act, which named no one but was obviously aimed at the Penner case. Soon after the Bracken government passed the law, the attorney general notified the City Council that Alderman Penner came under the provisions of the act and therefore had to be removed from council.

Some time after this, Norman Penner joined the army and claimed his mother as a dependant. He later received notice from the armed forces that unless he could prove that his father was physically incapable of supporting his family, he could not claim his mother as a dependant. It seems his commanding officer convinced the top brass that an interned man could not be expected to support his family. But as an

Jacob Penner
Winnipeg, Man.
June 1940 - September 1942

Public Archives Canada

interesting footnote, after Jake Penner was released and his son Norman was home on leave enjoying a family reunion, an RCMP came to the house, somewhat belatedly, to check on the status of Norman's claim to army allowance for his mother.

One day, as spokesman, Jake Penner informed me that I was to go to Calgary for a hearing. It was a surprise to me. I arrived in Calgary in the evening and was again placed in the RCMP cells atop the Post Office. As soon as I was settled in my cell, a soft-spoken, well-dressed civilian came up to me. "Bill," he said, "I came here specially to take a look at you. I have spent my life getting you and your kind behind bars and into the internment camps where you belong, and now because of our democratic society, I have to arrange for a hearing at which you might be released. Isn't that a disgrace?"

The man was obviously a highly paid security agent but he looked like an ordinary businessman. He was venting his anger and acute disappointment in having to participate in the possible undoing of his good work in getting me behind bars and barbed wire. I have often wondered where he would have stopped in persecuting our people if he had his own way.

Next day I was taken by a policeman to the hearing. My memory may be wrong, but I think it was Chief Justice Carter of the Supreme Court of Canada who presided. To my surprise, I also had the services of one of the most expensive legal houses in the city of Calgary. The lawyer told me that because I was a trade unionist, the United Mine Workers of America, CIO, and a number of labor organizations were paying for my legal defence at the hearing and he was their representative.

One of the first things my lawyer said when he took me aside was that his was a very prestigious legal house. Then he asked if there was any way he could say I was not a Communist. I said that was a very difficult thing to do because I had been in the progressive movement for many years and from about seventeen years of age had been publicly very active. I had been a provincial organizer for the Young Communist League in Alberta for a few years.

He told me that if I had been able to say that I was not a

Communist it might have made a difference, but as it was, there was probably not much he could do. He was absolutely right. When I came in front of Chief Justice Carter, the judge already had a dossier on me four inches thick. He first read to me the assessment of the security forces. "Bill is a well-built, 5 foot 7, brown-haired, green-eyed, likeable, well-kept, mannerly and friendly chap who is an effective Communist organizer, lecturer and propagandist."

The judge read on and then asked, "Were you, in 1931 and at seventeen years of age, a member of a delegation that met Vice Premier Reid of the United Farmers of Alberta government after the Hunger March of that year?" I said I was, but I wouldn't go into details; why fill out a police dossier?

That was a very important march. There were 10,000 people there. Being a "youth," I, along with other young people, was carrying a banner in the front line of the march. The police let the youngsters by before the RCMP on horses made a frontal attack on the rest of the marchers. At the same time the Alberta provincials and Edmonton city police pummelled the demonstration from all sides with broom handles and riot sticks. One man told the cop beating him, "But I am an anti-communist."

"I don't care what kind of communist you are," said the guardian of law and order.

Those who got away continued to march to the parliament buildings. When we got there, as the small delegation was going in, the leader of the group grabbed me and I soon found myself in front of the vice premier. With wheat at twenty cents a bushel and thousands of unemployed, it was an honor to be on the delegation.

The judge was not happy that I was not forthcoming with information. He read further, "You were one of the leaders of the restaurant strike when they shut down 26 restaurants in the city of Edmonton." I told the judge I helped the strikers get food for themselves and their families. I wanted to tell him that waiters and waitresses were getting pay that was hardly enough to cover their room rent, let alone uniforms and clothes.

"And then," said the judge, flipping more pages of the dossier, "you took part in the Corbin strike in British Columbia when miners struck that mine."

"I am not a miner," I told him, "but when the miners asked me to come, I went and spoke to their meeting." He wanted details but I told him a strike is a strike is a strike.

I'll never forget that trip into Corbin. The road is really only a mountain ledge with a cliff rising up on one side and a steep drop on the other. The mounties had set up a border checkpoint there and would not allow officials of the Mine Workers Union through. Fred, one of the miners, was allowed to come out of the town and load the back of his car with vegetables and other food. I was in one of the potato sacks. When we approached one of the checkpoints I stuck my head among the other sacks to look as much like the real thing as possible.

At that very moment I was seized with a coughing fit. As the driver pulled up in front of the police hut, two officers came out with flashlights and looked over the sacks while I nearly choked holding my breath. Our driver said he was in a hurry and he wanted to get back before it was too dark. They were just going to let us through when one of the officers told us to wait. I thought I'd been discovered but it turned out the guard just wanted a match.

Conscious of my coughing, Fred just reached into his pocket and told him he was fresh out of matches and stepped on the gas of the old Chev to get us out of there. A good thing too; I had got my nose so full of dust from the old sacks that I coughed and sneezed for a good while after that.

I remember the whole thing clearly because I celebrated my 21st birthday skating on a pair of borrowed skates on a tiny, improvised rink in the strike-bound town of Corbin. That afternoon in a jam-packed hall I was able to speak to the miners, telling them that the Canadian labor movement was behind them and that the American millionaires who were exploiting the mountain coal would have to settle with the union.

The judge mentioned a number of other incidents such as speaking to the Coalhust miners when a number of their mates were killed in an explosion at the mine, and speaking to a farmers' meeting protesting evictions. He finally ended up by saying that for a young man I'd really gotten around. "Your activities," he said, "would indicate that you are indeed a labor organizer and a Communist, and that therefore you are the kind of person that the Canadian government has decided must be interned."

I protested that organizing labor unions was not illegal in Canada and that to intern anti-fascists was a crime. The judge's mind was made up and no amount of arguing would change it. Then to my surprise his face softened. "I have a son your age," he said, "and all he is interested in is fast cars, fast horses and beautiful women. I've been wondering..." I think the judge was really trying to figure out what made some people interested in social affairs and politics. I didn't have any answer for him; the son of a rich man would have very little reason to interest himself in the affairs of beet workers, in their children working in the beet fields, or in waitresses earning $3 a week.

Back in Kananaskis, I reported to my comrades about the hearing. We were all clear that many things had to change before hearings would be useful and releases in sight. In the meantime I was learning a lot about how this society worked. You didn't get arrested only for fighting over hours, wages and working conditions. It was national and international issues that had plucked me off the combine. Historic forces moving tens of millions of people made my little problems seem insignificant indeed. Watching and trying to understand those forces was a real education.

Monotony is the cornerstone of any internment camp. You get up at 6 a.m., have breakfast at 8:00, begin work at 9:00. Lunch is at noon, then back to work till quitting time at 4:30. After supper it's free time for two hours, then lights out. The first couple of weeks there are new things to discover, but as the days, weeks and months wear on, with the same things over and over again, even the more interesting events get monotonous.

It reaches the stage where even a ball game is boring. The same players are as good or as bad as they were the week before. No amount of switching players around on teams revives the initial sense of competition. You can tell a week ahead who will win. You can almost guess what the score will be.

Ben Swankey and I used to play ping-pong. It started off as a fascinating game, but as time went on and I lost and lost and lost, the game got to be quite pointless. Some of the men got bar bells to build the body beautiful. They excercised, strained and sweated until they developed very fine chests and leg and arm muscles. But after they had reached a certain stage they just left bar bells alone and reverted to their old selves.

Some of us tried to study music. But after our comrades heard us play the same pieces a few dozen times, no matter how much we improved, they became less and less enthusiastic and would get up and go for a walk around the compound rather than hear us one more time. It is difficult to describe how tedious life becomes and how boredom stifles any efforts to use time constructively.

No one was successful in escaping from the camp. Once a few Germans tried but tracking dogs soon caught up with them and they quickly gave themselves up. The wide open spaces are a formidable fact in Alberta. That attempted escape was on the same night as one of the most moving and frightening events in the camp. It was a semi-religious ceremony organized by the Germans. Various groups marched back and forth on the parade ground in torch light parades. It caused a general hubbub throughout the camp. It wasn't till later that we found out it was done to cover the escape.

Bill Tuomi, Ben Swankey and I discussed escaping. It wouldn't have been particularly difficult. We worked at various sites outside the actual camp compound. But where would we go? And if you did escape you would be a menace to all your friends and comrades not only in the area but throughout Canada. Perhaps for military people, escaping was a matter of honor, for us it would have been foolishly romantic.

Many of the guards were friendly to us. One of them told us when there was a hut recently completed and empty. He suggested that before it was occupied we take matters into our hands and simply storm the place. Once we were in it it would be very hard for the commandant to get us out. And that's exactly what we did. One day, after we all came back from our field duties we grabbed our things and rushed down to hut 57. From then on we had our own hut.

The whole atmosphere of the camp changed for us as a result of our being together in one hut. We were recognized as a separate group in the camp with our own spokesman. It was much easier to have discussions on current events and issues. These were very important for us. It was like getting a university education.

We all worked to fix up the hut. Those men with a green thumb planted flowers around the hut. I remember Pat Lenihan asked his wife Anne to send some flower seeds. When we received them they were wrapped in the *Canadian Tribune*. He wrote her back saying the tribunias and petunias had arrived in very good shape. As a result of that we were also able to get caught up on current news.

Storytelling was a major occupation for everyone. After lights out the men regaled each other with stories and exchanged experiences. One of the Germans with whom I worked in the forestry told me about a very funny yet rather sad incident involving a young man who loved to tell about his exploits with women. Hans used to give detailed descriptions of his conquests and especially about his latest love, the daughter of a Protestant minister.

One day Hans came back from work detail to find a letter on his pillow. Like all letters to prisoners it had been opened and stamped "Department of Internment Operations." As Hans read the letter, his face dropped. When he finished it he stuffed the letter in his pocket and hurried out into the compound. He paced the compound for a while, then went to the camp canteen. Minutes later he was back at the hut with a box of cigars and a box of chocolates. "Boys," he said, "I'm a father."

Everyone congratulated him, although there was a great deal of suppressed giggling and laughter among the men in his hut as Hans began to enjoy the idea of being a father. He started to make plans to see the camp commandant and arrange an internment camp wedding. That's when the bubble burst.

"Do you know what day it is Hans?" asked some of his fellow prisoners. "It's April Fool's Day."

Hans looked blank. Finally, with some difficulty and a great deal of joking, the men managed to tell Hans that he'd been tricked. The disappointment in the man's face was tragic. He was very dejected. And the sad part for the men in the hut was that that was the end of Hans' titillating stories.

Another very interesting story was about Max. Max is an example of a non-political person who was railroaded into the internment camp. He was a bachelor of forbidding countenance, but a very friendly, down-to-earth sort of chap. Max had been an agent for a man who owned a big general store on an Indian reserve in the far north of Saskatchewan. According to Max, there was a man called Honest John who had a family of twelve children who lived close to the main store. John liked his wine but was careful about it.

He had a good understanding with the Catholic Church there. The Church knew that if Honest John was relatively satisfied, things would be quite peaceful and orderly on the reservation. However, if Honest John was crossed, all hell would break loose. So the bishop felt it was in the church's interest periodically to give Honest John some financial aid and other help for his large family.

This particular time John came to the bishop's secretary and said that his family was in dire straits and needed some help. The secretary suggested that John's oldest son, who was sixteen, should find a job. John protested that his son had no warm clothes to go into the bush and cut logs. The secretary understood the problem and said, "Well, then, you go to the store and I will write you out a note and they will give you what you need."

The note read, "Give Honest John what he needs." The secretary put the bishop's stamp on it and signed his name to it. John took the note to Max's boss and said: "You know, I need some pants for my son, and some shoes, gloves and a coat." Max's boss gave a long look at that piece of paper. Then he said: "Honest John, would you like my car? My house? My whole store? When I have a note from the bishop telling me to give you anything you want, then with all that money behind it you can have anything you want. Come into my office."

Max's boss got a gallon of wine, and sat in the office with John all afternoon, discussing this marvellous note. John's son got a complete line of the best possible clothes and went to work. Besides that, the whole reservation received clothes, including some of the hand-me-downs from the back recesses of the store. Old style ladies' hats turned up and button-up shoes and some of the men sported hats from 1910.

There was some wonder in the town as to why there was this sudden affluence on the whole reservation. Besides this, a fairly substantial number of gallons of wine turned up, very strictly kept in order by Honest John. Any wild whoop-ups took place in the far distant reaches of the reservation.

However, the state of euphoria didn't last forever. Finally the wine was gone, and so was the food. The clothes had begun to wear out. A few months later, Max was delegated to take a bill for $1,989.62 to the church secretary. As this bill was being delivered, Max's boss and his wife and two children had an urgent need to visit Mexico on a four-week holiday. Max dutifully presented the bill and the secretary looked at it in disbelief.

He said to Max: "What in the world is this for?"

"Well, in our store," Max said, "the friendly general store," (he had been carefully coached about the words he should use) "we received a note from the bishop's place that said, 'Give Honest John everything that he needs.' And so we gave it to him. Of course he wanted much more. But we only gave him $1,989.62 worth of goods."

Max was quite businesslike about the whole thing. The secretary was, of course, astounded. "The intention of that note was that you were to give Honest John a pair of shoes, a pair of trousers, a coat and a cap to equip his son to go to work," he told Max.

Max, as instructed, said, "Oh, no. The note said nothing about those things. That note, which will hold up in any court of law, said: 'Give Honest John what he needs.'" The secretary had a momentary faint spell. He pulled himself together and rushed over, holding his head in his hands, to talk to the bishop.

Max got on his bicycle and pedalled back to the store. He had barely arrived when the bishop's secretary jumped off his own bicycle and rushed into the store. Max told him that the boss was away and would be gone for some time, so poor Max had to bear the full brunt of the secretary's holy wrath. Max maintained that the note was quite legal and was in the safe, beyond his reach. There it was with the stamp of the bishop and the secretary's signature.

After that the bishop himself came and tried to remonstrate with Max about this bill. And then began a frantic checkup about the transaction. It was found that a bunch of trash had been sold.

Max pointed out that it had been bought and charged for on the advice of his holiness, as proved by the piece of paper.

Max was then treated to a display of the bishop's holy wrath, compared to which, said Max, the wrath of God was as nothing.

The thing that hurt him most, Max protested, was that his own personal honesty was held in question. He was the innocent victim of forces beyond his control.

About three weeks later, the boss phoned long distance from Mexico to find that the RCMP had picked Max up and taken him to the internment camp. Someone had to be the scapegoat and Max was on the spot.

Like Max, a few others were interned who had taken no part in politics—a janitor, a milk truck driver. There were injustices in that period that caused personal tragedy for many.

The Nazis in Kananaskis were quite convinced that it was simply a matter of time before the world was theirs. They used to sing the song *Heute Haben Wir Deutschland*. The main thrust of it is, "Today we have Germany, tomorrow the whole world." They used to entertain one another with what they were going to do when the "dung-heap" called Canada was theirs and they could re-arrange matters in their superior manner.

When Hitler marched into the Soviet Union, one of the Germans in our camp shouted out from his hut, "This proves to me that Hitler is not a socialist; he's a fascist and imperialist." He was immediately set upon by the others for treason. He was severely beaten and had to spend a couple of weeks in the hospital. There were no allowances for ideological deviation among the Germans in the camp.

After that there was a complete and dangerous turn in the way the Nazis approached us. While they were powerless to aid their forces in Europe, in Kananaskis they had strength. We were completely outnumbered by them. It soon became necessary for our spokesman to tell the commandant that if there were any incidents or any violence against our people we would hold him and the government of Canada personally responsible.

The result was that we were finally told that the anti-fascists were going to be moved. We bundled up our duffle bags and were loaded into the backs of stake trucks surrounded by platoons of Canadian soldiers complete with rifles and tommy guns. They were there to make very sure we desperadoes didn't go charging off into the vast spaces of the foothills of Alberta.

We were driven to the station at Seebe, not far east of Banff. Banff is truly one of the beauty spots of the world but there is not much joy in that beauty when you have a man standing over you with a gun. At Seebe we were herded into old immigrant railway cars. It was unsettling to see the cities go by. We were obviously moving east but we didn't have any idea where we were going.

When we finally reached Brandon, I think it was, the train stopped at a siding and John Navis recognized a man who was working on the railway section gang. He was a Ukrainian who belonged to the ULFTA. John knocked on the window and then dropped him a note saying that this train was likely going through to Winnipeg. Word had finally come from one of the friendly guards that we were going to an Eastern Canadian internment camp. Of course we couldn't know whether this information was true. People who were taken to the gas chambers in Germany were told they were going to some idyllic living place. Anyway, John told the man to phone Winnipeg and let people know we were coming.

As we approached Winnipeg, those with relatives there were very tense. They hadn't seen their families for months and now they were going through their own city. The train did not stop in Winnipeg but some of the men got little glimpses of their families as the train rattled through the station. It was a great joy to see each other alive and apparently well. But the tragedy was that an unfeeling government would not even allow the train to stop.

Peter Prokop

Winnipeg, Man.
July 1940 - September 1942

The Ukrainian Labor Farmer Temple Association was banned by an Order in Council on June 4, 1940. The official announcement in the Canada *Gazette* on June 8 listed a number of anti-fascist organizations, among them the ULFTA and its women's, children's and youth sections. However, the Labor Farmer Publishing Association was not banned. It published *Narodna Hazetta* (People's Gazette), the only Ukrainian daily paper on the American continent, and the weekly *Farmerske Zhyttia* (Farmer's Life). The publishing association was headed by the widely known leader of the Ukrainian progressive movement, John Naviziwsky (Navis).

I was one of the editors of the *Narodna Hazetta*, but at that time I was more occupied with my responsibilities as secretary of the bureau of the Ukrainian mass organizations and as recording secretary of the central executive committee of the ULFTA, one of the top leadership posts.

The first news that there would be a ban reached us through a news leak from a correspondent sympathetic to us on the Winnipeg *Free Press*. Up to that time there had been

83

no information on the radio or in the press. The morning after we heard, I had a meeting with John Boychuk, secretary-treasurer of the ULFTA, to discuss the matter. John, a well-known Communist leader among the Ukrainians, had been sentenced to five years in Kingston Penitentiary in the thirties along with Tim Buck, leader of the Communist Party of Canada, under the infamous Section 98 of the Criminal Code. We discussed the expected attack on our organizations, how to safeguard our meagre funds, and how to protect the membership lists and records.

In 1939 our organization had held a national festival of Ukrainian music, song and dance in Toronto, with participants from all over Canada. It was very large and the first of its kind ever held in Canada. We in Winnipeg had bought an autobus for the festival; because the bus needed lots of repairs, we later sold it for about $2,500. This money was in the bank and we were naturally concerned about saving it.

We decided to buy some Canadian bonds. When I went to a bank on Main Street they told me to leave the money with them and they would deal with it later. I realized that they already had information about the ban and that it was a trap. We would leave the money, and then, because we were illegal, we would not have any rights to it. I was right. On June 8, along with the announcements of the closing of the buildings of our organization, they also gave notice that our halls and all the wealth of our organization would be confiscated. We had to find another way to save that money.

The leadership realized that the ban would likely mean arrests as well. To avoid panic among our members it was decided to continue to issue our newspapers, which were not yet banned. Someone had to be in charge and make arrangements for the papers to come out. It was decided that John Naviziwsky, Matthew Shatulsky and John Boychuk, who were known leaders in the Ukrainian progressive community, should go underground. I was one of the younger ones so I was to be in a semi-underground position. The rest of the staff continued to work on the paper. I used to go to the office in the morning to arrange the details. Then I'd go home or to some other place to continue my work.

In the first week of June the police began to look for our people. First they arrested Alderman Jacob Penner. On that same day they came to the Ukrainian Labor Temple at Pritchard and McGregor looking for John Naviziwsky. John had already gone underground. They arrested him two days later on the road between Winnipeg and Winnipeg Beach. Jake Penner and John had their trial together. Their lawyer tried to get them freed on the basis of *habeas corpus* but he was unsuccessful. It was not the judge but the minister of justice in Ottawa who had the last word.

During that period I was hardly ever at home. I had to sleep out. It was not easy to hide because the people connected with our organization were intimidated by the fierce anti-labor propaganda. The establishment organized a hysterical campaign against the progressive anti-fascist movement. In addition, the progressive Ukrainian organizations were all viciously attacked by the Ukrainian nationalists. There was a general opinion among the nationalist leadership that all that was necessary was to arrest the leaders of our organizations and our members would run to them. The assumption was that the members were quite clueless, didn't know where they belonged, and that the minute they would hear the so-called "truth" they would go over to the nationalists. How mistaken the nationalists were!

It was a very difficult situation to work in. Many of the leadership were in hiding and had no contact with one another. The connections we had were through third parties. They know where to find me should the need arise. Nevertheless, our newspaper continued to come out right up to the day of the mass arrest of the ULFTA leadership on July 6. That's when I was arrested.

I was arrested around 5 a.m. I remember it as if it were yesterday. I was staying at Fred Mokriy's house. He lived alone upstairs; some Germans who were not sympathetic to our organization lived below. Fred told me to always come in before midnight. If the doors were locked I was not to knock. He would keep the door unlocked up to midnight. That way I could just walk in and go upstairs.

Friday night I got a message that Boychuk wanted to see me at midnight. I went to the address specified in the note. The people there seemed quite surprised when I arrived. The woman told me that Boychuk had left their place on Wednesday night. This news really upset me since I'd just been given the note that day. By this time it was late and I knew I'd have a problem getting into Fred's place, which was a long distance away. I hoped that he might realize I was delayed and leave the door unlocked.

I walked through the quiet night streets, but when I arrived at Fred's the doors were locked. I walked around the block, trying to figure out where to go at such an hour. Just then a thunderstorm started. I realized that it would look quite suspicious for a man to be walking around in the downpour so, having no other choice, I went home.

It was natural to worry about arrests any day, but that night I had a particularly uneasy feeling. I remember mentioning to my wife, Mary, that this is the kind of night the police like to make raids. It was on similar nights in 1920 in my homeland Lemkivshchyna that the police used to round up Ukrainian boys who were draft dodgers or who had deserted the Polish army, which was waging war against the Soviet Union. Although I was still quite young, just sixteen, I was already helping the deserters to hide. My family had strong feelings about the war against the newly established Soviet state.

But to get back to Saturday, July 6. We were jarred out of our sleep at daybreak by a very loud banging at the apartment door. When Mary opened it, four husky men, one of them in RCMP uniform, burst in and proceeded to our bedroom where I was sitting on the bed. One of the four left almost immediately; the other three remained.

In the doorway Mary also saw a civilian who looked like a member of our organization. He, it seems, had brought them to our door. According to information we later received from some of our members, he was busy that morning helping the Red Squad to round up our people. He had been a member of the ULFTA and on the board of the Winnipeg People's Co-op but had left in 1935, following a political struggle within our organization. He and a few others joined the Ukrainian nationalist organization.

When I think back, the scene seems almost comical. I was sitting on the side of the bed in my pyjamas. One of the officers barked out, "Peter Prokopchak, you are under arrest under Section 21 of the Defence of Canada Regulations. Get dressed and come with us."

"Prokopchak is not my name," I said. "My name is Peter Prokop." I swung my feet back on to the bed. I had cut off

the last part—"chak"—from my name when taking out my
Canadian citizenship. English people seemed to have trouble
pronouncing the long name and were always twisting it
around.

"It may not be the right name, but you are the man we
want," replied the officer.

I started to dress and they checked my pockets. All I had
was a handkerchief, a blank notebook and my pay envelope
containing around $20, my weekly pay at the time. The
officer wanted to take it away with him but Mary protested.
He examined the contents of the envelope and gave it back to
her.

Two officers, one in uniform and one in civilian clothes,
took me to the RCMP headquarters on Portage and
Broadway. One officer remained in the apartment to conduct
a search. He went through all the newspapers, books and
other materials. He took quite a few books and pamphlets
and even Mary's English Bible. He didn't find any
incriminating or so-called "subversive" materials as he had
no doubt hoped. Mary told me that he was quite rough while
questioning her. He got angry when she claimed ignorance
and refused to answer any of his questions. It appeared that
he was a bit under the influence of liquor.

They picked up nineteen of us in the early morning raids of
that day, some from home, some from friends' homes, some
from work. After a preliminary interrogation at the RCMP
headquarters, they took us to the provincial jail at Headingly
for further interrogating and fingerprinting. I can still see the
young officer who was so preoccupied with religious beliefs
that he couldn't deal with us non-believers. He soundly
lectured Matthew Shatulsky for living without religion.
When my turn came I was ready for his lecture, but our cold
eyes met and he proceeded to ask only routine questions and
fill out the required form. It must have been well into the
afternoon before they gave us our first meal of the day. It
was so bad I couldn't eat it; I don't think anyone did.

The next day, Sunday, we were all herded into a police
wagon. Some of us were manacled but they didn't have
enough manacles for everyone. We were taken to the CPR
station in Winnipeg and led through the basement passage so
no one would see us. There were always RCMP and
plainclothes men with us. Once we got on the train one of the

officers read us a lecture on behavior. If we conducted ourselves properly there would be no trouble. The next stop was the internment camp at Kananaskis. There we were: still no official charges or court appearance, nothing.

Naviziwsky and Penner were already at Kananaskis. Their numbers were 251 and 252. Our numbers ran from 290 to 308. There were nineteen of us Ukrainians, including one J. Pastuch, who was arrested in error. He was released and sent home just a few days after our arrival. Later they picked up Boychuk, Krawchuk, John Weir, Alex Miller, Bill Repka and others, all labor and progressive people.

When we arrived at the camp we had to strip. They took everything, including our watches. I never got mine back. It was a good watch and I'm sure someone recognized it as such. They gave us internment camp clothes to wear—blue denim pants with wide red stripes on the sides, shirts with a bull's eye on the back that looked like a big red sun, and caps with large red flashers in the middle to give an easy target in case of escape. Once we'd changed into our camp uniforms, we were marched out for an audience with the camp commandant. He treated us as worse enemies than the fascist internees. He read us the camp laws and threatened all sorts of reprisals "if we caused any trouble." There was an isolation jail inside the camp, where I spent two weeks on one occasion.

Then the commandant handed us over to the German Nazi spokesman. He made it clear that the Germans could do whatever they wanted with us. The Nazis, however, knew we were a disciplined and organized group. They decided to deal with us as fellow internees. The administration might like to see us fighting among ourselves, but the Germans seemed to realize that that way only the administration would benefit. They told us they knew we were working class and so would not fight us. What they were not aware of was that some of us knew enough German to understand roughly what they were saying amongst themselves.

We tried to have our own spokesman to represent us with the authorities, but at first that was impossible. The spokesman of my barracks was a German fascist from Winnipeg called Lohse. He always complained bitterly about how he had been beaten up in Winnipeg. He'd run into trouble when the German fascists had tried to take away the

Market Square from the workers who held meetings there. The workers would not stand for such an indignity and fought back. As the spokesman for my barracks, I had to go through him to deal with the outside administration. From him you had to go to the compound spokesman of all the internees, who was also a German Nazi, then to the sergeant of the guard, and finally to the commandant. It was a long process.

One of the camp rules was that we must salute all officers. Some saluted, while others simply ignored the rule. I could only bring myself to stand at attention. But Myron Kostaniuk always made a joke of the salute. I remember how he used to demonstratively click his heels together and swing his arm out and up in a salute. Whenever I witnessed that spectacle I always wanted to burst out laughing.

As soon as we got settled, everybody in Kananaskis was assigned to some kind of work. At first they gave us the job of cleaning up the compound. Later, we were assigned certain other tasks. The camp administration demanded that internees do all the work within the compound that was necessary to run the camp. We also worked on certain other projects: forestry, road building and carpentry in the camp. The request from the administration for work gangs for such projects would go to the spokesman of the compound. The organization and division of work was therefore in the hands of the Nazis. So all the best, lighter jobs that were paid for at twenty cents a day and were considered privileged were divided among the Nazis. Generally they shied away from the very hard jobs in road building and forestry. We were usually assigned to the hard or menial jobs which often weren't paid.

Soon after our arrival at Kananaskis camp, Jim (Dmytro) Petrash of Winnipeg and I were on a menial assignment, tearing up the grass on the gravel strip of no man's land between the two barbed wire fences and the two guard towers at the main entrance to the compound. As we were working, a lieutenant came up and ordered us to join the carpenter's crew to work on some urgently needed new barracks. The Nazis were in no position to counteract the lieutenant's order and get their own men on the job, and Jim and I stayed with carpentry until the end of the building program. We were the first among the anti-fascists to get paid work.

When the building project was completed we were assigned

to road building and forest work, also paid work. Then winter came and there was wood to cut, land to clear and fires to be kept burning. At first it was an all-day job but later we won the right to shift work—two shifts, morning or afternoon. The work was quite hard and dangerous. Men had to be very careful not to injure themselves or others.

I was glad to be on the half-day shift because it gave me the other half day to read and study English. Bill Repka was teaching English by that time. For me it was the first opportunity I'd had for regular study of English under supervision. In Winnipeg I had kept hoping to be released from some activities in the evenings to be able to attend at least night classes in English. However, the pressure of organizational work was such that I managed to make only one evening class. But in Kananaskis we had a good class.

As time went on, changes occurred in the various huts. In my hut a couple of the Germans were released. Matthew Shatulsky and Mike Biniowsky decided to move in. Without asking permission they just picked up their things and changed their address. The same happened in some of the other huts. Number 57 became a very special hut. It was one of the larger huts and it happened to become empty. So a number of our comrades moved in. After that we had a real meeting place where we were able to exchange news from home and have political discussions.

As time went on, there was tremendous pressure put on the government by our relatives and a growing public movement. They demanded our immediate release, and pending that, our segregation from the fascists. At the same time we were making our own demands from within the camp for segregation from the Germans. As a result, shortly before May 1 we were finally all given separate huts. May 1 that year was a double celebration for us.

Shortly after we had arrived in Kananaskis we in the camp and our families at home protested our arrests to the minister of justice. Our lawyer, Mr. Greenberg, made representations on our behalf. Late in the fall, hearings were arranged for some of us at the camp under Chief Justice Hyndman. It was a one-man commission with an RCMP assistant.

Greenberg came down from Winnipeg to represent us. He was not very experienced in dealing with harassment of labor people by the authorities. He did not ask any questions or bring forward any arguments or evidence on our behalf. At my hearing he just listened like a witness.

Those of us on the inside had no access to any written or printed materials for preparing our own defence. It was very difficult, especially for us Ukrainians with our limited knowledge of the English language, even to answer the judge's legal questions and especially to argue with him. We knew some of the ordinary workers' language but could not understand or express ourselves in legal terms.

We were all arrested under Section 21 of the Defence of Canada Regulations and, as the arresting officer told me, on the charge of membership in the Communist Party of Canada, which had been declared a subversive and illegal organization. At the hearing, Judge Hyndman threw all kinds of other ridiculous charges at me, at all of us, with some variations depending on what accusations had been made against us by the stool pigeons. They tried to say that I was a danger to the state because I was a member of the Communist Party which supported Russia, which had a non-aggression pact with Germany and therefore was an ally of Germany with which Canada was at war. This was one of the main accusations against all of us who were arrested on July 6.

After Germany attacked the Soviet Union in June 1941, we appealed to the minister of justice, pointing out the injustice of our arrest and continued internment. Our letter stated that "the accusations made that our opinions in regard to the Soviet Union make us allies of the Nazis and disloyal to Canada are proven by events to be unfounded and unjustified." We also pointed out that "reference to the stenograms of hearings before Chief Justice Hyndman in the capacity of an advisory committee will show that the main justifications given for internment were not any specific activities or acts on our part," but the existence of a pact between Germany and the USSR at a time when Canada was at war with Germany. This justified to them the use of the extraordinary powers in Section 21, on the grounds that wartime necessity required the adoption of precautionary measures against persons " 'who might be considered as actual or potential allies of the Nazis.' We have always been loyal to Canada and enemies of Hitler and Naziism in all its forms. We ask for our release in order that we might devote every energy. . . to aid in the destruction of Hitlerism. We are ready to do everything in our power to assist any measure directed to this purpose.''

The minister's reply stated that ''the fact that Germany attacked the USSR and that the United Kingdom and other members of the British Commonwealth promised aid to the USSR in defence of her territory in no way constituted an alliance'' and didn't change the reason for our internment. The minister of justice completely ignored the points we had made.

One of the more stupid charges made against me was that our organization, ''of which I was a leader,'' was fighting for ''the establishment of an independent Ukraine in Canada.'' I told him that he had his information mixed up, it was not we who were talking about an independent Ukraine but his friends, the Ukrainian nationalists. They even wanted independent Ukrainian regions in Canada.

John Naviziwsky and Jacob Penner, who were arrested before us, in June, went through a so-called court trial before they were sent to Kananaskis. They were already in the camp when we arrived. Jock McNeil had an experience similar to that of Mitch Sago and Tom McEwen. Right after Judge Corey acquitted him, he was snapped up by the RCMP and sent to Hull Internment Camp. I mention these three cases as examples of what courts and hearings and justice meant during that period of wartime hysteria when the RCMP ruled supreme.

All others who were arrested on July 6 went through the farce of a hearing before Judge Hyndman. Most of us knew that the hearing would be for appearance's sake only. However, we went along with it for several reasons. The wives of the internees were pushing for it from the outside—some because they really hoped it would release their husbands, and others, together with the Committee for Release of Anti-Fascists, because through the hearings it was possible to let people know what was happening in Canada (our arrests were kept quite secret) and to begin to mobilize a campaign for our release.

In February 1941 I remember that the Germans got quite excited about some news they received through the camp administration or other sources. The Soviet Union had refused to allow war materials to be transported across its territory from Japan to Germany. The news and rumors caused additional hostility towards us. I used to lie on my bunk and listen to their discussions as they raved against the Soviet Union. I gathered that things were not so good for Germany. They of course had access to news and information which we didn't, through sources sympathetic to them.

We did however become adept at getting snippets of news. I was lucky to receive as many letters from my wife as were allowed. The camp administration held many people's mail back. My wife and I, but especially Mary, learned to correspond in an Aesopian fashion. I am sure the censor must have thought that my wife was very stupid to write the way she did. She became quite ingenious at outsmarting the censors, and I got quite a bit of news from her letters.

When referring to meetings being held at the Ukrainian Labor Temple, which was at that time mortgaged to the Workers Benevolent Association of Canada (which had not been declared illegal), Mary wrote that friends and relatives got together at Aunt Tereza's place. From this it was easy enough for me to conclude that the word "Tereza" meant R Z T, the Ukrainian for W.B.A. Often names of people and places were translated from English to Ukrainian or twisted around in such a way that it made sense to me but not to the censor. So, though letters seemed innocent, and perhaps at times stupid, they brought precious news to all of us. On the other hand, any news written openly about the war or about the campaign for our release was usually cut out or completely blacked out by heavy black ink. There were times that the censors threatened to disallow Mary's letters if she continued to write about such matters. They actually withheld some of our mail.

Our daily newspaper, *Narodna Hazetta* (The People's Gazette), the *Fermerske Zhyttia* (Farmer's Life) and our publishing company were not declared illegal by the Order-in-Council that banned the ULFTA. But after our leadership had been arrested, the authorities handed the printing shop and *Narodna Hazetta* over to the Ukrainian nationalists. They continued to publish under false pretences in our own print shop at the Ukrainian Labor Temple and mail it out to our subscribers. The only change they made in the name of the paper was to add "Limited" so it read "The People's Gazette *Limited*."

Readers all across Canada immediately realized what had happened and began returning the paper at the sender's expense. Hungry as they were for news, they rejected the nationalists' lying newspaper. I heard about this from Mary. She wrote that the new people who had opened the mail order business at Pritchard and McGregor weren't doing well because people were beginning to return the goods, wrapped up with additional paper and even rocks or bricks, claiming that they did not order them. As a result, the Ukrainian nationalists' "People's Gazette Limited" venture failed completely and the government then declared the publishing company and its publication illegal.

Although we were always on our guard against all sorts of provocations, one day three of us became involved in an unfortunate incident. Alex Miller, a Norwegian, and I were asked to cart some parcels from one building to another. One parcel fell and broke open and a number of small items fell out. The guard from the store room who was accompanying us gave us a few small items. He gave me a toothbrush and a package of razor blades. Without giving it a second thought, I put the brush in my pocket and continued my work.

Later, to our great surprise, we were taken to the guard at the gate of our compound and arrested on the grounds that we had goods which were not allowed. The commandant sentenced us to two weeks in isolation on bread and water. We didn't put up a defence because we didn't want to point fingers at the man who gave us those items. We later learned that there was a routine pilfering of goods from the parcels, and those goods were being used or otherwise disposed of by soldiers and personnel of the camp administration. To divert attention from themselves, they framed us.

The isolation was not so bad. As it turned out, we were not on bread and water because as a payoff for not revealing the real culprits, the guards brought us good food—juicy steaks the likes of which we had never had from the camp kitchen. Also, while in isolation we were given the world news by the guards. The guards knew and trusted Alex Miller, who was a veteran himself and used to be in the Home Guard. He was also a veteran of the Spanish Civil War.

It was while we were in isolation that we first heard that Hitler had attacked the Soviet Union and that fierce battles were taking place on the Soviet border. It was exactly on that Sunday, June 22, 1941, that we were released from the isolation detention. We immediately informed the rest of our comrades about the German attack on Ukraine. After that the guards got to know us better and because Britain, Canada and the Soviet Union were now allies, they used to come and tell us about the progress of the war.

It was especially difficult for us to be locked up behind the barbed wire after we learned about the German attack. The Germans in the camp were spreading all kinds of rumors. They had a field day taunting us about how quickly "it will be kaput" for the Russians. They were so confident! Their spirits rose sky-high in their assurance of a quick victory. Oh, they were pleased with Hitler and themselves! They even began to learn Russian because they said they would need the language to manage the Russians in that vast territory.

I had one last discussion with one of them in the ablution hut. In a patronizing way he started telling me how fast the war would be over in Russia because no power could withstand the powerful German army. I told him that even if the Soviet troops are pushed all the way back to Siberia the Soviet army and the Soviet people would fight back against the likes of him. He was very surprised to find that I knew German and understood what they had been talking about all along but hadn't let on.

About a month later we were taken by army trucks to the train at Seebe and east to the internment camp at Petawawa, Ontario. All of us Winnipeggers were tense as we approached Winnipeg on the afternoon of July 22, hoping against hope to get a chance to see our loved ones, our friends. But it was not to be. We were on a special train which arrived in Winnipeg around four o'clock. Though it was a very hot day, we were not allowed to leave the train, and about 30 minutes later we moved on. But while our train was standing in the station we were recognized by some of our friends working outside and they waved to us. Mary told me later that by six o'clock that day there were about 2,000 people at the CPR station rotunda.

Mary Prokop

The events which I am about to relate happened more than 40 years ago, but I still have a keen recollection of them because I was so profoundly affected. The political powers that the Canadian government resorted to made me question our concept of democracy. By a stroke of the pen, these powers arbitrarily banned people's organizations and their press, confiscated their property and arrested and interned progressive trade union and left political leaders. We have no right to point fingers elsewhere; it can and did happen here.

By an Order in Council dated June 6, 1940, the Ukrainian Labor Farmer Temple Association (ULFTA), an organization with a Dominion charter, the Communist Party, and a number of other progressive organizations were declared illegal. On Saturday July 6, in the early morning hours between four and five o'clock, raids took place on the living quarters of the leaders of the ULFTA and the editors of *Narodna Hazetta*. Squads of RCMP rushed into homes and apartments, terrorizing the women and children, and arrested the men in a Hitler-like fashion. Those arrested were given no time to pick up even a toothbrush. They were spirited away in less than fifteen minutes—no explanations given, except that they were being arrested under Section 21 of the Defence of Canada Regulations. There was no time for husband and wife to exchange even a few words as to what she and the children were to do in this situation. One stormy morning of police terror and their lives were broken for over two years.

Nineteen anti-fascists were arrested in Winnipeg that day. Most were in their own homes, but some were taken off the street or from work. The raid on our apartment took place around 5 a.m. Four mounties came, one in uniform. One other man was outside in the hallway, a former member of the ULFTA who had turned renegade and became a police informer. He brought the police to our door. We woke to a very loud banging on the door and when I opened it they burst into the room. One went out almost immediately; two others including the one in uniform took my husband Peter away. The fourth, a Mr. Nicholson, stayed to do a search. In the next two years I was to see this Mr. Nicholson many times at all the various meetings and demonstrations.

These gentlemen appeared to have been drinking. I especially remember Mr. Nicholson's red face and bloodshot eyes as he searched our apartment. I had to argue with him to give me back Peter's pay envelope, which contained $18 or $20. I was so completely in shock that I have no idea how long the search lasted. While conducting the search, Mr. Nicholson questioned me about our organization and Peter's activity. Having discussed this possibility before, I knew what to do. I pleaded ignorance. That made him very angry. He tried to provoke me, calling me a very dumb woman. I just answered quietly that he had a right to his opinion. He then started throwing things around even more, the books and various papers and things from the dresser and suitcases. We just had one dresser so things were mostly in suitcases and a small bookcase. After he got through, the apartment looked as if a hurricane had hit it.

Finally a man arrived at the door and they left together, taking with them some mimeographed material, newspapers, pamphlets and books, including a Bible. When I asked why they were taking my Bible, he just glared at me. A few days later when I returned from work, the landlord gave me a package. A few of the things that had been taken were returned, together with the Bible. From what I learned later, similar searches took place in many other homes.

After the raid I sat alone in shock in the deadly silence. So many different thoughts ran through my mind. What to do? I must let the others know what happened. Were others also arrested? I wanted to go to them, but suppose they weren't arrested, I would be followed and probably lead the RCMP to others. Finally I went out and walked around the block a couple of times. Bilinski, one of our elderly members, came by on his bicycle. He was on the lookout for police cruisers which had been roaming the streets of Winnipeg for some time now. He informed me that some of the others who lived in our area had also been arrested.

Towards evening I couldn't stand it any longer. I went out and phoned the police headquarters inquiring about Peter and was told that he had been taken to Headingly Jail. Next day I phoned again and was told that they couldn't give me any more information but to phone back on Monday. On Monday we got in touch with our lawyer who enquired about all those arrested on Saturday. The police informed Mr. Greenberg that they would be interned in Western Canada. A couple more days of anguish and suspense followed as we wondered about the whys and wheres. Finally our lawyer found out that they would be taken to Kananaskis.

After those terrible few days it seemed that in north Winnipeg everything was dead, especially for us, the families of those interned. It seemed that a long, long wake or funeral had begun. It was especially hard for mothers. Their hearts were breaking and they had to continually answer their children's questions about why the police had taken their daddy and when was he coming home. I was spared this agony because I didn't have children at that point. The mothers explained as best they could. But how could they explain to the children what they themselves did not understand? Our husbands had been leading the struggle against fascism all those years, and then when Canada went to war with Germany it wasn't the German and Ukrainian fascists who were arrested but our husbands. "Representations had been made" that they were members of subversive and illegal organizations and were therefore enemies of Canada.

In the middle of the week the wives got together.

Uppermost in our minds was what would happen to our husbands. We immediately decided to protest the arrest of our husbands to the minister of justice and to demand their release. Secondly, we had to think of the children and our economic security: what to do? how to live? how to feed the children? No one had any savings, least of all those on organization pay. It was a week-to-week existence. Even though meat was fifteen or twenty cents a pound, you still had to have money to live. We could come to only one conclusion: the families, and especially those with young children, had to ask for government assistance. The government took our husbands away and now they would have to supply us with food and rent. Our children had to have shelter and food to eat.

The women got quite a runaround because the city said that they were not city dependants and told them that they were federal responsibilities. Eventually the question of jurisdiction was resolved and relief was granted. But only those who were unable to work or who were home with children got relief. Payment was not automatic; only those who requested it and qualified received payment.

I was working at the time in the needle trades for $8 a week. Our rent was $18 a month, so I had to move. We had very few possessions to move, but even so I had to find places for some of the furniture that we had acquired in our two-and-a-half years of marriage. Someone took a chair, someone else a small table, another a sewing machine and still another a sofa and some dishes. I had to sacrifice a second-hand desk which was a treasured piece of furniture. No one had any room for it, and I also wanted to hang on to the few dollars I had, so I gave it as payment to the man who moved my things.

I moved to a small flat to live with friends on Pritchard Avenue. They had only one bedroom and a living room themselves. A small sunroom served as a kitchen. Someone else brought me a rollaway bed and I slept in the living room. Every morning I would roll it away across the corridor into a storage cupboard under the low, sloping attic roof.

I couldn't wait until I received a letter from Peter and so I wrote to him first on July 10 to ask what things he needed. Peter's first letter was dated July 9 and I received it a few days later. He described the beautiful mountains around

Kananaskis and compared them to the Carpathians in his homeland in Poland. I remember that I was almost angry with him. Here I was worrying myself sick over what had happened to him and he writes describing the beautiful scenery of the foothills of the Rockies, the background of their concentration camp. He also asked me to send him two pairs of underwear, two pairs of socks, six handkerchiefs and a towel. Everything had to be new. Of course he had no time to take anything with him on that fateful day.

However, the first letters from Kananaskis brought us at least the news that they were alive and in Canada. After the brutal arrests by the RCMP we didn't know what to expect. We were even afraid for their lives. At least now we were able to write to them and they were allowed short letters to us once a week. All our letters had to be about family matters only. Anything else was blacked out or cut out by scissors. All through this two-year period the rules regarding mail, including heavy censorship, kept changing, harassing and irritating the internees and families at home.

The first letters from the camp came postage-free in brown envelopes, and in big black type at the top of the envelope was printed "Prisoner of War Mail." Thus not only were the internees branded enemies of Canada but also their families. Those markings resulted in many cruel insults to the children and made their lives really miserable.

We became very alarmed and scared for our husbands' lives when we found out that they were housed together with fascists—one anti-fascist per hut with eleven fascists. From the history of German fascism we knew that this could provoke some terrible incidents. We knew that we had to begin the struggle for their freedom. Fighting back fear and loneliness, we forced ourselves to look at our situation realistically. We became convinced that the struggle for freedom for our husbands and comrades would be long and hard.

Some of us were already working, others were looking for work. Those with small children had to stay home and live on the miserable relief they could get. I had gone to work a few months before the arrests and now was earning the grand sum of $8 for a 44-hour week sewing leather jackets. Those who had worked longer and were in union shops were earning $18 to $20 a week. That was about the going rate in the needle trades at that time in Winnipeg. It was possible to live on that when it was added to your husband's pay, but now it was the only money the family could rely on. And there was always the fear of losing your job through illness, or once it was revealed that your husband was an "enemy" of Canada.

But we did have friends; we were not abandoned. Two committees were organized: the Committee for the Release of Labor Prisoners and an aid committee to help the families. I'll talk more about the first committee later. The Aid Committee collected funds amongst friends of the labor movement and from time to time helped those who needed it most. Some families were helped by relatives and personal friends. But nobody likes charity. However, the continual tension, economic deprivation and cruel separation from our husbands had its effect on our health, especially on the older women. Their nerves were strained to the breaking point and some never regained their former health.

The Great Western Trust Company was made custodian of the confiscated property of the organizations that were declared illegal. Shortly after the men were interned, their agents made the rounds of the wives to take stock of their property and assess the riches we were supposed to have piled up from wages in the hungry thirties. Some of the women angrily declared that it was enough that they confiscated the organizational property. The trust company and government had no right to our personal property and they'd better keep their hands off it. Rose Penner took a broom to the man from the trust company. The trust representative came around to my place twice but I was at work and he never did catch up with me. In the end they gave up listing our "treasures."

For a year after Peter was arrested I was managing quite independently, helped by the fact that my friends charged me a very low rent. It was only in August 1941 when I landed in the hospital with an ulcer that I was finally forced to ask for government assistance. Mr. Macpherson came to St. Boniface Hospital to interview me and to check with the hospital as to my condition. He was from the federal government branch that was looking after the relief arrangements for the internee families. He was very sympathetic and a really decent man. He visited me a number of times at home after I left the hospital. They were routine visits because single women, if they were not sick, had no right to receive relief.

Mr. Macpherson used to come to the door and hear me pounding on a typewriter in my room, but he never questioned me about what I was doing. During this time, while recovering from my illness, I wrote many letters to the authorities in Ottawa and newspaper editors and prepared resolutions in connection with our continuing efforts to secure the internees' release. The National Council for Democratic Rights (NCDR) was already organized and was headed by Rev. A.E. Smith and Beckie Buhay, with its central office in Toronto. When my health permitted I was working as acting secretary for the Manitoba NCDR. I told Macpherson what I was doing for the release of our husbands, but he didn't cut me off relief. After I got stronger I worked in the NCDR office that was in the same building as the Workers Election Committee, the offices of Aldermen Jacob Penner and Joe Forkin.

As a single woman on relief I was receiving $8 a month for rent and $7.60 for food, a grand sum of $15.60 a month, and nothing for medicine. However, the federal authorities took care of the doctor and hospital bills. It was just as well that I was on a milk diet because $7.60 a month was hardly enough for food. Women with children received different amounts. Those in their own homes received payments for food only and a little for fuel in the winter. All needed additional help besides the relief they were getting.

As soon as the first shock of the arrests subsided, we women began to meet regularly once a week. We brought our letters from our husbands which we read together, discussed our problems and gave each other support. With the help of our friends we charted a course of action for the release of our husbands and all the interned comrades. This struggle was waged as a general campaign for democratic rights, for the legalization of the ULFTA and for support of the war effort against the fascist enemy. For more than two years we battled with the minister of justice for our comrades' freedom. First we protested the harsh arrests and demanded the immediate release of those interned. Second, pending their release, we demanded their segregation from the fascist internees. Third, we protested their classification as prisoners of war. That meant that they were branded enemies of Canada and lumped together with fascists. Fourth, we insisted that they be considered political prisoners and demanded political status for them.

We received replies to our letters from the minister of justice's secretary. They said that our husbands were interned because representations had been made (by whom was never stated) that our husbands were members of the Communist Party and other organizations that had been declared illegal. It would therefore appear, the letters said, that they were enemies of the state and this justified their internment. We wrote back that the Order in Council stated that after these organizations were declared illegal, if persons continued to meet in membership meetings and continued the activity of the illegal organizations, then they would be arrested and brought to court. The interned labor leaders did not have the opportunity to continue the activity of the organizations, because within a month after they were declared illegal, the leaders were arrested and interned. How could anyone belong to an organization which according to the Order in Council did not exist? We demanded that if the justice department had any charges against our husbands they should state them and bring those interned to trial or else release them at once. The justice department replied that the internments must continue because it was believed that, if released, the men would constitute a danger to the state.

Thus began our correspondence with Ottawa, arguing for their release. Over two years, day by day and week by week, we corresponded personally and organizationally. I wrote more letters than anyone else because I also wrote on behalf of a number of other wives who could not write in English. I also formulated, it seemed to me, hundreds of telegrams of protest from house gatherings. We used to call house gatherings from which we would send telegrams or letters demanding the release of anti-fascists. It often seemed that this correspondence was without end, and at times it was very discouraging.

A few weeks after the first protests to the minister of justice from inside and outside Kananaskis, the department of justice set up the Hyndman Commission, which consisted of one judge accompanied by an RCMP officer. The Kananaskis "hearings" in the latter part of 1940 were for appearance's sake only. We sent our lawyer, Sol Greenberg, to be present at the hearing but the outcome was never in question. Peter received a letter from the department of justice dated October 8, which read:

> Dear Sir:
> I have been directed to inform you that the Committee appointed by the minister of justice to deal with your objection to your detention has recommended that your detention be continued.
>
> Yours truly,
W.R. Jacket
for Advisory Committee on Orders of Restriction and Detention

I understand the same letter was received by others who had gone through the same farce of a hearing. The demand to be segregated from the fascists was also ignored.

Right after the arrests in July 1940, the Ukrainian Labor Temple at Pritchard and McGregor was locked up. Despite this, something kept drawing the wives of the internees to pass by this cultural centre where we had spent so many hours working for various worthwhile causes and enjoying our cultural life. One day, not too long after the arrests, I was walking along Pritchard Avenue in the direction of the Ukrainian Labor Temple when Bill Karpish stopped me and said I should see what they were doing at the Labor Temple. I quickened my pace and soon joined a small group of onlookers across the street from the Temple. Two police officers were standing guard as three men brought out books from our library upstairs. We had a very large and valuable library, one of the biggest of its kind for any ethnic organization in Canada. Their arms were loaded with our books: classical works of Taras Shevchenko, Lesya Ukrainka, Ivan Franko and many others, scientific books, novels. Some of the books were already torn by the rough handling. They threw them into a truck as if they were piles of wood.

At that moment I recalled reading how Hitler had burned books, and I thought that probably the same fate awaited our books. I was not mistaken because that is exactly what happened to our library in Winnipeg and in other cities. Most of the books were destroyed. We stood there frozen at the sight. I was so choked up with rage and sorrow that I couldn't utter a word. As more people began to gather around, the police asked us to move on. Frankly, I did not want to stay and watch this terrible sight any longer.

After our organization was declared illegal, the Ukrainian Labor Temples at Pritchard and McGregor streets and in Point Douglas were closed and guards placed around them day and night. The printing machinery and printshop at Pritchard and McGregor where *Narodna Hazetta* (People's Gazette) and other publications were printed was handed over to the Ukrainian nationalists, supporters of Hitler and our political opponents. In early winter they established the People's Gazette "Limited," but the paper they published still had our name, *Narodna Hazetta*. They hoped to fool our subscribers. Our members used to watch as the new editors and printers stealthily entered the print shop in the Labor Temple and quickly locked the door behind them. They used our building and our print shop and sent the paper to our subscribers.

Our subscribers learned very soon that although the name was almost the same, the content was very different. Besides, there was an underground paper, *Za Voilu* (For Freedom), which kept them informed about various goings on. As soon as our subscribers realized what had happened, they began returning the newspapers at the publisher's expense. But not just the paper—they would include pieces of scrap metal, an old shoe or a rock with it. The new publishers were unsuccessful in their attempt to fool our readers and by May 1941 this farce completely failed.

In Winnipeg, the black marias, as we called the police cruisers, continued to roam the streets night and day. There were more arrests under Section 21 of the Defence of Canada Regulations, more raids, and more intimidations. The homes and apartments of the wives and families of internees were especially watched. We women were shadowed as we got together for our weekly meetings or visited each other. However, in Winnipeg as throughout Canada, the underground leadership began to be active. In Winnipeg we already had the underground newspaper *Za Voilu*. Out west there was a legal paper being published in Smoky Lake,

Alberta, called *Holos Pravdy* (Voice of Truth) and on
August 7, 1941, a weekly newspaper began publication in
Toronto, *Ukrainske Zhyttia* (Ukrainian Life). With these
newspapers, leaflets, meetings and house visits, our people
were kept informed about the general situation in Canada
and in the war. As the war broadened, they began to draw
more and more courage from the struggle of the heroic Soviet
and British people.

Those were unforgettable days. The struggle for the release
of the labor leaders began to deepen and grow. The women
of Winnipeg and Point Douglas helped the wives of the
internees to organize house meetings and socials. As we got
out more information to the people about the internment of
the labor leaders, more people began to join in the struggle
for their freedom. Conferences and mass meetings were
organized, petitions were circulated and letters and telegrams
were sent to the department of justice in Ottawa. They
demanded the release of the anti-fascists and lifting of the
ban on the ULFTA. The high morale of the wives, and of
course our participation in the war effort, made it possible to
meet openly and enlist others in our campaigns. We tied our
efforts for the release of the men with our work for the
everyday needs of people.

In November 1940 we had municipal elections in
Winnipeg. What an election it was! The Workers Election
Committee organized public election meetings. Joe Forkin
was nominated candidate for alderman and Rose Penner for
the School Board. Those two, with Norman Penner, myself
and one or two others, constituted the committee. I
remember one work meeting at Joe's apartment. I had to go
to another meeting after that, but as I came out I noticed the
shadows of two men following me in the distance. Instead of
going directly to the meeting where I was expected, I passed
the house and went on and into the apartment block where I
used to live. I don't know how long they stood behind that
corner a little distance from the front door. I slipped out the
back door, through the school yard and on to my meeting.

We had a hard time renting an election headquarters.
Owners of premises were intimidated and our funds were
very low. We had problems raising money for printing the
election literature, which had to be paid for by cash on the
line. At first it was hard to get going because people were

intimidated. But as they saw Rose Penner and her son, Helen Krechmarowsky (whose husband was also interned) and myself working in the election headquarters our friends began, slowly at first and then more courageously, to distribute election leaflets.

Everyday we saw the black cruiser parked in front of our election office. When I would come in to open the office in the morning, I would find written threats under the door. When I answered the phone there was more abuse and threats. This made it hard to encourage people to come to the headquarters to work. Our enemies took advantage of the situation to threaten us. This angered us, but it was also a challenge. We wanted to show them that we could work under the worst conditions, and we did!

No leaflet distribution was allowed 24 hours before the election, but the night before the election an exceptionally vicious leaflet was issued by William Scraba, who wanted to win Joe Forkin's aldermanic seat. When this matter was brought to the attention of the electoral officers, there was supposed to be an investigation, but nothing came of it. Despite the intimidation and the fact that 40 per cent fewer people voted than in previous municipal elections, Joe Forkin and Rose Penner respectively received 3,012 and 3,200 first choice votes. They weren't elected, but under those conditions we considered it a big victory. We made a great deal of mileage that year in the election campaign. It was a double campaign: for election of candidates and for the release of anti-fascists, including Jacob Penner, who had been previsouly elected three times as alderman.

In spite of the very strict censorship, I managed to notify Peter about the results of the elections. I wrote to him that "Joe and Rose didn't get into the city on November 25 as they were celebrating because their aunt left $3,012 for Joe and $3,200 for Rose. They were her first choices." Writing in this Aesopian manner, I was able to slip bits of news past the censor.

That same fall we prepared for our usual cultural and educational activities. In Winnipeg the cultural club had to rent the Polish Hall on Prince Street, and in Point Douglas the cultural and sports club rented the hall over the Israeli Press building. In Point Douglas there was a band and at the Polish Hall there was an orchestra. Our concerts took place every Sunday in rented premises. Our cultural groups also performed all over the city in connection with the mobilization for the war effort and recruiting.

In 1941 the movement for the release of the internees gained more support in the west. In the east the trade unions got involved. By this time there were some 35 or 40 men interned and imprisoned in Western Canada and around 70 in Eastern Canada. Our Committee for the Release of Labor Prisoners became more widely known and gained influence. In Parliament one lone, brave voice, the voice of Dorise Nielsen, the MP for North Battleford, Saskatchewan, spoke up against Section 21 of the Defence of Canada Regulations and for the release of the anti-fascists. After many protests from across Canada, a parliamentary committee was set up in Ottawa to review the Defence of Canada Regulations. This committee was to receive delegations and written representations concerning these regulations. We knew that it was one more farce on the part of the government. But we all welcomed this step because it meant that the government was forced by public opinion to do something and it gave us an opportunity to involve more people in a greater campaign for the release of the internees.

In Winnipeg a conference and a mass meeting were held at the Hebrew Sick Benefit Hall on Selkirk Avenue near Main Street. The hall was packed with people. The meeting endorsed three delegates: Norman Penner, Helen Krechmarowsky and myself. People donated generously towards our expenses. On March 31 the delegation reached Ottawa and met other wives of internees from Halifax, Welland, Toronto, Port Arthur and Windsor. We had requested a hearing with the minister of justice and the parliamentary committee but up until our departure from Winnipeg we had not received a reply. As soon as we arrived we elected a steering committee. It was composed, as I remember, of Norman Penner, Kate Magnuson, Jenny Freed and others. The parliamentary committee that was set up to receive delegations categorically refused to see us. By telephone we told them we would not move from Ottawa until we got a hearing. We rented a room in the Windsor Hotel where, from our window, we could see the entrance to the Parliament buildings. People in Ottawa supplied us with sandwiches and meals in this hotel room and they opened up their homes at night for us to sleep in.

On Sunday we got in touch with the press and held a press conference. We got good support from the Toronto *Star*. The report stated that a group of wives of the interned labor leaders from all over Canada were crammed into one room at the Windsor Hotel without any money. The article stressed that we were standing firm on our position to get a hearing from the minister of justice and the parliamentary committee and that we would not budge without it. In fact, the Toronto *Star* printed practically word for word our whole brief which we had brought with us. The *Star*'s support brought country-wide recognition to our situation.

That in itself was a victory, for the government had tried to keep the internment a complete secret from the people of Canada from the very beginning. Up until that point the media, especially in Western Canada, had pretty well complied with that wish. In the east there was already some good publicity, particularly the news coverage of the Toronto *Star* and the large number of letters to the editor. After the newspaper and radio publicity and our messages home, we could see from our hotel window how busy the uniformed boys were delivering telegrams to the Parliament buildings. These telegrams were demanding that the minister of justice and the parliamentary committee give our delegation a hearing. With the help of Dorise Nielsen and the Rev. Hansell, MP, from MacLeod, Alberta, we were able to lobby 25 MPs.

Finally, on Tuesday afternoon, the minister of justice and the parliamentary committee relented. We were notified that they would hear us on Wednesday. They had given us the runaround since Sunday but nevertheless we were jubilant. It was the greatest victory yet for us. We saw that the people of Canada supported us in our stand for democratic rights. We made our representations to the minister of justice and the parliamentary committee, but they were not interested in our fate or that of the interned victims. They just kept barking at us from all directions that we were Communists and tried to provoke us into arguments on the policies of the Soviet Union. We refused to discuss that subject.

We stated firmly that long before this our husbands had fought against fascism and spoken against it. They had warned about it in our papers. They were not enemies; they were and continued to be anti-fascists, enemies of Nazi Germany. They should immediately be released to take their place amongst the people to help mobilize them for the war effort against the real enemy of Canada. Pending their release we wanted political prisoner status for them. Secondly, we wanted complete segregation for them from the German and Italian fascists. Third, we wanted the right of frequent and uncensored letters, and transportation paid by the government for monthly visits by wives and children. Lastly, we demanded the repeal of Section 21 of the Defence of Canada Regulations so that no one would ever again be a victim of that vicious section.

The minister of justice had some conversation in French with Madame McManus and Madame Bourget from among our delegation. He felt more at ease with them as his English was very poor. Among other things, he told us that he would take our representations under consideration, but that we should remember that he had received many delegations from the right that demanded stricter implementation of Section 21 against the Communists. That, of course, was no news to us. We knew who our enemies were from the right.

We returned from Ottawa to Winnipeg on April 5 and immediately plunged into the last weeks of the provincial election campaign, which was conducted under the same conditions of terror and intimidation as the municipal elections in November 1940. Our candidate was W.A. Kardash, veteran of the Mackenzie-Papineau Battalion which had fought for the republic in the Spanish Civil War. Kardash's election program called for total war against fascism in Europe, democratic rights and freedom for all anti-fascists at home, and economic security for the people of Manitoba. It was an exceptionally enthusiastic campaign. The last meeting held in Winnipeg before the election was attended by 3,000. In those circumstances it was quite a mobilization. Dorise Nielsen was one of the speakers at that meeting. On April 22, 1941, W.A. Kardash was elected with 5,889 votes. What a victory! Not just for Winnipeg, but for progressive people all over Canada. Then on July 18 we marked yet another victory. In the by-election for the aldermanic seat which had been held by Jacob Penner, Joe Forkin was elected with 3,632 first choice votes.

With these two elected representatives and Dorise Nielsen

in Ottawa, the campaign for release of the anti-fascists grew tremendously. We held successful meetings and demonstrations at the Market Square and at the Exhibition Grounds. More petitions were circulated and more telegrams and protest cards were sent to Ottawa. That was our everyday way of life. At the same time we continued to encourage people to support the war effort and the sale of Victory Bonds. More and more soldiers were in the streets, but in Europe it was still more or less a sitting-down war.

On June 22 Hitler attacked the western Ukraine and the whole of the Soviet Union. Churchill immediately declared support for the Soviet Union as an ally against Nazi Germany. But many months went by before the promised help arrived and three long years before the Second Front was opened. We increased our protests to Ottawa. If the internees were being held because, as we had been told, they sympathized with the Soviet Union which has a non-aggression pact with Germany, why keep them now that the Soviet Union was at war with Germany and was our ally? We quoted Chruchill: "Anyone who goes with us against Hitler is our ally and anyone who goes with Hitler against us is our enemy."

At the time of Peter's arrest I had enquired about when he would return home. I was told that he would be released when the Soviet Union entered the war on the side of Britain. We were now told that the internees' situation had not changed as a result of the shift in the international situation because they were not prisoners of war. There was always a way out.

In the late evening of July 21 I received a telegram from Sinefta Kizema in Calgary. The telegram stated, "Our friends are on the train going east." It seems that some railroad workers at the station in Calgary recognized some of our men at the windows of the train and immediately notified the Kizemas, who were members of our organization and also personal friends of ours. So Sinefta immediately shot the telegram down to me in Winnipeg to let me know what was happening.

First thing next morning I notified as many people as I could and they in turn notified others. I found out that the train was supposed to arrive in Winnipeg at the CPR station at 6 p.m. The news spread like wildfire through Winnipeg and by six o'clock there were close to 2,000 people there. Many men coming home from work with their lunch pails came straight to the station. There were also many police around.

We later found out that the men had been on a special train. Instead of coming at six o'clock, it had arrived sometime between 4 and 5 p.m. Some railway workers in Winnipeg recognized our men at the windows of the train and they notified comrades at the Co-op. They in turn immediately picked up Mary Bilecki and Helen Krechmarowsky who were working at the Co-op and went to the station. Helen and Mary were not allowed by the station guards to go up on the platform. Later I learned that Andrew Bilecki had written a letter to his wife that he had seen her and the children. In any case, the fact remains that by six o'clock their train had left. It was a cruel blow to all of us, especially the wives of the internees, that after a whole year of separation we were not allowed to spend even a few minutes with our loved ones on their way east.

As soon as we had grasped what was going on we shouted to the crowd that we had been tricked. We explained the situation and called on everyone to go to the Market Square. After a short demonstration at the station where we chanted "Release the Anti-Fascists," most of the people who had gathered at the railroad station came along with us to the Market Square. We held a very emotional and fiery demonstration. Norman Penner and some of the wives spoke. A telegram was sent on behalf of the meeting to the minister of justice protesting such a callous and inhuman act. The press did not have a word to say about this event, which shows how the media was regulated by the government. There was a complete blackout in the local press of any news concerning the interned anti-fascists.

We, the wives of the internees, were among the first to join our new organization, the Association of Ukrainian Canadians. We began to knit for Canadian soldiers and collect money for their comfort as well as aid to the Soviet Union in the war against Germany. Later we joined the campaign of the Red Cross to collect medical aid for the USSR. Our organization accepted a quota of $100,000 out of the total for Canada of $500,000. We took the attitude that aiding the Soviet Union was aiding Canada.

In the last week of December 1941 there was a lot of excitement in our progressive Ukrainian community. The Ukrainian National Organization (UNO) announced that on December 28 they were going to open their newly acquired *domivka* (home) on Euclid Avenue in Point Douglas. However, that *domivka* happened to be our own Labor Temple that the Canadian government had confiscated and had sold for next to nothing to the UNO, our political opponents. The former members of the ULFTA sent a delegation to the Winnipeg police department to protest this action and to inform them that there was going to be a big demonstration because these people were taking our building and some of them were outright fascists. On the Sunday of the opening our people came early and occupied the seats inside. There was also a big demonstration outside. When the demonstration got noisy the police came and ordered the nationalists to clear the hall. As they were coming out under police escort, some of our people attacked them. Coats were torn and some hats and galoshes were left behind. There were three or four arrests on the spot. In the next few days more arrests were made, making a total of thirteen. This meant more work for the National Council for Democratic Rights. We had to scout around for bail for those arrested and to prepare for their trial.

During the trial the whole story of the cruel injustice done to our organization came out and also the fact that some of the leaders of the UNO were fascists. Joseph Zuken, who was defending our people, provided evidence of the links between the UNO and Nazi Germany by quoting from articles in the nationalist newspapers.

Demonstrations similar to the one at Point Douglas took place across Canada in front of our halls which had been confiscated. There were about a hundred such halls. The one Labor Temple which was not confiscated was at the corner of Pritchard and MacGregor streets in Winnipeg, although it was closed. It happened that the Workers Benevolent Association (W.B.A.) had a large mortgage on it. After a long process of negotiations, on May 28, 1941, the government finally notified the W.B.A. that it could take over the building. We had no quarrel about the Labor Temple with the W.B.A. They allowed us to rent it any time we wanted. After a hard battle, legality was restored to the

ULFTA which then paid up the mortgage and took possession of the Labor Temple in Winnipeg.

More and more of our members and sons of members were joining Canada's armed forces. Among these were Zane Navis, Eugen Boychuk, Kosty Kostaniuk, Johnny Sawiuk, Harry Lysets and Norman and Roland Penner, all sons of the internees. Imagine how the mothers felt with their husbands behind barbed wire and their sons joining the army! The sons had picked up the battle against fascism where the fathers were forced to leave off. These young men were ready to lay down their lives against fascism even though they carried very deep hurt against the Canadian government for denying their fathers their freedom. As it turned out, Zane Navis and his father John never did see each other again. Zane was shipped out before his father was released, and died in battle overseas. When the boys were leaving Winnipeg for their various training camps all of us were there bidding them farewell and we cried as if they were our own sons.

At the end of 1941 and the beginning of 1942 permission was finally granted by the government for us to visit our husbands in Hull jail. This didn't help us in Western Canada because we couldn't afford the travel costs. By the beginning of 1942 some of the internees were being released, one by one, two to three weeks apart. Every time one arrived in Winnipeg, there always was a big demonstration of welcome at the CPR station. That, by the way, is where I always saw Mr. Nicholson, who did such a thorough search of our apartment when Peter was arrested.

I remember especially the return of Michael Sawiak in January 1942. He was so ill that he was taken from the CPR platform on a stretcher and into an ambulance and driven home. He did not want to go to the hospital and his family complied with his request. He was just a skeleton of the man he was, and when he died he weighed only 50 pounds. It is just unbelievable that the authorities could be so cruel to another human being. He had been sick for over a year but they would not release him until they saw that he was going to die, and they did not want that on their record. They finally released him only after hundreds and hundreds of demands for his release were made by his family and others. During July 1942 his son Johnny, who was in the army, was home on leave. His father was already very ill and Johnny wired for additional leave so that he could stay with his father. He was not permitted the extra leave and I believe he was shipped overseas, because he was not there for the funeral.

On February 22 and 23, under the auspices of the National Council for Democratic Rights, an all-Canada conference took place in Ottawa in the Chateau Laurier. Although the conference was called by the NCDR, it was endorsed by hundreds of activists throughout Canada—Members of Parliament and other elected representatives, union leaders, church people, lawyers and so on, representing over 140,000 Canadians. It was the largest conference of its kind ever held in Canada on the question of the defence of democratic rights. There were 200 delegates present. A delegation of 25 was elected to interview and present a brief to the minister of justice and the parliamentary committee on the Defence of Canada Regulations, which were still on the books. From Winnipeg our delegates included School Trustee Joseph Zuken, Thomas Bain, a railroad worker and a long-time trade unionist, Jock McNeil, also a railworker, and myself.

Quite a large number of Ukrainian delegates attended the conference in Ottawa, and on the last day we got together to interview the Secretary of State Norman McLarty on the issue of legalizing the ULFTA and returning our buildings. At first it was difficult for me to speak, but once I got going there was no stopping me. I just told Mr. McLarty what a terrible injustice they had done to us Ukrainians. I pointed out to him that we were working people and these buildings were built with nickels and dimes contributed by working people and were the centre of our cultural life. They were the places where our children learned music and dancing, and where we conducted other activities that kept our children off the streets.

Mr. McLarty congratulated us, but especially me, because, he said, "Although you haven't got a written brief as the others have, you have told us more verbally then we ever heard about your organization before. My secretary has taken all this down and I will get back to you." Unfortunately, he died soon after this delegation.

When we returned to Winnipeg in April we had a big job ahead of us. All of Canada was preparing for the plebiscite to authorize the government to bring in conscription if necessary. Our organization was working all out amongst the Ukrainian people in support of this plebiscite. Bill Kardash and some others of our people were on the main committee that endorsed the plebiscite. The vote took place on April 27, 1942.

After our return from the conference in Ottawa, the department of justice again set up an advisory committee of three people to review cases of those who were interned in Hull. The hearings began and continued until late May. The parliamentary committee finally recommended the release of all the anti-fascists. Even then it took a long time before all were released, and in the meantime we continued supporting the war effort.

On September 1, I finally got word from Peter that he was being released. Once the interned men were released and sent home they had to report regularly to the RCMP and they were not allowed to leave the locality without permission. I at once sent a wire to Peter at the jail to proceed to Toronto because I had a job there and Peter was also to work in Toronto on the Ukrainian paper *Ukrainske Zhyttia*.

Before I conclude I want to pay a warm tribute to all the other women, wives of the internees with whom I worked so closely during that trying period. Although not all were politically prepared for the harsh conditions we faced, we stuck together and generally the morale was high. Our regular meetings and mutual support and the support of our friends was what kept us going. Our correspondence with our husbands, although heavily censored, also gave us much encouragement and strength.

For me, those two years of life and struggle were like a crash course in university. I remember reading the book *How the Steel was Tempered* by M.O. Ostrovsky. My life was tempered in those years of hard struggle. Our reunion on that happy Labor Day when Peter met me at Union Station in Toronto closed an important chapter in my life, but the events and lessons were not forgotten.

Peter and I both plunged into the immediate tasks on the agenda for all democratic Canadians. Through our paper, *Ukrainske Zhyttia*, and the new organization, the Association of Ukrainian Canadians, Peter devoted all his energies to mobilizing Ukrainian Canadians for the war effort. I went into war industry as a machine operator at John Inglis making components for the Bren gun. I was a steward and then a chief steward in the Steel Workers Union and a representative on the Labor-Management Committee. I worked for the welfare of the workers and for increasing production of weapons for the Canadian armed forces and our allies. In between I did Red Cross work and worked for the sale of Victory Bonds.

Of course, both Peter and I continued our efforts for the legalization of all the banned organizations, including the Communist Party, and the restoration of our confiscated properties. The ban on the ULFTA was finally lifted on January 25, 1945. Most of the property was restored, and compensation for the rest was agreed upon in April 1946 through lengthy negotiations and a lot of compromises on our part.

II
PETAWAWA

Bruce Magnuson

Port Arthur, Ont.
August 1940 - August 1942

When the war started in 1939 I was living in Port Arthur, Ontario. I was the president of Local 2786 of the Lumber and Sawmill Workers Union and Secretary of the Port Arthur Trades and Labor Council. We had over 6,000 members in the union and paid a large per capita tax to the Trades and Labor Congress. We sent a big delegation to various central bodies, including the labor councils in Port Arthur and Fort William and other smaller towns around northwestern Ontario. We published our own paper, the *Timber Worker*, and subscribed to the Communist Party paper, the *Daily Clarion*. Being a member of the Communist Party, I worked to publicize the position of the Party with respect to the war.

Before the war was declared, we had called for an anti-fascist alliance with the Soviet Union and for collective security in Europe. After war was declared, we criticized the Defence of Canada Regulations under which the government arrested people and held them in jail or internment without any trial or charges being laid. There was a campaign to remove progressive people in the labor movement by arrests, harassment and internment. It affected me early in 1940.

My first experience was a raid on our union office by the Port Arthur city police. They confiscated a bundle of the *Daily Clarion*. As I walked in with a briefcase in my hand, the secretary was at the desk and there were two policemen going through our files. I realized at once what was going on. In my briefcase I had some drafts of a leaflet that I didn't want them to get. I wheeled around, told the secretary that I had forgotten my mail and went back out through the door. On the street I met an elevator man I knew and handed him the briefcase. I told him the situation, and then returned to the office with my mail in my pocket, where it had been all the time.

The Labor Council and various unions at the Lakehead made a big protest about this raid and similar occurrences. At the same time, some members of the Labor Council tried to find some excuses to have me removed from my office as union secretary, but without success.

My next experience was with the RCMP. Early one morning in August 1940 I was sitting at my desk in my shirt sleeves, with my coat hanging on the chair and my pipe in front of me in the ash tray. I was doing some writing when a very well-dressed gentleman walked in the door and asked for me. I identified myself. He asked to have a word with me in private. I went outside with him and discovered another gentleman behind the door. I was politely told that I was under arrest.

"What for?" I asked.

"Never mind. Just come along with us," they answered.

They didn't take me to the Port Arthur police station, but the one in Fort William. I wondered why they did that—later on I thought perhaps it was done to confuse people who would be looking for me. At that time my wife was out in the country, about three miles from town, doing some mimeographing in a farmhouse. I had no way of communicating with her; there wasn't any phone where she was, and they wouldn't let me use the phone anyway. With no explanations they put me in a dirty old cell where they had had somebody the night before. It hadn't been cleaned up and it was in a terrible mess.

It was six hours before the president of the Labor Council was able to get in touch with my wife and bring her down to the police station. He had been notified by my office secretary. They eventually found me through a policeman in Port Arthur who knew me and told them where they could find me. I only had a brief discussion with them, and then was kept there overnight. At 4 a.m. the RCMP came and took me on to the train to Petawawa. And that was it.

We left Fort William station about seven o'clock. We stopped in Port Arthur, but there was no way I could communicate with anybody except the RCMP constable who accompanied me on the train. I had to sit with him all the way to Petawawa, a trip that took almost 24 hours. When we got out for coffee and a sandwich, he bought the food and I had to sit and eat with him. I wasn't even allowed to walk around on the train. We reached the Petawawa station about three o'clock the following morning. Petawawa is on the Ottawa River between Pembroke and Chalk River, about 100 miles up river from Ottawa. There was a military jeep at the station that picked us up and took us to the camp, which was in the centre of the Petawawa military training camp. That was August 7, 1940.

I was first taken to a hut where there were a few people I happened to know. Then I was asked to come to the commissary. We were supplied with prisoner-of-war clothing—blue jeans and a jacket with a big red circle on the back—for a target in case we tried to run away. I got army boots, work socks and underwear. Once I got this paraphernalia on, they took away my own clothes. I didn't get them back until I was released, over two years later.

The camp was by a little lake in the woods. I was quite at home there because I had worked in the bush a great part of my life, both in the old country [Sweden] and later on in Canada. Camp life was not new to me. The only thing that was different about this camp was that it was surrounded by two rows of barbed wire which had, at certain intervals, watchtowers or guard towers in which there was an armed guard walking back and forth with a loaded rifle. There were soldiers everywhere and they had all kinds of military equipment.

In Petawawa we had to go out on work parties. They would take ten of us out at a time. The work that we did on the road around Petawawa was exactly like what we did on the trans-Canada highway during the Depression under the Bennett regime. We loaded gravel onto wagons with shovels, and it was taken out to the road with teams of horses. In the winter time we worked in the bush, and that was of course my trade. It was cold and wet, and we did not have proper clothes. The blue denim clothes we wore got wet very quickly and froze, and this made it miserable. You had to keep on working to keep warm. When you had work to do, the time went reasonably quickly. If you had a trade and could work at it, there was some satisfaction in doing something well. Sometimes we held competitions to see who could saw a log the fastest. The worst part of the internment was when we had nothing to do. If the weather was too miserable we stayed inside.

The people in the camp had widely different views about society and the war. Labor activists like myself—Communists and other anti-fascists—had been opposed to war and fascism all our lives, and were also critical of imperialist countries like Britain and France. They had practised a policy of appeasement towards Hitler and Mussolini in the hopes that Hitler would attack the Soviet Union.

This was used as the excuse for an attack in our country on the working-class movement. I was reminded of the words of Pastor Niemuller, a minister of the church in Hitler's Germany: "When they came for the Communists, and I was not a Communist, I remained passive. Then they came for the Social Democrats, and I was not a Social Democrat, so it didn't bother me. Then they came for the Catholics, and I wasn't a Catholic, so it didn't concern me. Finally they came for me..." and by then who could he look to for support?

This was very much like what was happening here. Communists were being harassed, arrested, and interned, but along with them were prominent trade union leaders, people who were not much concerned with Communism, or even with politics. They were being harassed for the work they were doing. The trade union movement was particularly the target, and where there were Communists leading a trade union, every effort was made to remove them from their positions.

Some people in camp were interned because they were sympathetic to fascism and Hitler's Germany. There were German seamen who had been captured and were interned for the duration of the war. There were also Italian fascists from Montreal and Toronto. It was "interesting" that when we were on work parties, people like the millionaire Franceschini, the Montreal industrialist, and Maciola, the big construction millionaire from Timmins, were the foremen. Class divisions were maintained in the camp very much as on the outside. The wealthy Italians were also able to get certain privileges. They could pay people to do their chores in the camp.

Camillien Houde, mayor of Montreal, was interned with us because he had opposed conscription. This was quite common in French Canada. He was a very big, stout man, weighing 350 pounds. The first thing we did when he arrived in camp was to build a structure of boards for him to put his stomach on so that he would be able to turn over on his narrow iron bunk without too much discomfort. Houde wanted to work so he could lose weight. He worked with me and another man; between the two of us we helped him lose 50 pounds in about a month, sawing logs.

There was also a group in the camp headed by the fascist Adrien Arcand from Quebec. Their deputy leader was a fellow from Toronto by the name of Farr. These people were in a hut by themselves. I remember they constructed a throne for Arcand. When they conducted drills they would set up guards, one on each side, with a broomstick held upside down. They would pretend that they were in charge of the camp and that they were just waiting for Hitler to win the war so they could take over the country. They were just a bunch of dreamers behaving in an infantile and immature fashion.

It was difficult the first year in camp because Communists made up a very small group in relation to the large numbers of people that were politically our enemies. By the spring of 1941 the war had begun to change as the Germans occupied France, the Low Countries, and most of Eastern Europe. Finally on June 22, they attacked the Soviet Union. Our relations with the fascists worsened. We began to have difficulty when we went for meals; there was always the potential for a fight.

Now there was absolutely no reason for the government to continue our incarceration. There had never been a valid reason for it, and now there was no justification whatsoever as the Soviet Union became Canada's ally.

We wrote a brief to present our case to the government and

presented it to Colonel Pense, the commandant at the camp. About a month afterwards, the Communists who had been interned at Kananaskis were brought to Petawawa. We compared our statement with a similar statement that they had produced in Kananaskis, 2,000 miles away. We discovered that the two documents were so alike that you would think that one person had written both.

The arrival of our comrades from the west did a lot to boost our morale.

Charlie Murray

In 1939 I was the director of organization for the Canadian Fishermen and Fish Handlers Union of Nova Scotia. I was attempting to negotiate with a number of companies to get some of them to sign an agreement with the union and others to renew the one-year agreement which they had signed the previous year. In June I received the following letter from the minister of labor of Nova Scotia, Leslie Currie.

Dear Mr. Murray:

I have good reason to believe that you are again endeavoring to stir up labor trouble at the fish plants at Lockeport, and I must tell you that my patience in this is exhausted. I am convinced from your actions throughout this whole business that your motives are entirely selfish and that your paramount desire is to keep a job for yourself. If your desire was to organize the fish workers in a strong, respectable labor organization, you would not have adopted the tactics which you did at the very beginning, and now that the fishermen have organized themselves into unions you would at least wait a reasonable time to see if the fishermen were getting a fair deal from the fish companies.

Apparently you have no such desire and your desire now is to again stir up trouble. Well, let me tell you that you will not be permitted any longer to disturb industrial relations in the province of Nova Scotia. Up to the present everyone has been unduly patient with you and your ilk. No matter how many denials and protestations to the contrary you may make, you are a Communist and as such you deserve to be treated in the same manner as I would be treated if I endeavored to carry on in Russia as you are doing in Nova Scotia.

I warn you now to desist from your efforts to create industrial trouble and I warn you too that your conduct will from now on be very carefully watched and examined and if I find that you do not quit this sort of business, then it will be most certainly the worse for you. I am giving you this final warning. My advice to you is to get out of Lockeport and stay out because you have never from the moment you entered the place been of any service either to the Fish Companies or to the workers.

Yours very truly,
L.D. Currie

Disregarding the warning, I went down shore and assisted the fishermen in making preparations for the negotiations which were expected to take place in early October. On Sunday, September 29, 1940, I was arrested at my home by the RCMP under Section 21 of the Defence of Canada Regulations. I was home at the time because my wife was pregnant. I was standing by to take her to the hospital as soon as the labor pains began. With no concern for my wife, the RCMP took me to Halifax. She had to get in touch with her doctor after I'd left and it so happened that the baby was born the next morning.

The mounties wanted to take me directly to the internment camp. I was angry and accused them of persecuting me, my wife, and our unborn child. They could have picked me up any time. All my movements were well known. I think the two mounties who picked me up were genuinely shocked at the timing of my arrest. They seemed quite disturbed when I accused them of using Hitler-like tactics in Canada. They took me to a commanding officer of the mounties in Halifax.

When I told him the circumstances of my arrest he called the doctor and found that my story was true. He arranged for me to spend the night in the local jail and to see my wife and the baby the following day. I was permitted to see my wife for a few minutes, but just in the presence of the officers, never alone. That evening I was taken to the train and escorted to Petawawa.

The mountie who escorted me was instructed by the commanding officer that he should wear civilian clothes and avoid all appearances of a prisoner-escort. During the whole train trip he sat in civilian clothes but with the butt of his gun sticking out of his shoulder holster. A good deal of the time he kept repeating, "Oh, how I would like you to make a break for it so I could shoot you down, you red bastard."

However, I arrived safely at Petawawa and was taken to the hospital because I had a spot of impetigo on my leg. While I was in the hospital there was a celebration held in the compound, commemorating an Italian fascist holiday. A throne had been built for Adrien Arcand. He was formally seated on the throne and he announced the names of the fascist cabinet who were to accompany him on his march to Ottawa as soon as Hitler won the war. Others who were present reported that Arcand made it clear that he not only had an agreement with Hitler directly, as his *Gauleiter*, but he also had an agreement with people in Ottawa. Arcand believed that his Ottawa friends had sufficient authority to open the gates of the compound and the doors of the Parliament buildings in Ottawa. This information has never been made public. I believe that it is quite possible that somebody, somewhere, has the list of that cabinet.

I came through the guard house into the camp still carrying my small jack knife. So far as I know it was the first such knife permitted in the camp. In the next few days, Scott McLean acquired parts of a handsaw blade. He fashioned a handle for it and produced a usable handsaw. He also acquired a file or two. One was used to keep the saw sharp, while others were sharpened to make chisels. These tools were used for woodworking. With them, our group of anti-fascists in Hut 7, the International Hut, organized a handicraft project. Some of the handicrafts were sent out and sold and the money put into the camp fund.

Other items were sent out as gifts for friends or relatives and used for propaganda purposes or sold to raise funds for the campaign for our release. It was important that we got together, cooperated and helped each other to make the artifacts, especially in that trying situation. Scott McLean played a very active role because of his knowledge and skill with woodwork. He had a great deal of natural ability, and he was also a millwright, which meant he was able to do almost anything with wood.

We established a price on all the artifacts on the basis of the labor involved. Twenty cents a day was our rate. A great deal of macrame work was done; one of the popular items was a belt. This led me to specialize in getting bones from the kitchen and making bone buckles to further the hut's camp fund.

Like others, I also volunteered to work daily in the bush and contributed my twenty cents per day to the fund. So far as I know, Bruce Magnuson and I were the only anti-fascists in the camp who had experience as lumberjacks. A number of times a dangerous work situation arose when trees were left notched and partly cut off, or cut off completely but left hung up in other trees. Whenever one of these situations would occur, Bruce and I would be called over to take out the dangerous snarl. This also meant that we spent a good deal of time building fires for the soldiers who were in charge and standing around the fires talking to them.

On one occasion, in the spring of 1941, one of the soldiers that we got acquainted with proposed that he would give us a map of Vulcan Park, where the Petawawa camp was situated. On this map the lodges were marked which were stocked with food and fuel for the benefit of people who got lost. He suggested that we do a disappearing act some morning as soon as we got to the woods and he would make sure that the alarm would not be given until the gang was rounded up to go back to the camp in the evening. We never made use of this suggestion.

Later in Hull jail we had a little radio sent in and it needed an aerial. We all knew that the front part of the roof of the jail was patrolled, but no one knew whether the back part was patrolled. In order to find out we took a nut off one of the iron beds which was not in use, tied a piece of string to it and from the airing court threw it over the roof till the nut hung down on the other side, leaving the string across the roof as an aerial. Then we sat back to see what would happen.

In a very short time the sergeant major and his group made a rush into the jail, up the stairs to the second floor, and began searching the rooms. In the second room they entered they spied a piece of string hanging out the window. They pounced on the string and pulled in a beautiful piece of salami. At any rate they did not find our aerial because the end of it had been let go and it was just blowing in the wind.

Muni Taub

Montreal, Que.
June 1940 - September 1942

I would like to start with my activities in the left-wing political and trade union movements in Montreal before the war. During the 1930s, Premier Maurice Duplessis, head of the Union Nationale government, passed the infamous Padlock Law. This law was designed to eradicate all opposition from the left. The law permitted the padlocking of any hall or house from which so-called communist literature was disseminated. The provincial police raided a number of houses, confiscating all books on Marxism and Socialism. At that time I was active in the Communist Party, in my union and in fund-raising drives for Dr. Bethune's blood transfusion unit in Spain. It was not very surprising that my home was raided a couple of times without any search warrant. Once, the police even climbed into the house via the back stairs in a commando-style raid.

There was wide-ranging opposition to the Padlock Law by trade unionists, CCF people, Communists, Liberals, lawyers and others. My family and I were very active in this struggle. At this stage many newspapers started publishing stories about the Padlock Law, the closing of halls and the attempts to padlock private houses. The police informed me one day that they had orders to padlock our house so we had better get out by a certain date or we would be thrown out. We had no intention of moving; we had a six-month-old baby and the winter weather was freezing cold. Many people came to our home on the day it was scheduled for padlocking. As many as could get in sat inside the house while the police waited outside. Everybody was very tense, but no one on either side moved. As a result, the house was not padlocked, but the threat remained.

A committee was established on the initiative of the Civil Liberties Union to combat the Padlock Law. One of the members, R.L. Calder, a prominent Liberal lawyer and a strong supporter of civil rights, was determined to fight the law in the courts. That was not easy, since no individual citizen could challenge the government in court. This did not stop R.L. Calder. In my case, the house we lived in belonged to my father-in-law, Louis Fineberg. Calder proposed that Fineberg take me to court, demanding that his son-in-law, daughter and grandson be evicted to save his house from being padlocked, which would deprive him of rental revenue. I was then able to contest his action on the grounds that the Padlock Law was illegal.

After many briefs, hearings and sessions in provincial court, the judge ruled, in a very lengthy judgment, that the Padlock Law was constitutional and the government had the right to padlock a private home. As there had emerged a strong opposition to the Padlock Law, we decided to appeal our case to the Supreme Court of Canada. However, in the meantime the war broke out and this overshadowed the issue. The case did not reach the Supreme Court, our house was never padlocked, and the Duplessis government was defeated in the provincial election of early 1940.

I had also participated in a very bitter strike of the Independent Dress Cutters. Our victory subsequently led to the final organizing drive of the Montreal dressmakers who later joined the International Ladies Garment Workers Union (ILGWU). I was a cutter in one of the striking shops, a member of the union executive and of the strike committee. The dress manufacturers tried to break our strike with goons and strike breakers. Pitched battles took place in the garment district almost every day. Some strikers, including myself, were arrested. They charged us with attempting to kill and maim and with spitting on the sidewalk and the scabs. A number of us were sent to jail. I spent ten days in Bordeaux, which gave me a criminal record.

What irked the police more than anything was the deal a few of us made with the hired goons. Strikers would go to hospital as "beaten" victims. They would be released, properly bandaged, after the goons had collected their fees from the manufacturers' agents. It was a mutually satisfactory deal, carried out with the cooperation of a sympathetic hospital staff who were ready to bandage people to forestall injuries. The victims of the phony beating then appeared in public with bandages as incontestable evidence that the goons had done their job. The police learned about the deception only after the strike was settled.

As you can see, by the time the war broke out, the police had a number of counts against me. When the War Measures Act was proclaimed, a member of the Red Squad took the opportunity to assure me that the time would come when they would settle accounts with me and my kind. Frustrated at being unable to find the leaders of the Communist Party, the police decided to pick up whoever they could lay their hands on. The three they arrested in Montreal were Sydney Zarken, Kent Rowley and myself. Zarken was the elected business agent of the Amalgamated Union and worked each day in the union office. Kent Rowley, of the textile union, was also around every day. I worked in a garment shop. The RCMP could have picked us up any day at work, but in order to make it sensational, they came to our homes around three in the morning when we were alseep.

There was a big story the next morning in the newspapers, with our pictures, stating that the police were searching for people who were a danger to society. They accused the three of us of being Communist leaders and detrimental to the war effort. They had to have something to show for all their searching. We were not given a chance to be interviewed or to answer the charges. It was June 28, 1940, and we were taken to military barracks, searched and kept incommunicado. In a couple of days we were taken to the prisoner of war camp at Petawawa. The Civil Liberties Union immediately raised an objection. They protested that these arrests were made without a warrant or any charges being laid. They charged that the police had violated the elementary democratic laws of the country when they turned us over to the military.

In Petawawa we were put to work at such duties as chopping wood. Many of us were not accustomed to that kind of heavy work, even though most of us were workers with trades. Some became sick and were not given proper treatment. Sidney Zarken contracted Burger's disease and in the end had to have his leg amputated. Matthew Popovich subsequently died of a heart attack and Sidney Neal, the editor of the left-wing Finnish newspaper, subsequently died of TB. These tragedies could have been averted with proper medical treatment.

I got to know Sidney Neal very well because I took care of him. He was placed in a separate room when he developed TB. They asked for volunteers among us to be his nurse and stay with him. I volunteered because I knew a little bit about it as I had had TB in 1929. I knew that, although it's a contagious disease, if you take care of yourself you can look after a person without catching it yourself. So we slept in the same room. I'll never forget him; he was a very intelligent scholar. He knew a great deal and I used to have difficulty keeping him from talking. He constantly talked to me about history, philosophy, Marxism and the history of trade unions. He was a walking encyclopedia and I learned a great deal from him. He was a remarkable man; he was very proud and insisted on working right until his death. He was a carpenter by trade and he worked in the barracks both before and after he was moved to the isolation room.

When the colonel would come into the room, everybody would have to stand up, to comply with military procedures. But Sidney was too sick to get up. I remember once the colonel and his adjutant came into the room, and of course Sidney couldn't get up from the bed. I reminded them that he was sick and should be taken to a proper hospital. The colonel signalled for me to be quiet; he wanted to talk to Sidney himself.

"I have nothing to say to you," Sidney said. "You are an inhuman beast and if you don't get out of here I'm going to throw you out."

I burst out laughing. Here was Sidney practically on his death bed, telling this tall colonel with his sergeant that he's going to throw him out. I couldn't help laughing. The colonel blustered a bit and finally turned around and walked out. A few days later Sidney was sent to hospital in the city, but it was done in a shameful manner. They woke us up in the middle of the night and carried him out. They practically stole out with him so that nobody in the camp would see. That was the last I saw of Sidney Neal. He died shortly after.

It happened similarly with Matthew Popovich. Matthew was also a very fine scholar. In addition to his knowledge of general human history, he was particularly acquainted with Slavic literature, history of the Ukrainian people and Canadian history. He had a very weak heart, and I took care of him to some degree as well. He too was taken out from the camp shortly before he died.

The bitterest struggles took place in relation to Sidney Zarken's health. Sidney knew the worsening condition of his legs was Burger's disease. It is a sort of gangrene that develops in the tip of the foot due to a lack of circulation. It is so called because a Dr. Burger discovered that particular disease and also discovered medication that would relieve it to some extent. The local doctor who examined Sidney hadn't even heard of it. He certainly had never had a case like that and he didn't know what to do. No matter what Sidney would tell him, the doctor ignored him.

One day, Sidney asked me to come with him to see the colonel. I went with him because he was walking with a cane and was in great pain. Frankly I did not have much faith in what the colonel would do. I had seen how he treated people, but I decided there was nothing to lose. An appointment was made through the sergeant. It took days and days before we convinced the sergeant to pass on the request for an interview. It took more days before the colonel agreed to see Sidney. We finally got into his office. It's an experience I'll never forget.

Sidney told the colonel what was the matter with his leg and that he needed medical attention immediately. He explained that otherwise the disease would spread and eventually kill him. Sidney said that the local doctor had already examined him and given him all the medication he knew about but nothing had helped. Sidney said he needed to see a specialist. I told the colonel that this was something that had developed many years before and that it was getting worse in the internment camp, particularly because it was winter. The colonel listened, asked a few questions and told us that he would send in a report. He said this was the customary way of doing things in the army and that he would have a reply for us in due course.

At that point Sidney lost his temper and picked up his stick. I thought he was going to hit the colonel, but he started to bang the table and said, "Mr. Colonel, you listen to me. You are looking at a man who is in danger of losing his life and you're asking me stupid questions. You are going to send in a report. You are going to wait for an answer. You have already got the report from your own doctor. Who are you going to send the report to? What reply are you going to wait for? I insist that you phone the prime minister of Canada right here and now."

The colonel looked at him as if he was crazy. "I can't do that," he said in all seriousness.

"I don't give a damn who you call," Sid shouted. "Call the minister of justice. You tell them right now that you have Sidney Zarken here who refuses to leave this room without a decision."

Sid dragged himself over to a chair and said, "I can't stand up any longer but I'm not going to move from this office until I get an answer. I want a promise that you are going to take me out of this camp and to a hospital where I will receive proper care."

The colonel was squirming and hemming and hawing. He looked at me inquisitively as I must have appeared to be chuckling at his predicament.

"The man is right," I said. "What are you going to do? It's actually very simple. Send him out of here, get him to a hospital."

The colonel was quiet for a moment and then he told us that Sid would have an answer by the next day and that action would be taken promptly. At that we left his office.

As we walked away, two guards watched Sidney as if he was going to run away. With his condition! Very shortly after that Sidney got worse and was taken out of the camp. Eventually his leg had to be amputated. This need not have happened if he had had proper treatment in time.

After he was released Sidney went back to Montreal. He was again active in his union and a very beloved leader among the needle trade workers. He was elected business agent in his cutters' local of the Amalgamated Clothing Workers Union. In need of a milder climate, he later moved to Vancouver. He still lives there. One of his hobbies is wood carving, which he started at camp. He has created some beautiful carvings which have been exhibited in Vancouver. He has also written a book in Yiddish, a history of the trade union movement in the old country and Canada and his participation in it.

I remember a big fight between the Italian and German fascists. It's an event that's really stuck with me. I liked the idea of the fascists fighting among themselves. They were usually very friendly to one another, but in this case things blew up. The Italians were in charge of the kitchen and they helped themselves to the best of the food. Our meals became worse and worse. It was discovered that the Italian kitchen staff had parties in the evenings and that they ate the best of the steaks and the salamis. After an investigation we found out that they even smuggled back some food in garbage cans, in collaboration with the soldiers that brought in the provisions.

There must have been a few leaks from some of the Italians who apparently were not given an equal share. When the Germans found out, they didn't like it at all. They held a meeting with a delegation from their barracks and the Italian staff that took care of the kitchen and the preparation of the food. A real fight broke out and a couple of the Italians had their hands and legs broken. One German or Austrian captain was thrown off the roof of one of the barracks. Finally the military officers stepped in, stopped the commotion and rounded up the people involved in the fight. The kitchen staff was changed and the food became a little better. But it all became German-style and for us that was not such a great improvement.

One fine day an Italian professional boxer issued a challenge to anyone that wished to box with him. We had no boxers in our ranks. However, we did have a man who we were convinced was a stool pigeon sent in by the RCMP. Nobody knew him personally and the story he told us sounded suspicious. When we suggested he take on the Italian he said it would be no problem, he'd handle him.

The whole camp was waiting for this boxing match. We all

arrived in our separate groups. The Italian boxer walked up and down the ring showing off his muscles, dressed in a silk gown as if he was appearing in Maple Leaf Gardens. Everyone was waiting for the man nobody knew, who was going to challenge this Italian boxer who had a chest full of hair, huge muscles, and looked like a real dynamite.

Finally this lanky young fellow appeared. He walked into the arena, looked over the Italian and sat down in his corner waiting for the bell. The bell rang and the Italian guy came out swinging, right and left, right and left. All the lanky fellow did was stick out his long, left arm. The Italian couldn't hit him; it was physically impossible for the Italian to hit our man because his arm was so long. Two minutes passed as the Italian boxer sweated away. Then the bell rang and the two of them sat down. Everyone was watching, wondering why the guy didn't try to hit back.

Second round was exactly the same, only instead of turning the right way the cop turned to the left. Now he had his right arm out. The Italian boxer kept trying to hit him. All we saw was swinging, right through the third round. People were getting impatient but the tall guy paid no attention.

In the fourth round, all of a sudden, out of the blue sky, the tall blond guy started swinging from the left and right, from back and from front. The Italian didn't know what hit him. It didn't take more than fifteen seconds before the professional boxer was lying on the ground. He got up but in a few seconds the tall, lanky guy knocked him to the ground again. Finally the bell rang. This time the Italian was actually bleeding. Our man was obviously a trained boxer.

Right after the bout we asked him where he had learned to box. It turned out that he was trained by the RCMP in their school in Regina. He told us that on looking over his opponent and seeing that he had short arms he knew he would be able to handle him even though the Italian was supposed to be a professional. He was going to teach him not to be a showoff. Besides, "our boy" was no lover of Italians. He had made a derogatory remark about Italian "wops" and said he'd wanted to beat one of them up.

Shortly after, we told him, "It's time for you to leave here, because if you don't we'll beat *you* up. We are quite a few and would not worry about going by the rules." Within a few days our boxer friend left the camp. That was the end of that.

Later we were transferred to a jail near Hull. We were very angry to find we were being put in a jail, not a camp. Our spokesman, I think it was McManus at the time, stepped forward and announced to the military that we were not moving in unless a few points were cleared up, namely that we didn't want cell doors locked, that we intended to administer our own internal affairs, that we wanted to be in charge of the cooking of our meals, and that there should be no limit on parcels allowed in. We made it clear that if those conditions were not agreed to we were not going into the prison. We figured that they could not very well force us physically, being so close to Ottawa and to the media. After all, we weren't isolated as in Petawawa a hundred miles away where they could do whatever they wanted.

We did win our demands. We moved in and the cell doors were left open. We appointed our own cooks and we had a spokesperson. We demanded a lawyer, and subsequently J.L. Cohen came to visit us in order to start proceedings for our release. I was released after 27 months of internment.

Shortly after my release I got a job in a fur shop, and in 1945 I was offered a position as organizer in the International Fur and Leather Workers Union in Winnipeg. I worked there for ten years, and was only squeezed out during the merger of the AFL and the CIO. The fact that I was an elected official made no difference to the heads of the unions concerned.

Louis Binder

I was arrested in Ottawa with some anti-war leaflets I had in a baby carriage. I wasn't distributing them at the time. Someone had given them to me in a hurry to get rid of them. Art Saunders and I were tried and acquitted in police court on charges of printing and distributing leaflets attacking the government's war policy. We were told that we would be released. They let us out through a side door, not the regular gate. A small sidewalk led from the building to the outer wall, and as we got to the front gate there were two plainclothes men waiting for us. The minute we saw them we knew that something was up. They flashed their RCMP badges, put us in their car and drove us up to Petawawa. This was in June 1941.

We had no idea where we were going. We spent the evening in a cell on the outskirts of the camp. We could see people walking around inside the fence with targets on the backs of their clothes but we didn't know who they were. We were a bit afraid. I remember discussing it with Art and wondering where we were and what was going to happen to us in the morning.

The camp was a huge area enclosing a series of large huts. We were placed in a hut with a lot of Italian Canadians who had been arrested in Canada. We were worried about what our reception would be. They clearly outnumbered us and we didn't know how they would treat us. Their leaders soon approached us. They told us that they knew who we were and didn't want any trouble with us. They wanted to be sure that we would not give them any trouble. We were quite happy with that arrangement.

Later other left-wing people, some of whom I knew, were brought into the camp. We were all put on work details. We bitched about it, but it was a way of getting out of camp and it wasn't very hard work. We had to load gravel onto a truck and then we waited twenty minutes until the truck came back for the next load. The main thing I complained about was that after we had done a day on the work detail, we would often come back and find that the cooks hadn't saved anything for us to eat.

One day after coming back from work, we washed up and walked over to the cook shack for something to eat. They gave us a bowl of minestrone soup. I picked it up, walked over to the gate, and said to the guard, "This is the kind of bullshit they are feeding us."

I held it out for him to look at, and then threw it over the inside gate between the two wire fences. Then I turned around and walked back to the hut. Within five minutes a detail of soldiers took me out and locked me up in a jail on the outside of the compound. It was very small, about 6 feet by 4 feet, just room enough for two bunk beds. The lower part was wood and the top was wire, so I could see out to the compound.

Outside my cell was a sergeant. I can see him to this day. About 7 or 8 p.m. he got out a bottle of whisky and began to drink it with a couple of soldiers. He kept calling me all kinds of names for the things I supposedly did to his commander, who he claimed was a very fine fellow. I got the idea that these guys were liquoring themselves up and were going to come and visit me. I jumped on top of the bunk and took off one of my shoes that had steel cleats on the back. I told them that anyone that came in the cell would get whacked with it. On the opposite side of the cell there was a peephole where I could see through into the compound. When one of our fellows came past, I told them the situation. Anyway, the soldiers never did come into my cell.

A day or so later Joe Wallace was put in a cell next to me. The boys started to demonstrate a bit. They marched around and hollered and shouted. I could see them but I didn't know what it was all about. The next thing I remember was the evacuation. Some friend came and told me that we were being moved out. I was scared. I thought that they might leave me as I had not received official notice about moving. The day of the move, all the trucks lined up and the prisoners marched out and got on. No one as yet had said a word to me about moving. I was still very worried. But just before the last truck moved, the sergeant came along and opened the door and told me to get on a truck. I asked about my clothes and he told me that they were already on the truck.

They moved us to a brand new jail near Hull, Quebec. Time passed much more quickly there as we were able to organize many activities. My mother came to visit me there. We were allowed in the same room, and I don't think that there were any soldiers there. We only had about half-an-hour. They rushed it because there were a lot of other visitors as this was the first time visits were allowed.

I was one of the first ones released, perhaps because I was the youngest one there. I visited my brother, who had been sent to Kingston Penitentiary, and then went home to Winnipeg. I had been in the army before my arrest so I went to Ottawa and joined up again. I joined the Signal Corps, took my basic training and finished the advanced training. When it came time to go overseas, they took me off the draft and put me on a job teaching wireless. I was changing tapes and things like that. Then I was offered a posting to Vancouver. Very stupidly, as I thought later, I turned it down.

By this time my brother was out of the penitentiary and was overseas. I wanted to get overseas and join him. I kept asking the CO for an overseas posting, but he refused until one day when the inspector general visited the camp. Anyone had the right to take a grievance to him. I asked for an appointment. The CO of my company wanted to know why I wanted to see the inspector. I said I wanted to complain about being taken off the draft and not allowed to go overseas.

"If we put you back on the draft, would you still want to see the inspector general?"

"No," I said, "I'd have no reason."

So they put me back on the draft and I went overseas about three weeks later.

C.S. Jackson

Toronto, Ont.
June 1941 - December 1941

My case was exceptional in that I was interned following the passage of Orders in Council which prohibited internment without trial. I was picked up for my labor activities. It was a critical time for unions throughout the country.

The sharp recession of 1937 brought to a halt the growth in union membership initiated by the CIO; there were massive layoffs across Canada. It wasn't until after Canada declared war against Germany on September 9, 1939, that industries again started to increase production. Even then the startup was slow due to the "phony" nature of the war. Canadian and British troops didn't see any action until after the fall of France and the subsequent invasion of the Soviet Union by Hitler. When war production began in earnest, the Canadian corporations refused to accept a five per cent limit on profits, as suggested by the government, and held out for a "cost plus" agreement.

By mid-1940 workers in industry after industry, pressured by rising prices, eagerly joined unions. They were also encouraged by the tremendous growth and success of the CIO organizing drive in the United States. Industry leaders were brought into government commissions and the War Measures Act was used to block union organization. Pat Sullivan, head of the Canadian Seamen's Union on the Great Lakes, was whisked away from the bargaining table and interned. Fred Collins, who led the battle of the Stratford furniture workers, was also held. This was the case across the country as union leaders, under the allegation of being "dangerous Communists," were detained. The leaders of the Ukrainian Labor Farmer Temple Association and active members of the Communist Party were also arrested in an attempt to thwart the rising demands of the working people for the right to collective bargaining and union contracts.

As war orders came into the Canadian General Electric plants at Davenport and Ward Street in Toronto where I worked, organization of the workers by the United Electrical Workers (UE) was gaining momentum. By early 1941 UE represented a majority of the workers at the Davenport plant. Growth at Ward Street was much slower because of the workers' hesitancy to join the union—most were women in industry for the first time. At that time the UE in the United States had already achieved a national agreement with General Electric.

In early 1941 we sought a meeting with the company to start negotiations for a collective agreement. The manager at Davenport, a Mr. White, refused to meet with the union. A noon-hour meeting was called for June 6 at the open field across from the plant. The anger of the workers at the company's refusal to meet the union expressed itself in a vote to stay out of the plant until the company agreed to meet. That was the start of a week long "holiday." Although the War Measures Act prohibited strikes and theoretically provided for conciliation under the Industrial Disputes Investigation Act (IDIA), which had been on the books since 1927, it had seldom been applied.

Our union was attacked daily in the media and threatened with every kind of penalty for injuring the war effort. The IDIA carried penalties of $100 a day for every day a worker stayed away from work and $1,000 a day for the union leader. The union called on the government to set up a conciliation board, but got no response. The press continued to hound us. At the end of the week's "holiday," charges were laid against seventeen stewards and officers of the local and against me as president of the union. Trial date was set for Wednesday, June 24.

We held a membership meeting at the end of the week and had a lengthy and heated debate on whether to continue our walkout. Late that night we decided to return to work and keep the pressure on the government for a conciliation board and recognition of the union. At the same time the union, on the crest of a new wave of organizing success, was seeking recognition at the Westinghouse plant in Hamilton.

Following the return to work at Davenport on the weekend of June 20, I attended a general executive board meeting of UE in New York City. At the end of the meeting I was informed that the RCMP were awaiting my arrival in Toronto to pick me up for internment. I was advised to fly to Buffalo instead of Toronto. It's significant that the day I spent at the Hotel Buffalo was Sunday, June 22, the day that Hitler invaded the Soviet Union. Churchill announced at that point that Britain and the USSR were now allies against Hitler.

In Buffalo I hired a small private plane and arrived at the Toronto airport about five o'clock on Monday. The union planned to have a large number of union members congregate at the airport. We came in over the Toronto airport as planned, only to see a long line of autos streaming away from the airport. I assumed something had gone amiss, but on landing and clearing customs and immigration, I found a large demonstration of UE members outside the airport. The autos I had seen leaving were carrying public figures who were at the airport to celebrate the opening of a Toronto-to-Buffalo air service. At the airport I was told that I should go into hiding and appear at the trial of the stewards and myself to fight the internment order. But the best laid plans of mice and men...

My car, which I had parked at the airport when I left for New York, would not start. Instead of speeding away to a hiding place, here I was trying to start my car. My wife and I and Harold Kinsley, a UE staff member, climbed into Kinsley's old Ford and started to tow my car away from the airport. We were met on the airport road by armed RCMP and Toronto police. They took me into custody. That's when I learned that they had removed the distributor points from my car.

I was taken to my apartment while Detective Mann of the Red Squad searched the place. He was particularly interested in my library. Any red-covered book, or copies of *Hansard* which had underlining, were seized. Mann had already told me I was going into internment, so I amused myself by quipping at him incessantly as he scrutinized my books.

From the apartment I was taken to the police headquarters on College Street, photographed and finger printed, and then locked up. Around 10 p.m. I was taken under RCMP escort to Union Station to catch the 11:30 train to Ottawa. I had had no supper, and only on my insistence was I allowed to eat at the counter under guard of two plainclothes RCMP. We arrived at Ottawa in the early morning and were met by four uniformed RCMP who were to take me to the internment camp at Petawawa. They were in a hurry to get going. Again I demanded to eat and was allowed the pleasure of breakfast at Murray's surrounded by four mounties.

En route to Petawawa I requested an opportunity to urinate. For a while they kept on driving, but finally they stopped out in the country alongside an open field. I was allowed to get out and walk a few paces out into the field. My four guards surrounded me while I relieved myself. It struck me as ridiculous. Did they really think I might try to run away in that open field where they could pick off a rabbit at 100 yards or more?

Arriving at Petawawa, I was issued a prison uniform and put in a hut with interned Italian Canadians. I subsequently discovered that I occupied the bed that had only recently been vacated by Franceschini, the big time contractor who had just been released. After two days I was transferred to the unionists' hut where 83 anti-fascists lived. We were the most crowded hut in the camp. The huts were wooden structures about 70 feet by 25 feet, with double bunks and straw palliases for mattresses. In the middle was a large barrel stove.

Each hut had its own committee. Ours was an elected committee responsible for representing us in job allocation and housekeeping. Each hut had to supply a quota of workers every day for work inside the compound, such as the clean-up of the grounds, latrines and so on, and another quota for work outside the compound. On work gangs outside the compound the pay was twenty cents per eight-hour day. We discovered that the contract for outside work was held by the Franceschini who had been an internee, and that he was getting $3 to $5 for our labor. We rotated the work days among our group which amounted to about three days or 24 hours work per week.

Among our group I was the most fortunate in receiving regular parcels. The union had arranged for each UE local to make up a parcel in turn. The contents of these parcels were distributed by the hut committee so that everyone benefited from the UE contributions. The YMCA provided us with books and sports equipment. An ironic touch was that the library included books by Marx and Engels, for use by people who had been interned for, among other things, having such works in their private libraries.

With time on our hands, most internees tried to work at one craft or another. Woodwork was favored by a number, and some beautiful pieces were turned out, including inlays of all kinds. Others worked on bones from the cookhouse that they boiled, bleached, and then carved. The tools were homemade, using the camp cutlery. Some used the cellophane from cigarette packages to make belts, while others used wool sent in from the outside. It is truly amazing what talents surface in time of need.

Our group carried on a consistent struggle to win political prisoner status instead of being regarded as prisoners of war. Petitions from inside the camp and from organized groups outside were regularly sent to the government on this issue. Our campaign came to a head in the late summer of 1941 when we held a strike which resulted in our being transferred from Petawawa to a new but unused jail in Hull, Quebec. The transfer arrangements were high drama, indicating the government's hysteria about us. We were taken to the railway station at Petawawa in army vans, with eighteen men in each van accompanied by two armed guards. Motorcycles, armed with machine guns, drove between the vans. We entrained for Hull, again under very heavily armed guards.

It's ironic but a few weeks later we read that the army had transferred about 300 Nazi prisoners of war from Belleville to the north with only a small handful of guards. The government obviously considered us anti-fascists more dangerous than the real prisoners of war.

Under the War Measures Act, the custodian of enemy

property had the authority to seize the assets of an internee and cut off phones, other services, and credit to the wife remaining at home. In my case, my car was seized, my phone cut off, and my bank account with a balance of $83 impounded. When I tried to get even that paltry sum released to my wife, the custodian withheld 10 per cent of it to meet the so-called cost of administration of the transaction. After three months of incarceration, they wrote to me requesting my approval to sell my car, against which they would charge storage. My wife would not receive a cent out of the sale. Naturally I refused. Upon release I found that my car had been returned to my garage, and that they had "fixed" it. The RCMP had sugared the engine and it was a write-off.

As I indicated earlier, I was interned following the passage of Orders in Council which prohibited internment without prior trial in court. Unfortunately that order had not been gazetted before I was picked up. The Toronto *Star* printed an editorial protesting my internment under these conditions. The international UE carried the fight for my release to the British and Canadian embassies in Washington. The week I was interned the Westinghouse local of UE organized a one-day walkout at the plant. They included the issue of my release with their demands for a conciliation board to win union recognition and a collective agreement. The growing public demand for the release of the political prisoners resulted in the government ordering individual hearings to be held in the camp, in order to furnish evidence to justify our internment.

It was evident from the charges presented against me by the government committee of Taschereau, Lapointe and others that they had no case to justify my internment. The main concern of the examining judge was my knowledge of the legislation on trade union rights. It was clear that they were only focusing on the "illegal" strike at the CGE plant and that they were interested solely in protecting the corporation. This was borne out subsequently, some 38 years later, when justice department files were made available to the public.

In several letters to the minister of justice, the minister of labor stated the following:

The same gentleman who succeeded in creating the

strikes at the Canadian General Electric plants in Toronto has now moved into Hamilton, and last night and the night before called meetings of the workers in the Westinghouse plant. This plant, I am advised, is about as important as any in Canada in connection with our war work. I apprehend, unless something can be done, that he will be able to foment a strike within a week...

Jackson was detained on the 19th June, 1941, in accordance with the order of the Minister of Justice...

Jackson's case is at present (19th November, 1941) under consideration by an Advisory Committee appointed by the Minister of Justice pursuant to the provisions of the Defence of Canada regulations, and it is anticipated that a recommendation will be made shortly.*

Several points in the above are interesting. First, the order of detainment apparently was issued on June 19, 1941, but is written as if I was already detained. The fact is that it was Monday, June 23, that I was picked up. The rule was, evidently, detain, then investigate.

During my internment, CGE at Davenport held secret meetings with the local negotiating committee in an attempt to buy them off. On December 19, 1941, they called the committee to a meeting of which no union officer was notified. Management told them that I was going to be released from internment the next day, and that, if they wanted wage increases they had better sign an agreement between the company and the committee—not the union—that day. They signed. A select group of workers including the committee, got increases, and the union did not get recognition—a real company union set up! It is important to note that I had no notification that I was going to be released until around noon on December 20, but CGE was informed in time to get an agreement signed before my release. Government/corporation cosiness was never clearer and the culpability of CGE in my internment became

*There is much more in justice department memos. See files in Privy Council office RC2, Series 18, Vol. 2, File D-15 in the Public Archives of Canada.

apparent.

Later events gave even more evidence of the activities of CGE in trying to smash or buy off the UE. Within a couple of months of my release I received a call from the vice president of CGE asking for a meeting with George Harris and myself. At that meeting Turner, after a few crude jokes, got down to business. He said that he knew that we young fellows were anxious to have a union in the electrical industry and that we were working hard at organizing but hadn't had much success. He suggested that he was in a position to remove obstacles to our organizing the industry. All he was asking was if we would be willing to cooperate with him. When I said, "How do you spell cooperation?" he got the message that we weren't in the company union business. End of meeting.

In 1980 one of the retired top executives of CGE voluntarily offered the information to an enquirer that he had personally requested the justice department to intern me to get the union out of the company's hair. It is quite clear from my case, and that of many other union leaders, that the Canadian corporations, concerned about the rapid growth of unions, pressured a willing government to use the War Measures Act to try to stop the organizing drives. The Canadian Congress of Labor leadership, steeped in anti-communism, did not lift a finger to help the interned labor leaders in our fight for release. On the contrary, they actually aided the government and the employers by supplying "evidence," as revealed in other government records available in the Public Archives of Canada today.

I was released after six months, one of the shortest periods of internment. This was due to two things: first, the public role played by our union in both Canada and the United States; and second, the course of the war and the rising public antipathy against the government's policy of internment of labor leaders. It's interesting to note that at no time was I charged with being a Communist.

Ben Swankey

The highlight of our stay in Petawawa was, undoubtedly, the series of events flowing from the visit to the camp of Timothy Eden, brother of Anthony Eden, Britain's foreign minister and Prime Minister Churchill's right hand man. He was apparently on a tour of inspection in his capacity as an official of the British government. When he came to our huts, one of our group, Joe Wallace, spoke up.

"We are not enemy aliens," Joe said, "we're Canadian anti-fascists."

Wallace was a poet, a Communist, a practising Catholic, and in his youth had been a protege of Prime Minister Wilfrid Laurier. The camp authorities looked on this action with consternation. He was immediately arrested and put into a jail cell in the internment camp.

We held a meeting and decided to protest his arrest. We agreed to stage a protest march around the camp. The camp commandant, in something of a panic, called in the army from the military training camp nearby. The troops arrived, armed with machine guns, and took up strategic positions around the camp perimeter. We were given an order to either disperse within a certain time limit (I think it was ten minutes) or be shot. We marched until the last few seconds and then dispersed and went to our huts. It was touch and go as none of us knew if a trigger-happy officer might give the order to fire at any moment.

When we returned to our huts we were ordered to stay inside. The camp commandant then immediately had a barbed wire fence built around our huts. So there we were surrounded by barbed wire in our own special internment camp within the larger internment camp also surrounded by barbed wire. We then embarked on a campaign to be moved out of Petawawa into a camp of our own as an interim measure prior to our release. We managed to get word out about what had happened, and considerable publicity was given to the incident and our demands.

Before long we received word that we would be transferred to another camp. We looked on this as a victory but we let the authorities know that we wouldn't move unless Joe Wallace was also transferred with us. He was still being held in a jail cell within the camp. Our demand was granted. When we were transferred, Joe came with us.

While Joe was in solitary confinement, he composed a number of poems. This one particularly appealed to me.

Your Arm Is Strong Enough

Your arm is long enough
  To reach the stars.

Your arm is strong enough
  To break all bars.

Your arm has skill enough
  To set all wheels in motion,

To skim the sky with ships,
  To mine beneath the ocean.

And yet your golden guests
  In their eternal south

Swear that your arm's
  Too short,
  Too weak
  Too lame,
  To reach your mouth.

Tony Bilecki

When we came to Petawawa we were again locked up with fascists, this time Italians. There was a lot of discontent at the camp because the rich Italian internees had special privileges. They didn't eat with us in the kitchen. They ate separately at a special table, served by other Italians. They had a lot of money to throw around and even the guards were very nice to them.

When work was assigned, we were the ones who got the hardest jobs. For instance, I was assigned to the crew that hauled gravel. They placed most of us anti-fascists on this job with a man standing over us, yelling at us to work faster and faster. Naturally we didn't respond to his yelling. We just did our job in an ordinary manner. What could they do to us? Fire us? Put us in jail?

There were about 100 of us anti-fascists so we were able to do things that we would not think of doing at Kananaskis. Although we were still forbidden daily newspapers, sometimes we received news through friendly guards or by reading the papers the rich Italians had delivered to their huts. When good news came from the Front, we immediately staged a demonstration. We would all buy cheap two-for-five-cent cigars, light them (even those that did not smoke), and then parade around the camp. We wanted everybody to know that we were winning at the Front and that we were celebrating.

This angered the fascist leadership of the camp. They tried to punish us indirectly by giving us the worst possible food. They served us macaroni at every meal. Even if our day's work was not very hard—like swinging a shovel full of gravel and loading trucks in the fresh air—it was enough to give you an appetite. So what did we get? Macaroni again, with some pieces of fat that none of us could eat.

Once, the food was rotten and smelled so bad that we just could not eat it. We found maggots in some of the macaroni and decided that we would not take it any longer. When Louis Binder was thrown into a jail cell for protesting about the soup, we launched a protest demonstration. At one point we decided on a hunger strike, "Remove us from Petawawa or we starve." Shortly after that the order came for us to get ready to move.

William Repka

When we reached Petawawa we were taken off the train and loaded onto trucks, accompanied by French-Canadian soldiers carrying tommy guns. The trucks made their way to the camp in a convoy with jeeps bearing machine guns driving ahead and behind. When we got there we were ordered to get off, to line up and be counted. Then we marched into a large barracks. I distinctly remember that we scrambled for partners for upper and lower bunks. As soon as we were settled, we became acquainted with the other anti-fascist hut. In it were Misha Cohen, Norman Freed and many others who had been interned from Eastern Canada. We spent the first few days exchanging experiences.

The dining room at Petawawa was much older and dirtier than the one at Kananaskis. They both had the same system; you lined up to get your meat and potatoes, and whatever, and then went to a table. In Petawawa we had to eat in shifts because of the smaller size of the dining room. The most terrible thing for me in Petawawa was that my stomach did not agree with the water, or the other way around, and I had a terrible time with stomach pains. Whether it was from the change in the water, or the stuff they put into it, many people developed various illnesses after the move.

The main advantage of Petawawa was the hut arrangement. We had two huts of roughly 50 men apiece, joined by a washroom, ablution huts and toilets. This was much better than the small twelve-man huts and primitive facilities in Kananaskis. Most important, we were immediately brought into the anti-fascist hut and separated from the Germans and Italians.

The Germans were very sports-minded, and they organized boxing matches among themselves. However, the Italian defeated the German champion and then challenged our group to a match. The Italian was a muscular, hairy-chested barrel of a man, with a jaw like a cement block, arms like tree branches, and the neck of a gorilla. They wanted us to put up a man to fight him. This posed a problem for our group of editors, writers and union organizers.

It so happened that there was a clean-cut Canadian youth, perhaps 25 years old, in our hut. He was constantly on the parallel bars and the rings, doing exercises for hours. He was in absolutely perfect physical condition. Some of our people immediately suspected him to be an RCMP plant. After much discussion somebody had an inspiration. Why not put the cop against the Italian? The man agreed, in fact he seemed eager, provided Norman Freed was the referee.

When the two stood in the ring, it was a clear illustration of the difference between a lightweight, fast-moving athlete and a brawny gorilla. If the gorilla had even swatted the cop once, he would have flattened him. But for all his lunging, the Italian could never get near the cop, who was fast and light on his feet. He kept jabbing and banging at the Italian until the bigger man became exhausted, stumbled and hit out blindly. Norman Freed declared the fight over to save the Italian from further punishment.

There was also a chess tournament in the camp. The Germans and the Italians played each other and this time a German won. The champion was blonde, 200 pounds, 6 foot 2 inches, and a perfect specimen of humanity and the master race. He challenged one of us to a match. Here our problem was a good deal simpler. Saunders, our champion, weighed 110 pounds, was about 5 feet 4 inches, and had thick glasses—clearly one of nature's inferior specimens. The Germans were all chuckling that their super race, as exemplified by their champion, was going to mop up the floor with this Jew in the chess tournament. But to the amazement and chagrin of the master race, Saunders, a mathematician, wiped the floor with the blonde giant.

Meanwhile the fascists in the camp were becoming increasingly hostile towards us. It became obvious that if we remained in the camp, violence could erupt and somebody could get killed. It is hard to describe the fanaticism of some of the Nazis. The sun rose and set on Hitler, *Der Fuehrer*. They were positive that they were going to win the war, and emphasized this with their song *Morgen Die Ganze Welt*—

Tomorrow the World. These fanatics represented a real danger to the anti-fascists in Petawawa as others like them had in Kananaskis.

Another problem was that the camp commandant at Petawawa was a nervous wreck. He had not gone overseas because of a severe nervous condition. Thus we never knew exactly what he would do under pressure.

The whole situation in Petawawa came to a head when Anthony Eden's brother was visiting the camp. He was escorted through the gates by a platoon of soldiers as he looked the camp over. Pointing to our hut, he asked the officer in charge who we were. The officer replied that this was the Russian Communist hut. Joe Wallace happened to be sitting outside the hut. He was a Catholic who never swore but he couldn't resist denying the slander.

"That's a god-damned lie," he said. "This is the Canadian anti-fascist hut."

The officer in charge immediately said, "Arrest that man." Joe was put in a jail inside the compound. There was an Italian fascist already in the jail who was stir crazy and talked loud and without stopping. It didn't help matters that Joe didn't understand Italian and so didn't know what he was talking about. The whole episode was very upsetting for Joe.

In spite of this Joe wrote a beautfiul poem while in the jug.

How High, How Wide?

My prison window is not large,
Five inches high, six inches wide,
Perhaps seven.
Yet it is large enough to show
The whole unfettered to and fro
Of heaven. How high, how wide, is heaven?
Five inches high, six inches wide,
Perhaps seven.

Soon after Joe was jailed, our youngest internee, Louis Binder, threw his bowl of soup over the fence near the guards to protest about the food. He too was immediately arrested and joined Joe and the Italian in the clink. We recognized that these events arose out of the changed international situation and the growing tensions. This was a very sensitive situation and we had to do something about it. Our hut organized a march around the jail. We sang "Solidarity Forever" and "Hold the Fort For We are Coming" and various labor songs to cheer up Joe and Louis in their incarceration.

I have been on many picket lines, but I must say that this one was special. The commandant reacted in a fury. He sent his soldiers on running drills between the outside and the inside wires. They carried rifles with bayonets fixed, tommy guns and rounds of shells. He was obviously prepared for anything. All the Germans and the Italians in the compound were instructed to lie down on the floor so they would have less chance of picking up stray shrapnel and bullets. We were blithely swinging along behind Norman Freed and Fred Collins, singing our heads off. I think I sang loudest of all to hide my nervousness. It was a very dangerous situation. We were afraid that the commandant might order the guards to fire, or that someone might get nervous and fire without an order.

After parading for some time we returned to our huts. At once a small army of soldiers came into the compound on the run and surrounded our two huts. Trucks pulled in with stakes and more barbed wire, which they quickly strung out around the huts. Before we knew it, we were interned inside the internment camp. We learned later that the commandant had sent for flame throwers, tanks, bazookas, heavy machine guns and an army of men from the nearby military base to make very sure that these unarmed bolsheviks would stay behind the barbed wire.

We were now effectively isolated from the Germans and the Italians. For several days we had our meals by ourselves, in our own hut. Acting as our spokesman, Gerry McManus of the Seamen's Union told the commandant that if we weren't taken out of the place we were going to walk through the barbed wire. At that time Prime Minister Mackenzie King was in England. No one in Ottawa could decide what do with the revolting prisoners. Finally, one afternoon, some trucks pulled into the compound, guarded as usual by platoons of soldiers. They were followed by jeeps with mounted machine guns. We were told to pack our duffle bags with our few things and load them onto the trucks.

We were not told where we were going, but we were certainly leaving. We left that evening, under cover of night, in the convoy of trucks and jeeps. We were then packed on a train, with windows covered with brown paper. We rode off into the night, wondering what next.

Poet Joe Wallace was interned from March 1941 to September 1942.

Peter Prokop

At the Petawawa camp there wasn't the same pressure for everyone to work. Some worked, but others, after a check-up by the doctor, were exempted. There were only about seven from our barracks who worked regularly. I was one of them; I worked loading gravel. On the day of the demonstration I was quite a way from camp.

I remember that coming back from work that day we saw truckloads of army troops, artillery and machine guns on the road. We wondered where they were going. It became clear later that this detachment had been brought from the military camp close by to put down the demonstration in our camp.

At the entrance gate the guards separated us from the other workers and arrested the Norwegian chap and myself. We wondered what in the world was happening. When the rest of the men from our work gang had gone in, we were told that our barracks was surrounded by barbed wire and that no one was allowed in or out. They made it clear that since we did not participate in the demonstration we would not be punished and that we did not need to go back with our fellows. I immediately told them that I was going to join my own people, and the Norwegian came with me. Together we went straight to our barracks, which was now surrounded by barbed wire. There we learned the reason for the demonstration. It was a dangerous situation.

Our spokesman sent demands to the minister of justice through the commandant. We wanted to be immediately and completely separated from the fascist prisoners at Petawawa and to be given the status of political prisoners to which we were entitled. We also stated that of course the easiest and most just solution would be our release from internment. In presenting this demand to the commandant, our spokesman Gerry McManus informed him that if this demand was not met our men were ready to march out through the barbed wire. The commandant realized that this was not an idle threat. Consultations took place with Ottawa and we were soon taken to the internment jail in Hull.

Norman Freed

Toronto, Ont.
September 1940 - August 1942

I was enjoying a game of chess with friends in Toronto when all of a sudden three men walked in. They told us they were from the RCMP, the provincial police and city police respectively. When he saw me, the RCMP fellow said, "Well, well! We didn't expect to see you!" They had come to arrest somebody else and had found me by accident. The RCMP man said to one of the others that he'd better go downtown and get a warrant for me.

When they came back with the warrant, they went through a brief ceremony of arresting me. I asked them what the charges were and told them that I wanted a lawyer. They advised me not to bother with a lawyer since I would not be appearing in court. They would not even tell me what I was charged with. I was just under arrest, period. They took me into a waiting car and rushed me downtown to RCMP headquarters. After fingerprinting and a few more questions, I was taken to a place in the west end which I later learned was the horse shed of the T. Eaton Company.

At the horse shed I found other people I knew. We found ourselves in very uncomfortable circumstances, confronted with soldiers who were quite brutal. They were from the militia that had fought in World War I. A few of them were decent individuals who even sympathized with our point of view and were quite helpful. Others treated us with contempt and acted like the Gestapo. They used to have nightly beer-drinking orgies with their friends. Often they would deliberately spill a glass of beer on the floor and then make us get down and wipe it up, all the while showing off to their lady friends what great power they had over their prisoners.

The conditions in the horse shed were indescribable. We were kept there like pigs. We were not allowed to see our families, nor to have newspapers or radio. We did manage to send out and receive some letters through some of the decent soldiers. This made our stay there a little more tolerable. At one point things became so bad that we worked out a plan to escape. We didn't care too much whether the plan worked or not. We were just determined to draw the attention of the public to the conditions under which we were forcibly detained.

As word began to get out, there were public protests. Finally, we were taken out of this dungeon and sent to the camp at Petawawa. When we got there we found some 90 other Canadians from different parts of the country who held similar opinions. In the camp we were still under military guard. They were apparently following the agreements reached in Geneva on the treatment of prisoners of war. These agreements usually referred to prisoners captured from the enemy in the field of battle. We were not in that category and we did not accept the idea that we were prisoners of war in our own country. Whether the Geneva agreements covered prisoners like us, we did not know.

After getting into one huge building where we could be by ourselves, we utilized our time to organize for our release. We wanted the right to appear in court, and if no charges were made against us we wanted to be freed. We also began to fight for the right of visits from our relatives.

We decided first of all that we needed a committee to supervise our work there and also our leisure time. We elected a camp leader, a person in charge of education, a person in charge of food, a person to look after a library as soon as we were allowed to receive books and newspapers, and a secretary. We chose a person to encourage cultural activity, which included songwriting, singing and writing stories and poems. We had among us some very able musicians and songwriters, and even a few comedians. We assigned people to take care of our hut. We also decided what hours we would work, what hours we would play and what hours we would give to creative work.

We found that we were entitled to army rations, which were pretty good and made well-rounded meals. They included all kinds of meat, fruit and vegetables. The Italians and German fascists who made up the majority in the camp collaborated with the quartermaster about the food that came into the camp and its preparation. They assigned the cooks among themselves and the food naturally had a distinctive German and Italian flavor.

We eventually learned, to our amazement, that the people who were collaborating with the quartermaster were also involved in black marketeering. Some of the food that we were entitled to never reached the camp. Apparently an arrangement was made whereby some of it was sold and some of it was shared among some of the internees and officers. We were never able to prove this but it was widely rumored that this was the case. It was borne out by the fact that quite often, for days on end, we were unable to get oranges or other fruit that we were entitled to. The story was that the order got lost somewhere on the way. We agitated to have the right to assign one or two people to have some say in the preparation of our food. We wanted to make sure that we received all the food in the variety that we were entitled to. Eventually we won this fight.

It was quite natural that the first committee that appeared in the fight for our release was composed of our wives. I am very proud of the fact that my wife Jennie was elected secretary of the committee. In 1941 they called a special conference at which they established a Committee for the Defence of Canadian Democracy and called for the immediate release of all internees. At this very first conference a resolution was adopted which served in the continuing campaign for our release. The resolution, which received great publicity at the time, was addressed to the Right Honorable Ernest Lapointe, Minister of Justice, and to Prime Minister Mackenzie King.

WHEREAS there are in Canadian concentration camps at present over a hundred labor and progressive Canadians, most of whom have been active anti-fascists, both in views and in actions;

AND WHEREAS all these individuals have been interned without trial under Regulation 21 of the Defence of Canada Act;

AND WHEREAS Regulation 21 of the Defence of Canada Act destroys every right and liberty known to the British peoples since the Magna Carta and gives complete authority to the Minister of Justice to arrest and dispose of any individuals, put away without trial or right of appeal to anyone but the Minister of Justice: in fact whereas Regulation 21 is an outright fascist law such as is practised in Nazi Germany;

AND WHEREAS labor people interned under this provision are branded as prisoners of war and subject to all the regulations that come under that classification, isolated from society, not permitted to see their families, their belongings confiscated, housed together with open fascists and generally subject to petty persecution and punishment, particularly in reprisal for any punitive actions against British and Canadian war prisoners in Germany;

AND WHEREAS the families, particularly the innocent children of these labor internees, are made to suffer intense hardships because of these conditions, being victimized because of the brand of Prisoner of War with which fathers and husbands are labelled;

AND WHEREAS they receive totally inadequate relife and in some cases are at the mercy of all forms of injustice and persecution from local relief authorities;

THEREFORE BE IT RESOLVED that this organization or assembly registers its strong protest against this condition of affairs, regards the use of Regulation 21 and the evils flowing therefrom as the very negation of all democratic, humanitarian principles, and calls upon the Dominion Government to take immediate steps to:

1. Repeal Regulation 21 of the Defence of Canada Act.

2. Release all the labor internees incarcerated under the said Act.

Pending these major reforms, we urge the government to effect an immediate improvement of the conditions of the labor internees and their dependents by acceding to the following:

A. Return of confiscated belongings of the internees to their families.

B. Permission for regular visits to internees from families and friends.

C. Labor internees be given status of political prisoners and receive privileges as such.

D. Uncensored mail, freedom of letters be permitted for internees and unrestricted receipt of newspapers and other printed matter.

E. The families and dependents of labor internees be given decent and adequate maintenance without discrimination.

The resolution was sent to trade unions and mass organizations of various kinds. In response, literally hundreds of letters were sent to newspapers. Resolutions were adopted by many church, union and community groups. They declared that the application of the Defence of Canada Act had cut deep into the basic liberties of the Canadian people. The unlimited power assumed by the government under these regulations was criticized as a harsh and arbitrary measure. Under the tremendous pressure of this campaign, the government established an all-party committee to investigate the regulations.

According to a statement released by the Committee for the Release of Labor Prisoners (CRLP), this House committee stated that the government's stubborn determination to hold on to its dictatorial powers was a danger to our democratic traditions. The government was determined to retain Regulation 21 even though the committee of the House considered that it was being administered unjustly. The CRLP concluded that as long as this Regulation 21 remained in effect, no person in Canada was safe from arbitrary and unjust detention. Regulation 21 gave the minister of justice absolute power to intern any person for what it called preventative reasons. It made very little difference whether the committee which reviewed the cases consisted of one man or three men as was now proposed. As long as that committee had no power to release an internee, the government would continue to operate under the so-called Provision of Preventative Arrest.

It appeared that even when the government-established committees of one recommended the release of a labor prisoner, Minister of Justice Mr. Lapointe invariably reversed the finding. He finally admitted that in most cases he did this because the police advised him that, despite the findings of the judge, the person should not be released because he constituted a danger to Canada. So it was the police who were running Canada. It was the police mind that was deciding people's fates, not a judge or the courts. The minister of justice possessed such arbitrary powers that he did not have to heed the advice of anybody, including judges, and he could arbitrarily keep a person interned on his own personal whim.

The CRLP pointed out that there was nothing said in the reports of the House committee about the other sections of the regulations which drastically curtailed the freedom of speech, press and assembly. Nothing was said about the people who were languishing in prison as a result of these regulations. Nor was anything proposed to rectify the injustice which had been perpetrated against the 100 anti-fascist and trade union internees.

The committee noted that a year earlier, on June 14, 1940, in a judgment handed down in the case of *Kunutsky Goudoc*, a Russian-language newspaper, Mr. Justice Deniston had declared that "in wartime, Parliament may take from the courts the judicial discussion and substitute for it the autocracy of bureaucrats."

And in a judgment handed down in April 1941 on the application of Pat Sullivan for a writ of *habeas corpus*, Mr. Justice W.T. Henderson declared, "This country is in a state of war and therefore we cannot review the actions of military authorities who are in charge of the affairs of Canada today."

These statements and the actions committed during this period bear testimony to the fact that there had grown up in Canada a military dictatorship which had usurped from the courts their judicial functions and from Parliament its legislative functions. It instituted rule by Order in Council which exercised complete control over the lives and destinies of the Canadian people.

After the Soviet Union became our ally in June 1941, Canadians became even more indignant with a government that continued to keep anti-fascists interned. Committees for the release of the labor internees and for the restoration of democratic rights began to spring up all over the country from Halifax to Victoria. At that time the National Committee for Democratic Rights (NCDR) was founded and had on its executive two outstanding Canadians, the Rev. A.E. Smith and Miss Beckie Buhay. This was a very broad committee comprised of people with different political opinions. Membership came from various sections of the population and particularly from the labor movement. They all agreed on one point, that the war for democracy must pertain to our country as well.

The NCDR issued an appeal to Canadians to urge Parliament to promptly restore the rights of interned Canadians. The overwhelming response reflected the anger and indignation that existed among Canadians from coast to coast. Two other events that occurred in 1941 contributed to this indignation. James and Leonard Franceschini, two notorious millionaires and self-confessed fascists, received their unconditional release. Apparently it was now considered safe to allow them to go free, even though they continued to support the Italian and German fascist governments that were killing Canadians on the field of battle.

The other event was the acquittal in a court in Montreal of Teles Foredomin, 27 years old, of Bordeaux, Quebec. He was charged with membership in the fascist party in Quebec, which had been declared illegal under the War Measures Act. This self-confessed fascist told the RCMP, and they declared in open court, that he believed in the principles of fascism. He stated that he would continue to be a member of the fascist party after the war and to fight for that kind of social system in our country. Yet, like the Franceschini brothers, this man was unconditionally released. As a matter of fact, he was never interned. The attorney general of Quebec couldn't stomach this outrage and appealed the decision to a higher court.

The Toronto and District Trades and Labor Council were fed up with the continued detention of labor activists. They contacted Tom Moore, President of the Trades and Labor Congress of Canada, to ascertain what steps had been taken by the parent body. It was decided unanimously to ask the minister of justice to release J.A. (Pat) Sullivan, president of the Seamen's Union (CSU). Dewar Ferguson, acting president of the CSU, claimed that Mr. Sullivan had suffered six heart attacks while interned. Despite the union's efforts, the authorities refused to allow a doctor to examine him. He pointed out that they had also tried to arrange for Mrs. Sullivan to be allowed to visit her husband. This too was refused. Mr. Ferguson also noted that Pat Sullivan's son was overseas with the Canadian army and one could well imagine how he must feel about being ready to give his life while his father was branded an enemy alien and held in an internment camp in Canada.

J.W. Buckley, secretary of the Trades and Labor Council, read a letter from the Association of Technical Employees, protesting the arrest of J. Murphy, chairman of the broadcast division of their union. Murphy was arrested on May 23, 1941, by the RCMP and interned. A letter was read, signed by the national secretary of the Technical Employees, stating that Murphy had been arrested on his return from Ottawa where he had been discussing details of a dispute between the CBC and broadcast division members.

The council came to the conclusion that when anyone started negotiating for labor in its fight for better conditions and higher wages, they were simply arrested and put away. The so-called Preventative Arrests Provision of the War Measures Act was being used to prevent workers' efforts to defend their social and economic interests. The council came to the conclusion that the false cry about Communist and disruptive elements was used as an excuse to suppress the efforts of labor people seeking better conditions. It was pointed out at the same meeting that a Canadian Manufacturers Association representative had urged the government to intern any radical who dared to call a strike.

Mr. A.B. Johnston, the leader of the Restaurant Workers Union and a delegate to the Trades and Labor Council, declared, "One of my very close friends was placed in an internment camp some months ago. I considered it from many angles and then held my head low because I figured the government must be right or it would not do such a thing.

However, recently I had a change of conscience when I learned of the release of the Franceschini brothers. I reasoned that if the government was right in interning them in the first place, then it was wrong in releasing them. I feel that it is our duty to urge the government to state the facts of the case and not act one way for the rich and the opposite way against the working people and the poor.''

Similar reactions were found in other parts of the country. In Vancouver a committee was established to aid persecuted labor leaders. They addressed a letter to Justice Minister Lapointe, demanding the release of the interned labor leaders. Their letter insisted that even prior to the Nazi invasion of the Soviet Union there was no reason or excuse for the internment of these people. Referring specifically to Fergus McKean, Bill Rigby and Bob Kerr, three outstanding British Columbia labor leaders, the letter said,

> For many years they were among the first to propose a collective security agreement with the Soviet Union while others in higher places advocated a policy of appeasement with fascism. Yet the people that sought to appease fascism are in power and the people who fought against the appeasement and for the establishment of a collective security pact with the Soviet Union against fascism are being kept in internment camps.

In April 1941 the Toronto *Star* carried a report, date line March 31, 1941, that a deputation of nineteen wives of internees had arrived in Ottawa with the aim of interviewing cabinet ministers and seeking the release of the labor internees. They requested the abolition of Regulation 21 of the Defence of Canada Act, and pending the release of their husbands, that certain concessions be granted to them to make their life a little easier.

The government refused to hear them, asked them to leave their written petitions and advised them to go home. The deputation appealed to private MPs. It was with the aid of the Rev. E.C. Hansell, CCF member from MacLeod, Alberta, and Dorise Nielsen, MP, from North Battleford, Saskatchewan, that a gathering of MPs representing all parties received the delegation in a committee room of the House of Commons. According to the report, the delegation received a very sympathetic hearing and a promise by the members to do whatever they could to release the prisoners. They also agreed to assist the delegation to get an opportunity to appear before the parliamentary committee that was sitting at the time in Ottawa investigating the War Measures Act and its regulations.

The deputation stressed the list of demands from the CDCR resolution printed earlier. Mrs. McManus of Montreal, whose husband, a leader of the Seamen's Union, was interned, told members she had seven children from two to seventeen years of age. The oldest boy was earning $11 a week. The total assistance she received from the government was $1.80 a week food allowance and $14 a month for rent. She also said that she had not seen her husband since he was interned on June 6, 1940, because rules did not permit visits from wives or children.

Mrs. Jean Bourget of Montreal had five children, three to twelve years of age. She stated that she received $4.95 a week in allowance from the federal government and $10 a month rent. Her rent was $13 a month so she had to make up the other $3 out of the other slim allowance. Some women described how their husbands were spirited away in the middle of the night and how they had no idea where they were until they got the first letter from the internment camp months later.

All the delegates insisted that their men were being kept in internment without sufficient cause. They were determined to continue the battle with other Canadians for their release. Pending release they wanted some amelioration of their conditions in the internment camps, and changes in the defence regulations. They were very certain that they were expressing the consensus of opinion of large sections of the population.

The wives of the internees made a very important contribution to the campaign. They were not only fighting because their husbands were interned. They were fighting because of their own convictions and their own role in the labor movement. Many of them were members of labor, cultural, political and women's organizations. Those of us who were interned are very proud of the part played by our wives and other women. My wife Jennie played a persistent and inspiring role in the battle for justice in that dark period of history. She appeared quite prominently as secretary of the committee and displayed great courage and initiative. She understood that she was fighting not only for her husband but for every Canadian who was concerned with democratic rights.

One morning, after we had been transferred from Petawawa to a jail outside Hull, we got up and looked out the windows to see what the weather was like. To our surprise we saw a group of twenty or thirty women standing outside. We immediately opened the windows and heard, to our delight, the words of "Solidarity Forever." Many of us recognized our wives among the women.

The wives and the rest of a delegation that had visited Ottawa had decided that before they returned home they would make one more effort to come and see us. They were flatly refused by the military authorities. They decided that the next best thing was to stay there all night. Of course, we knew none of this, but when we saw them in the morning we were thrilled beyond words, and encouraged by this noble action of our wives and the rest of the deputation. We joined in with them from the windows, in singing "Solidarity."

We were proud to hear the voices of our beloved women. They were singing to encourage us to keep up the fight so that the gates of our internment would soon be opened and we would return to normal life and take part in the direct struggle against fascism. We will never forget that morning in April 1942 when we heard the sweet voices of our wives calling upon us inside and the people outside to keep up the battle for a democratic, free Canada.

Jennie Freed

When the Communist Party was declared illegal we moved to Montreal. When we discovered that we were being watched we moved out and lived in the country for five months. The men lived separately in hiding and the wives lived—just lived. Occasionally they would come to visit us. It was a bad period for all the wives because we never knew when the men would be discovered and picked up. All we could do was to wait and hope.

When Norman was arrested in Toronto I was in Montreal. I heard on the radio that he had been picked up, but I didn't know where he was. One of my friends in Toronto found out that he was in Lansdowne Barracks. I had a great deal of difficulty getting permission to visit him. There was a lot of red tape and when I did see him I was really shocked. He was practically in rags and looked awful. He was very surprised to see me, but there were soldiers standing guard, so we could not do much talking.

I saw Muni Erlich at the same time. They both came out together. It was because of Muni that Norman was arrested. It was in the evening and Muni had gone out to see a girl friend. The police followed him back to the house. When they came to the door, someone noticed and told Norman to hide in the cupboard on the third floor. He said he would feel foolish if they opened the cupboard and found him there. They never did look in that cupboard, so he could have got away with it if he had hid. But he thought he would look silly, and I can't blame him.

The next time I went to visit they told me Norman had gone to Petawawa. They just whisked him off without telling me anything about it. They wouldn't let us visit Petawawa. This period was very hard on the wives, especially if there were children. We had to go on relief. I didn't get any cash, just vouchers. I was not able to work because I had a little boy who was only three years old when Norman was arrested. The first year I was so busy just trying to get to see Norman that I didn't have time to work. After that it was difficult getting a job until I was able to get the little boy into a nursery. Then I worked off and on for about a year.

When I lived in Montreal it was easier for me because I lived with my mother-in-law and she helped me out. We got a number of wives together and hitch-hiked to Ottawa; we didn't have any money for the bus or train. We thought we could do more by going to Ottawa personally than by sending letters. We went a few times, six or seven of us, hitch-hiking each time. Dorise Nielsen, MP from Saskatchewan, helped us. She tried to get other Members of Parliament to listen to us. These MPs would reluctantly promise to look into it.

After the men had been moved to Hull we started a campaign to get visiting rights. One day when we went to Ottawa and couldn't get a hearing, we went to the jail but were not allowed to visit the men. So we stood outside and started to sing "Hold the Fort." We could wave to the men up at the windows. We went back the next day and they chased us away. They wouldn't even allow us to be on the grounds.

In February 1942 there was a big conference in Ottawa of the National Committee for Democratic Rights, the organization that was formed to get the men released. Most of the wives were there at the conference. We were received by the minister of justice in the Chateau Laurier. After the conference we campaigned extensively for release on the grounds that the men were not against the war. Finally in the spring they agreed to let us have visits twice a month.

I went to visit Norman but they wouldn't let me see him alone. The commandant was in the room while we were talking. I asked to be allowed to bring little Lennie along to see his father, but Lennie didn't want to come. The first time he did come he was quite upset by this strange man who was his father. Fred Collins was the gardener at the camp and looked after the flowers. When Lennie started to cry at the sight of his father in prison uniform, Fred took him out in the garden so that Norman and I could talk. One day, some time later, Lennie told me that he'd told a friend that his father was a guard at the jail. I used to explain to him where Norman went and what was happening, but of course he could not understand the whole thing. Poor little fellow, he had to find some explanation for his father being away.

III
HULL

Mitch Sago

Winnipeg, Man.
October 1940 -
August 1942

In reminiscing about the war years and our internment, it must be clearly stated that first and foremost all of us were identified on the public record with the Canadian and worldwide struggle against the rising tide of fascism on the European continent and the growing danger that it posed to people everywhere. There can be no mistake about where we stood on this life and death issue, or the organizations and public activities with which we were indentified. We were active, often in leading roles, in the mainstream of the struggles against the fascist danger and the threat of world war.

The same could not be said about those running the country. The prime minister, who also led a secret life as a mystic, seemed favorably impressed by Hitler after meeting the dictator prior to the war. As long as Hitlerism was aimed at the liquidation of communists by whatever means, and was geared to the avowed destruction of the Soviet Union, it was an acceptable or tolerable evil to most western leaders. This was indicative of the sick mentality of the time that shut its eyes to the monster it helped create. Only when their own

179

survival was threatened did the western leaders finally concede the danger of fascism and decide to do battle with it. Even at that, while human and material resources were committed to the battlefields, there was a continual persecution and imprisonment of Canadian anti-fascists for the first two years of the war. We were robbed of two years of freedom, and the opportunity to serve our country in the war against fascism.

War was declared in Europe on September 1, 1939; Canada entered the war nine days later. On June 8, 1940, the *Canada Gazette* published an Order in Council, dated June 4, outlawing the Ukrainian Labor Farmer Temple Association and other working-class and anti-fascist organizations. On July 6, the RCMP, with the assistance of local police, raided the homes of many leaders of the progressive Ukrainian organizations and whisked them off to the Kananaskis concentration camp. In Winnipeg, the offices of *Narodna Hazetta* (People's Gazette) and *Farmerske Zhyttia* (Farmers' Life) were sealed and the Ukrainian Labor Temple was seized by the authorities, as were the halls of the ULFTA across the country.

Warned by the ban on left-wing organizations, I took precautions against possible arrest and went into hiding a few days before the police raids. A police officer told me some years later that nearly 300 homes were raided by the police looking for me and Bill Ross, who was also in hiding. Many of these raids were reported on the radio news, and it soon became widely known that we were wanted men. The three months in hiding was a difficult and painful experience not only for myself, but also for my wife and family and for those who gave me cover. The raids and newscasts helped create an atmosphere of terror in the progressive community, as no doubt they were intended to do.

Those who provided a hiding place were brave people. They knew that if they were caught putting me up in their homes, they would be arrested and jailed. But they were anti-fascists and were shocked and outraged at the persecution of anti-fascists. If this was the law then the law was an ass—and break it they did. Generally I only stayed a day or two in one place and then moved on. Time and again I would move from one house to another just in time to miss the police.

I remember one such occasion. I had been warned that in the evening a police raid would be made on the place I was staying. I was rushed to another home to stay overnight until another place was arranged. My hosts were a young married couple who worked in the daytime. Mid-morning the next day I received a frantic phone call from the young wife at work: she had phoned and told her mother a "secret"...that a man wanted by the police was hiding out in her home. She thought she could share the secret with her mother, but instead her mother told her she was calling the police and hung up.

I had to leave immediately. As I walked along the sidewalk, I found myself moving toward a police officer at the corner. He was looking in my direction. My face was well known in Winnipeg because I had been a candidate in municipal elections. I wondered if he'd recognize me but I knew I had to take that chance. I casually walked up to him and asked for directions to a street in the area. He explained how I could get there. I thanked him and kept on my way to the next hiding place. I learned much later that the mother was as good as her word. She did phone the police, and the house was raided. The young couple were questioned by police, but denied there was any truth to the telephone tip.

I recall another incident while hiding in a home outside the city. The family knew I was in hiding and they were concerned that someone in the area would recognize me. It was agreed that I would keep out of sight if any visitors came to the house. They had a young school teacher as a boarder. I kept out of her way and rarely spoke to her. It didn't take her long to tell the people I stayed with that I was a "queer fellow."

One day, when the family was in town on a shopping trip, three young men came to see the man. Upon finding the teacher home alone, they made some brash and obnoxious remarks to her. She became very upset and they left. It was obvious that I should have intervened, and probably would have if matters had gotten worse. But in the situation I did nothing. For the few remaining days that I stayed in that house, she held me in contempt. Only after the war, when I ran into her on Main Street in Winnipeg, did she tell me that she finally found out who I was and why I had acted so strangely. We laughed about it.

Tom McEwen and I decided to rent a couple of rooms together. Shortly after we moved in, on a bright, crisp morning in late October, I was startled by a loud pounding on the front door down the corridor. I had just lathered my face in the bathroom on the main floor. I heard the running footsteps of the landlady as the pounding continued. I knew it was the police. This was quickly confirmed when a loud male voice informed the landlady that the police had a warrant to search the premises. I looked out the bathroom window into the backyard, and saw a police car with more officers walking towards the house. The police had surrounded the place. As I tried to get my thoughts together, there was a pounding on the bathroom door with orders to open up and come out. I could also hear the footsteps of police climbing the stairs to our rooms on the second floor.

I opened the door, lather and all, and faced the officer. He told me to get a towel, wipe the lather off my face, and accompany him upstairs. He didn't recognize me, but the inspector at the top of the stairs, whom I knew from previous encounters on many picket lines, yelled in disbelief, "Not you, Mitch! I thought you were somewhere out of town!" When I asked him who or what he expected to find, he told me that they were under the impression that this house was an important literature dump, nothing more.

The police were already at work, turning the place upside down as they searched for papers. They began stacking stencils, books and clothing into three large cardboard boxes for delivery to police headquarters. Through all the commotion, I could hear the angry protests of the landlord, and the tearful voice of his wife. Tom and I told the police to leave them alone, that they had no idea who we were, and that they were simply renting rooms to us. As Tom and I were led to separate police cars for the trip to Rupert Street jail in the Winnipeg police building, we could see the landlord being pushed and half-dragged to yet another car. He kept shouting at the police in great anger, and only when they slammed the car door on him did his voice die out. His wife had already been taken to the police station for questioning, but she was released after a few hours. Our hapless landlord was sentenced to six months in prison.

I was in the inspector's car. He was still in a state of euphoria about having netted, in his words, "two big fish" in what began as a routine police raid. He told me during the ride that Tom and I would be surprised at the evidence they had collected against us. There was no doubt in his mind that we would be convicted and receive lengthy prison terms. For three or four days, Tom and I were held incommunicado in the police cells. We were also held in isolation from each other, and from any contact with other prisoners. Days passed before we could get word to our lawyer and to our families.

We went on trial before Magistrate R.B. Graham in police court on November 8, 1940. We faced charges of membership in an illegal organization, the Communist Party of Canada. I was also charged with publishing the Party's illegal paper. A senior police officer told us, with undisguised relish, that we could look forward to at least four years in the penitentiary. Tom made an eloquent statement in court on his right to belong to a party that served the interests of the people and that played a leading role in the struggle for peace and against fascism. He saw no need to defend his right to belong to the Communist Party, but attacked those who challenged that right. The court had no difficulty, in view of his statements, in finding him guilty of membership in a party that the government had seen fit to outlaw.

My own position, when I came up on that charge, was similar to and yet different from that taken by Tom. I pleaded "not guilty" on strictly technical grounds, leaving the burden of proof on the crown prosecutor. I was an officer of a cooperative organization subject to a highly organized and well financed red-baiting campaign. For purely tactical reasons, and at my request, my membership in the Communist Party had been suspended. However, I told the court that I had no differences with the Party, that I believed in its program and policies, and that I planned to continue my participation in its activities.

The crown prosecutor could neither shake my statement nor come up with evidence to the contrary. When the magistrate asked the prosecution to bring forth evidence in support of the charge or withdraw it, the prosecutor walked over to one of the large boxes from the raid on our domicile. He reached into the box and pulled out a pair of bedroom slippers, and then some articles of clothing. The court roared with laughter as the magistrate told the flustered prosecutor that this was not enough to prove membership in an illegal organization. The charge was dismissed.

The dismissal had no bearing on a reduced prison sentence. I knew already that I was going to prison, and so did Tom and our lawyer. I was found guilty on two charges of publishing an illegal paper for a party that had been declared illegal. I had been in the process of preparing a mimeographed paper for the Party when my room was ransacked; the court made the point that it was possible for a person to be found guilty for publishing an illegal publication without being a member of the illegal organization that was its sponsor. Tom and I were sentenced to two years less a day at hard labor. That "less a day" sent us to Headingly Jail in Manitoba rather than to Stony Mountain Penitentiary.

We served most of our time in Headingly in Cage 2, where prisoners under the Defence of Canada Regulations were quartered, including a number of fascists. We were told that behind the wall at the end of our cell block was the pit of the execution chamber on the floor above. On the other side of the wall, the plunging body of a condemned man sputtered its last breaths of life at the end of the hangman's rope.

There was one hanging while we were in Headingly: the execution of Nick Sikha. Nick was a young lad who, we were told, was mentally retarded. He had killed a harvester while robbing the victim. Only a few dollars were involved but, in the end, it cost two lives. Until the sentence of death was passed on Nick, we would often see him escorted by a guard in the corridors of the prison. Stories trickled down to the prison population that he was not aware of what lay ahead. But the shadow of the noose was unmistakable. The place seethed with a silent anger against the inhumanity of capital punishment.

Tom was one of six or seven prisoners who were taken to Vaughan Street jail the day the court sentenced the lad to death. On their return to Headingly, with all of them handcuffed to each other, the full impact of what had happened in court finally hit Nick. He broke down and wept like a child. Tom was visibly shaken. On the day of the execution, the prisoners were all confined to their cell blocks. A pall of silence hung over the place. I had never experienced such silence—unnatural, almost physical in a strange and inexplicable way. The one sound that would break the silence, minutes after midnight, was the muffled boom of the sprung trap door in the execution chamber.

Two days after the execution, Mickey from the prison laundry came to Tom and me in the adjoining tailor shop where we worked and asked if either of us wanted the black hood used in the hanging of the condemned man. I was appalled at the idea, but Tom suggested that I pass it outside for future use as an exhibit against capital punishment. I dreaded the thought of handing the grisly article to my wife on her next weekly visit.

The next time I was taken to the visitors' room I had the hood in my shirt. The prisoners, as always, were seated along one side of the long table, with the visitors opposite and facing them. At the far end of the table was a guard, perched on a high seat for an unobstructed view of those present. There was a low barrier down the centre of the table to prevent touching of hands and the passing of contraband.

I told my wife Frankie that I had a piece of cloth that Tom wanted her to keep for him, and that I would flip it over the barrier at the first opportunity. I asked her to leave the article beside her purse until visiting time was up, and then to casually pick it up as she rose to leave. She insisted that I tell her what the article was, and I kept evading the question. Finally, with visiting time running out, and because I had other things to discuss before she left, I told her.

She recoiled from the table with a look of horror. She was so visibly shaken that I was sure the guard would notice that something was wrong. I pleaded with her to get a grip on herself or I would end up in the isolation cell for passing contraband. Why would Tom want such a terrible thing, she asked, as she struggled to compose herself. I explained in a few words. When the guard announced that visiting time was up, Frankie rose, picked up her purse, and gingerly took the black hood off the table. She told me later that the black cloth in the closet had caused her many nightmares. In time, it was sent to Tom.

At another point Tom and I were in the remand cage awaiting the decision of the Supreme Court of Manitoba on an action for *habeas corpus*. One of the guards asked if we wanted to see the inside of the execution chamber. Hesitant at first, we finally agreed. That visit haunted me for a long time, as did the guard's stories about some of the executions he had witnessed during his years at Headingly.

As a footnote to this recollection, I remember a visit to a newsstand years after my release. I was looking for some periodical and noticed a detective magazine. Its front cover featured "The Story of the Pock-Marked Killer" and the picture and name of Nick Sikha. Some hack writer presented the youth as an inhuman monster. It was an exercise in cheap sensationalism typical of yellow journalism. Many years have passed since that dark and disturbing episode in prison life, and fortunately capital punishment has been abolished in Canada.

While we were in jail our wives and many of our friends on the outside were not idle. They spearheaded a public campaign for the release of their husbands and all interned anti-fascists. Not only were they bringing the truth of this injustice to thousands of people in cities across Canada, but they also made representations to the federal government. In March 1941 a delegation of fifteen women, wives of the interned men from Regina to Halifax, met with the minister of justice in Ottawa. They demanded the release of their husbands and all anti-fascists. This marked the first stage of a national campaign that would rally broad circles of public opinion and support.

In the spring of 1941, some months after Tom and I began serving our sentences, we were informed that a federal commission had been appointed to hold closed hearings into the cases of those who had been interned under the Defence of Canada Regulations. We knew that the commission had the job of white-washing the government's action and of creating the illusion that the cases had been duly considered under the law, and thus that justice had been done. Time would prove our assessment right. At first we decided to refuse to appear before the commission, and we informed our friends on the outside of our decision. But as we were repeatedly urged to appear before the panel, we reluctantly, and under protest, agreed to do so.

We were taken to the Vaughan Street jail in downtown Winnipeg for the hearing. Tom was the first person to appear. In an opening statement, he told the judges that he would not participate in what was nothing more than a kangaroo court. He was back in his cell within the half-hour.

As the guard came to escort me to the courtroom, Tom shouted, "Good luck."

I faced a panel of three judges. After the preliminaries, during which the chairman of the commission read me a few samples of the questions they planned to put to me, I asked for the right to make a statement. I told them that my position was identical to the one expressed by McEwen. I said I had no intention of helping them fill out their police dossiers (the sample questions had indicated that to be their prime goal) and I was not prepared to participate in a hearing that was actually a whitewash of an injustice. I was dismissed from the courtroom and taken back to my cell. Tom had a big grin on his face. "For a minute there I thought they let you go," he commented wryly.

Hitler attacked the Soviet Union on June 22, 1941. The war had now entered a new stage. New and powerful forces were engaged in what was a total war to defeat the Nazi drive to enslave the world. The attack on the Soviet Union changed the relationship of forces between the countries at war, and within each country. Colonel Burritt, governor of Headingly, came to see Tom and me the following day. He was all smiles. He informed us that we were being transferred to the so-called honeymoon suite—to the spacious quarters of the isolation hospital that were unoccupied and available. The surroundings were indeed a big improvement over the stark confinement of the cells. We even slept on regular beds. We were spared the daily searches, we were never frisked, and the door to the corridor of the cell block was not locked.

McEwen and I had served about half our two-year sentence when our lawyers filed an application for *habeas corpus* before the Supreme Court of Manitoba. This action was taken on the grounds that the magistrate who sentenced us had wrongfully included "hard labor." Our lawyer contended that this was in excess of the Defence of Canada Regulations under which we were charged and imprisoned. During these court proceedings it was revealed that shortly after the committal papers were issued stipulating "two years less a day at hard labor," the court and the attorney general's department discovered that the legality of the sentence was vulnerable to a challenge by the defendants. Another committal paper had been issued dropping the stipulation of "hard labor," but this doctoring of the papers could neither cover nor validate the original order.

The Supreme Court decision that ordered our release on these grounds was something of a cause celebre in Manitoba jurisprudence. But the order for our release never got off the paper it was written on. Whatever the outcome of the court case, another order had been prepared by Ottawa for continued detention—an order for our internment. Some time in July of 1941, Ernest Lapointe, the federal minister of justice, signed an order for the detention of both of us in case we won the court action or served out our sentences and qualified for release. There was never any question of justice or freedom for us. Our continued imprisonment was essential in the eyes of the government.

We awaited the court's order for our release in the remand cage at Headingly Jail. We had no illusions about freedom. The prison authorities also knew that when we finally left Headingly it would be under police escort, and that we would be taken as prisoners of war to an internment camp. Word of our release came on the eve of the Christmas holidays. I remember the sense of outrage with which Colonel Royal Burritt informed us of our departure the next morning. He knew, as we did, that a court order for our release would be a cynical formality, and that internment would follow. Moreover, he could not understand the total lack of compassion in taking us outside the reach of our families at that particular time of the year.

Tom and I were taken to the Vaughan Street jail where the court order for our release would be served. After stalling for more than an hour, while waiting for the RCMP to arrive, an official finally unlocked our cell door and informed us that we were free to leave. As we walked to the front doors, we could see two RCMP officers waiting outside. We knew they were there to serve the order for internment. The jail guard had no sooner opened the door to the outside than the older of the two mounties stepped forward and asked us our names. He then proceeded to read the order for our internment under the Defence of Canada Regulations.

I had sent word to Frankie that we would be at Vaughan Street that morning. She and our small daughter looked on as the drama at the jail door unfolded. I will always remember my daughter's frightened cry: "Why have they put those irons on Daddy's hands, Mother?" I was not the only one deeply affected. Even the young mountie, who was one of our escorts to Hull, Quebec, would upon his return to Winnipeg pay a visit to my house and express his distaste for the job he had to do that day.

Following the court's decision in our case, an editorial in the Winnipeg *Tribune* expressed a growing public concern with the way the RCMP had become a law unto itself. It said in part:

> Authorities in charge of the enforcement of the Defence of Canada Regulations would do well to consider that they cannot have it both ways except at the risk of creating serious public alarm and inviting a sense of injustice. This procedure of attempting to get convictions in the regular courts reflects the Dominion Government's timidity in the handling of one of the most important wartime problems. It is unfair to the courts to use them as "first resort," and then, if the court's action fails to meet the unrevealed desires of the Defence authorities, to make use of the "last resort" of holding for internment persons whom the courts have just found "not guilty." The evasive, equivocal mixture of peacetime and wartime procedure is definitely harmful to public morale, and should be stopped.

The real concern of the Winnipeg *Tribune* was not with the issue of justice, wherein anti-fascists were the victims of persecution and imprisonment in a war against fascism. The concern was with a system of double-dealing that ran "the risk of creating serious public alarm and inviting a sense of injustice."

The train trip to Hull was long and tiresome. The older of the two officers wondered if we should be handcuffed during the station stops along the way, but the idea was abandoned. At one point during the trip I shared a seat with an RAF officer who had been in training in the west and was returning to England. After I'd made a couple of trips to the washroom at the end of the car, he asked me if I was aware that one of the mounties always followed me. I told him that I was and explained the situation. He was deeply shocked and said that in his country people like us were either in the armed forces or working in production. He could not, for the life of him, understand what was wrong with Canada where people like us were locked up and denied a chance to serve their country.

We arrived at Hull jail some time near midnight. We were brought to the office of the camp commandant, who was waiting for us. He looked the typical officer of the British Imperial Army, in which he had served at one time. His uniform was impeccable, riding boots polished to a fault. He could have been a movie stereotype. He paced up and down for a moment as Tom and I watched in silence.

Finally he picked up the detention papers on his desk and asked Tom McEwen his name. When Tom told him, the commandant looked annoyed and asked for his real, Russian name. He found it hard to accept the fact that a Communist had a Scottish name. After Tom repeated his name a few times, the commandant told him that it really didn't matter since he would henceforth be known and addressed as H4.

After giving the commandant my name (its foreign sound vindicated his backward theories), he advised that I would be known as H5. I was numb with fatigue and my first impulse was to tell him to shove it. Instead I told him I had a name and would continue to answer to it. He replied that I would behave according to the rules, or else. It was obvious that we were not going to see eye to eye on this, or any other, issue.

We were then escorted down the corridor to the heavy metal door of the prison inside. We heard voices lifted in song on the other side of the steel door. It was a song I had never heard before, and it moved me to tears. These were our friends and colleagues singing the Kananaskis song, a Canadian adaptation of the stirring song of the German prisoners of fascism—"The Peat Bog Soldiers." The commandant had given our boys permission to stay up and greet us upon our arrival. I remember the crowd of fellows gathered at the door as we entered, the greetings, hugs and handshakes. And I recall one of the boys shouting over the bedlam, "Geez, what took you so long?" It was an unforgettable moment.

The prison camp was a whole new world, gray and claustrophobic. Time was two-dimensional: inside and outside. Inside, each day was confined by stone and steel, barbed wire and bayonets. There was a sense of waste, of suspended animation. Outside, humanity fought for its life and its future. All of us were garbed in POW uniforms with the red circle on the back of the jackets as insignia and target. We were marked men, prisoners of war, in uniforms decreed by international law. We had consistently opposed the enemies of our country, in return for which we had been imprisoned behind stone and barbed wire.

One of the great burdens of doing time in a concentration camp, in addition to the deep sense of injustice, was the indeterminate nature of the sentence. The question of "how long" had no answer. There was always hope that public opinion and protest would give that answer or that the war would end soon in victory for the allied cause. These were our only two doors to freedom.

Our overriding concern was with the war and the smashing of fascism. This was inseparable from our concern for freedom and our own participation in that struggle. We suffered with news of every setback and cheered with every victory on the battlefields of Europe, Asia and Africa. We urged our countless friends and supportive groups on the outside, by whatever means were open to us, to do all in their power to strengthen the war effort at home and abroad.

This spirit pervaded life in the prison camp. It was expressed in many ways, and in a variety of modest creative ventures. There were the beautiful poems by J.S. Wallace. Joe was already widely known as a great and talented labor poet. A number of his poems on the war against fascism were set to music by Ben Swankey and myself. While in prison he wrote many others on the theme of man's inhumanity to man and on life in prison. Joe and I became close friends in Hull, and upon my release I took copies of most of his poems to try to arrange for their publication. I arranged for his first book, *Night is Ended*, to be published by Contemporary Publishers in Winnipeg. It was published in the fall of 1942, with a foreward by Margaret Fairley and an introduction by the poet E.J. Pratt.

Flame of the Future

Our country's young and our army's young.
    But we hurl at our foes defiance!
For we march as heirs of heroic years,
    And we march in a world alliance.

For we march as heirs of heroic years,
     And we march in a world alliance.

Our hopes are high and our hearts are high,
     As we march to the final battles!
But if die we must, better deathless dust—
     Than the life-long death of chattels.

But if die we must, better deathless dust—
     Than the life-long death of chattels.

A people in arms, we fight on as one,
     The flame of future inside us!
While the glorious dead march on ahead,
     And the women we love beside us.

While the glorious dead march on ahead,
     And the women we love beside us.

Hull jail, 1942

A representative of the International Red Cross came to
check conditions and to list materials and equipment we
could use for recreational and cultural activities. There were
many requests by our committee and individuals. I asked for
an easel, paints, brushes, paper and canvas for art work, and
for a supply of plaster of Paris for a project I had in mind.
The commandant assigned the cells on the main deck as
studios or workshops for those who needed space. I was one
of four or five who accepted the offer.

My first project was to paint a number of posters for the
war effort. I had no idea if they would ever be used or even
see daylight, but I went ahead anyway. When the
commandant saw me working on the first poster, "The
Nutcracker," he became excited and asked if he could take it
to Ottawa for the consideration of the wartime information
people. I told him I would be happy to see it used, or even if
it suggested an idea to one of their artists.

The work was slow. After I had completed two more
posters and they were sent to Ottawa, I asked Major Greene,
the commandant, if I could get photocopies of my work as
keepsakes, regardless of what ultimately happened to the
posters. He promised to try to arrange it, but nothing came
of it. Only after I was released did I find out that two of the

poster ideas were used and published.

I also made poster-size sketches of my family from photographs and mailed them home. I made quite a few for my colleagues from their photos. After many weeks at the easel, I turned my attention to a project with plaster of Paris that became quite popular. I set out to make ash trays modelled on a caricature of Hitler's face. First I made a master copy, which had an elongated open mouth for ashes and cigarette butts; "Butts Here" was lettered on the chin. Ben Swankey and I devised a system of mass production and manufactured hundreds of the Hitler ash trays. Not only did my colleagues take a few to send outside, but hundreds were taken by officers and guards—even by a representative of the Red Cross.

There were two other projects in plaster of Paris that gave me many hours of pleasure, and also many headaches, and which helped occupy the time. I decided to make bookends from a reproduction of two hands that would give the impression of holding a row of books together. I selected a model with hands best suited for the purpose, and from which a plaster mold would be made. On the first attempt, we couldn't remove his hand, which was encased in a box of plaster. As we wrestled with the problem, dinner was announced. The model walked into the dining room with this clumsy box at the end of his arm. There were many good-natured jibes by those seated at the tables. When we got back to the problem at hand, some twelve sets had been made before the forms finally chipped and broke. We added a base and gilded the hands to complete the bookends. They looked attractive and we had many requests for more, but the one-armed diner incident discouraged other models.

The last plaster project was a bas relief mask of a facial profile. I decided to experiment on my own. I used highly refined sand as the base for the mould, and it worked. I mounted the copy on a polished wooden plaque and sent it home. I found out later that it was never displayed at home because my mother saw it as a death mask. I made another bas relief profile of John Navizivsky. He was good-humored about the whole thing, and quite cooperative. He also sent the finished product home to his wife. The detail was remarkable. Some years later, when I met the sculptor in Kiev who was preparing a bust to John's memory, I remember thinking how useful that bas relief might have been.

During this period, when arts and crafts were a feature of life in the prison, a number of fellows turned to woodcraft with surprising results. Painstaking weeks of work went into the production of tea trays and jewellery boxes, with intricate inlays of specially selected pieces of wood. Then came the stains, lacquers, and a high polish that gleamed like glass. Some of the army officers asked if they could buy the finished articles, with offers of $100 to $150 for a beautiful tray or jewellery box. My wife still has the jewellery box that Tom McEwen sent her as a gift.

The climate inside and outside the prison camp changed as time and the war moved forward. Not only did we feel that our release would soon be ordered, but so did the military officers and guards at Hull. Attitudes were changing. This could be seen in the way the guards on duty outside the small compound where prisoners could enjoy the sun would peacefully snooze with their rifles stuck in the ground on their bayonets. We'd wake them up when we saw an officer approaching. Public pressure was mounting for our release. People from every walk of life were demanding an end to the injustice. The first to be released, beginning in the early summer of 1942, were the critically ill. The authorities did not want any of the prisoners dying on their hands. But a number of the sick who were released died shortly after their return home.

A judicial commission was set up to effect the release of anti-fascist internees. The government had already made the political decision to free us. The commission would make it appear that we were released by due process of law. Our legal counsel, J.L. Cohen, advised us to appear before the commission and go through the motions of a formal hearing. This would be a different exercise from the one in Winnipeg a year earlier. That one was a whitewash to justify our internment; this was a formality that would authorize our release.

There was a relaxed atmosphere at the hearing. The questions were few and straightforward. In reply to one of the questions, I stated that I had been married three days after my nineteenth birthday. There was laughter when the commissioner commented that "according to the record, you were a young man in a hurry." My lawyer, in a brief statement on my behalf, requested that the commission grant me an immediate release on compassionate grounds. My mother-in-law was dying and the family wanted me home. She died on the day the order for my release came through—on August 6, which is also my birthday.

One memorable incident on the trip home to Winnipeg was the unexpected appearance on the train at Schreiber of my uncle, Steve Borysko. He had received word that I would be on the train and came to welcome me to freedom. We embraced, with tears streaming down our faces, and then settled back and talked our heads off until he left the train in Fort William. My arrival at the CPR station in Winnipeg, where family and friends awaited me, was a highly emotional experience.

All of us, upon our release, had our freedom circumscribed. The RCMP informed us that we would continue to be classified as "enemy aliens," with orders to report twice monthly to designated barracks. This procedure was followed for a few months, and then gradually we were allowed to ignore it with the unwritten consent of the police.

Within weeks of my release, I went down to the military recruiting office to join the armed forces. John Dubno and Archie Gunn, who were also with me in Hull and were recently released, accompanied me to join up. I was the first one out of the office—with a medical certificate that placed me in a category that would keep me out of the army. Dubno and Gunn came through the door as members of the Canadian armed forces. The Winnipeg *Free Press* carried a front page story on this visit for enlistment. A short time later both friends left for training and service overseas.

Later that year I was appointed to the speakers' list of the Victory Loan campaign, teamed with a prominent figure in Canadian business and finance. We addressed many factory meetings in the needle trades industry with appeals to the workers to buy Victory Bonds: The response was always generous, for they saw it as part of their jobs in the national war effort.

Upon our release from Hull, every one of us—health and age permitting—either joined the armed forces or worked for victory on the home front. We had been robbed of two years of freedom and service to the country, but it had not changed our commitment. The war against fascism had to be won.

Bill Walsh

London, Ont.
December 1940 -
October 1942

At the time that the Communist Party was declared illegal, I was stationed in Windsor and was active in helping to organize the autoworkers. The auto plants in Windsor were then being organized into the UAW, which was part of the CIO in the United States. The CIO as such did not yet officially exist in Canada. The Communist Party organizers went underground, but Party members working in unions generally did not.

Arrests were being made, and we went into disguise. Most of us adopted the same disguise—long mustaches, dark glasses, hats and trench coats. Charlie Weir, my brother-in-law, was the exception; he wore a raccoon coat. I went underground and left the place in Windsor where I had been living with my wife Anne. I moved out to a farm near Leamington. I slept in the barn, where I installed a hand printing press which I bought from a firm that was going out of business. I had to ink the roller and roll it over each sheet by hand.

We were all very isolated at this time. I had no connection with the Party except for a couple of members who knew

196

where I could be contacted. Once in a while we would get a letter from the centre of the organization. It usually consisted of the slogans they had decided upon. This was a very difficult time for me; I found it very hard to know what was the right policy in the time of the phony war. One of the slogans that came in one of these letters was, "Every bomb dropped on Britain frees a million Indians." I could not see how I could use a slogan like that in my paper. The one I used which seemed to best fit the situation was "Bring the Boys Home." Another was "Stop the War."

I sent this paper out, first by hand delivery and later by mail, to all the Party members and supporters. As that would make it very easy for the members to be singled out, I padded my list with well-known people like David Croll and George Burt. Both David Croll, the mayor of Windsor and a man very sympathetic to workers and the organizing of the UAW, and George Burt, head of the UAW, supported the war, so we were on opposite sides. I also sent copies to union members and some anti-union people. I even salted in some names taken at random from the telephone book. I had a list of about 700 names to whom I sent our hand-printed *Windsor Clarion*. The Communist Party's official *Clarion* had been banned and was not being published at this time, but many local papers that were started by different members were also called "Clarion."

The UAW was organizing Chrysler and Ford and I wanted to send my paper to the UAW members. I went with a union member to the union office on a Sunday afternoon to get the list of members. We decided to send a special letter to the UAW members, and to print it right there on the union mimeograph machine with the UAW letterhead. We even mailed it out with the stamps that were there in the UAW office. In the letter I was critical of George Burt for his support of the war. Later on he took a very active part in the campaign for the release of the interned labor leaders. At one meeting I was told that he said he strongly supported our release but he sure didn't want that so-and-so Walsh released, who had used his letterhead and his stamps to criticize him to his own members. Who could blame him?

We were in a very difficult position in regard to the war and we were all trying to come to grips with it. At an earlier point in Montreal my main work had been organizing the

Friends of the Soviet Union. Later it was the League against War and Fascism, which subsequently was changed to the League for Peace and Democracy. I had always been against war and fascism—the two were linked together—and supported peace and democracy. At this point we condemned the war, but if we were to regard England as the main enemy as the imperialist exploiter, we found ourselves in the position of seeming to side with the fascists. We never supported fascism and we also opposed our own capitalists, but the lines were not clear and many people were confused. Many people left the Party at this time. Many of us wrestled with the problem on our own. I was certainly one of those very troubled Party members, but I carried on.

Dick Steele and Charlie Weir were the Party organizers for Hamilton and the Niagara peninsula respectively, and we were all very good friends. I arranged for us to get together to discuss these questions. It must have been very late in the fall of 1940. We were all disturbed by the unclarity of our position on the war. We were all involved in putting out papers in our areas and brought copies to the meeting. We were concerned that if one of us got pinched, the people in our area would stop getting the paper. We agreed to get together again when each of us would bring extra copies of the mailing lists. This way if one of us got picked up the others would see to it that his mailing list still received papers.

We agreed to meet on New Year's Eve on a street corner in London. Anne was not well at the time, so I came up early to see her. I had been told of a printer who could give me a supply of paper and stickers, and I had gone to see him a day or two before Christmas. He was a middle-aged fellow who had a little print shop which was not well equipped, and he obviously was not doing well. I ordered about 2,000 stickers with the slogan "Bring the Boys Home" and perhaps 10,000 sheets of blank paper. I arranged to pick them up on New Year's Eve. I was meeting Charlie and Dick about 6:30, and arranged to meet the printer at eight o'clock.

On New Year's Eve I met Charlie, in his coonskin coat, just about the appointed time and we waited for Dick. It was snowing heavily. When you're underground you don't like to stick around and wait on a corner on New Year's Eve for very long in unusual clothes. I didn't want to wait until 8:00

to go to the printer. I wanted to go earlier—just a sort of sixth sense I had—half to three-quarters of an hour earlier, in case the place was being watched. After half an hour or so we went down the dark street where the print shop was and circled it a couple of times. Everything seemed all right. You couldn't really see, the alley was so dark. The printer was inside playing cards with a young lad and an older fellow, and he seemed very casual. I was unhappy about the other people being there but I went in and Charlie stayed outside.

I asked the printer if he had my order. He answered yeah and told me to open the trunk of my car and he'd bring out the stuff. Since there was no one around when I opened the trunk, I told Charlie to come and help me carry out the stacks of paper. I loaded some on Charlie's arm and asked where the other stuff was. The printer told me that it was in the safe and that he'd get it out while we loaded up the rest of the paper. We had just got outside when it seemed like a million cops jumped us—RCMP, provincials and the London municipal police. There were maybe nine or ten of them. They went in and got the stickers and the rest of the paper. I never saw the stickers. They put Charlie in one car and me in another, but there was enough time for me to remind Charlie that he had nothing to do with it, that he was Anne's brother and was visiting her because she wasn't well.

During the war we had national registration. Everybody had to register. We all registered in our own names, but I knew I couldn't go around with a registration card saying Bill Walsh. I was known as a Party official. I needed to register again in some other name. Somebody had a bunch of blank registrations—they weren't too hard to come by at the time. I remember looking for a name. At an old historic cemetery at Niagara Falls I found a tombstone with the name Charles Potter. I think he had died about 100 years before. I filled out a national registration card with that name on it and kept the card in my pocket. The idea was that I wouldn't carry the Bill Walsh card when I was doing Party work; I'd carry the other one. When I met Charlie and Dick on Christmas Eve, I told them about this. I gave each of them registration cards, and they made them out in the same name, Charles Potter. That way we'd know what name the others were using.

But now sitting in the police car after being pinched, I thought, God, here I am with two registrations in my pocket and Dick and Charlie and I all have cards in the same name. It was dark in the car, and there was an RCMP in the front and another sitting beside me in the back. I put my hand in my back pocket and felt my wallet. I could feel the two registration cards, but I couldn't tell which was which. One way or another I had to get rid of one of them. I shoved one card down behind the seat.

They brought us into the Mounted Police headquarters. I was asked for my registration card. I looked around but I couldn't see Charlie anywhere. I took it out and the RCMP looked at it.

"Oh," says he, "Bill Walsh. A big Communist, eh?"

"No," I said, "I'm a Communist, but not a big Communist."

Charlie was brought in just then and they asked for his registration card. He hadn't brought the other card so he handed them his Charlie Weir card—quite right, for he was visiting his sister. I was craning my neck to see if Dick was there, but I couldn't see him. It turned out that because of the snowstorm he hadn't come. But I didn't find that out till a long time later.

They brought in the printer and asked him which of the two of us he knew. He pointed to me as the one who had ordered the stickers and the paper. He told them that that night was the first time he'd seen Charlie. He identified me and not Charlie, but they locked us both up. After a wait, they finally brought us something to drink, a cup of tea. I remember smashing the metal cup so that it had a sharp edge and then carving on the wall: "Steal a loaf, go to jail. Steal a million, go to the Senate."

Charlie was shocked. He was revolutionary but he did things in an orderly and law-abiding way. When the warden finally came in he told me I'd have to pay for the wall being plastered and repainted. But it never came up.

We were moved to the London County Gaol, a place that at one time held prisoners arrested in the Rebellion of 1837. The jail was very old, really obsolete. I think it's still there—a horrible place. There were rats running through it. We were kept in the death cell for about a month before our trial. Fortunately, Charlie and I were in neighboring cells.

We had lots of experiences in the jail. We were in with hobos, drunks and thieves. There was a piece of paper on a wall about a Geneva Convention and political prisoners. I asked to see the warden. I tried to tell him that I was a political prisoner, that I wanted books, newspapers and decent food—the food was ghastly. Some of the first poems I wrote in there were about the food.

Eventually we had a trial. They charged us with being officials of an illegal organization and attempting to print for distribution literature likely to cause disaffection to His Majesty. Not sabotage of any kind, but to undermine the war effort. The lawyer the Party got to represent us at the trial was Mr. Dave Goldstick. My wife Anne and Charlie's close friend Louise were both there. By that time I'd had a couple of short visits with Anne but always through the grill.

At the trial the RCMP gave evidence. They told what happened but they never mentioned that the printer didn't identify Charlie. They only said that we were both caught picking up the stickers. One of them testified under oath that Bill Walsh boasted that he was a big Communist. That got me mad; it had been the other way around. They were twisting everything. Earlier they'd asked me if I knew Tim Buck and when I told them that every Communist knows Tim Buck they translated that back during the trial to say that I'd said I was a personal friend of Tim Buck's. I wanted to get on the witness stand and make it clear that they were telling a bunch of bloody lies but my lawyer wouldn't hear of it.

"Listen," he said, "if they ask you if you're a member of the Communist Party, an organizer, what are you going to say?" Because he knew what we'd say he wouldn't let either of us take the stand.

The RCMP had found a couple of copies of my old leaflets on Charlie. The judge said that two copies of two different leaflets was not evidence of "leaflets for distribution." They couldn't prove anything and in the end the judge found Charlie not guilty. Right away the RCMP asked the judge whether he was going to intern him anyway. When the judge said he couldn't order Charlie interned when he'd just found him not guilty, the RCMP said right there in the courtroom, "Well it doesn't matter, we're going to intern him."

They found me guilty of one charge and asked if I had anything to say. I answered yes. I took the opportunity to say what I thought of the War Measures Act until, after two or three attempts, the judge finally stopped me. I was sentenced to six months and a $300 fine or three additional months. Both Charlie and I were taken back to the London County Gaol and a few days later Charlie was taken to Petawawa Internment Camp. The RCMP was right, they could intern him even after he'd been found not guilty.

Two or three months later they took me to Guelph. I was driven there with other prisoners—crooks, vandals, rapists. I was a bit older than the average prisoner. They regarded me as an unusual fellow. The other prisoners were in for rape, motor manslaughter, theft, high-grading, receiving stolen goods and so on. They used to compare what they were in for. Almost everyone claimed he was framed; most blamed the frame-up on a girl. When I told them my story they didn't really understand what I was talking about. When I mentioned "illegal organization," most thought I was talking about the Mafia. Even though they couldn't quite figure me out, they did come to like and respect me. I became the confidant of many of the prisoners and used to do things like write letters for them.

When we first got to Guelph I was on what they called the bull gang. We were a work gang that was closely guarded. Each day we were taken to some place in the rear part of the jail grounds. We dug up what seemed to be heavy wet clay from a hole and shovelled it into a pile. I never did find out if there was any practical purpose to the work or if it was just a way of putting us to hard labor. It was physically very, very hard work.

I don't remember how long I did that but next I was promoted to the marmalade gang, which worked under excellent conditions compared to the bull gang. The 5-pound cans we made were sent to various officials in the provincial government and to provincial institutions, hospitals and such.

After that I was promoted again. This time I was made a trustee on the garden gang. By now the weather was fairly good. About fifteen of us worked in groups of two or three on the different grounds around the vast Guelph jail. There were one or two easygoing guards in charge of us, but we were left pretty much on our own. We just wandered from place to place where the flower beds needed weeding, digging, tidying up or replanting. If there are still lovely gardens around Guelph jail, well, some of them go back to the days when we worked on them.

Even though things were lax, I still had the impression I was watched more than the others. I was fairly familiar with the Guelph area. I had a number of quite close friends there, and it would have been relatively easy for me to have gotten to the home of one of them, where I would have been hidden or helped to make a further escape. However, I talked with Anne about the prospect of escaping, and after she talked with the Party, the word came back that they didn't want us to break out. There was a campaign going on outside to get us all released.

After the garden gang I was put into a real soft job—a real "good go" as we used to call it. The upholstery gang was made up of just one chap who was going to be released, and me. There was also a guard, an old war vet with one eye. He used to close his one eye and go to sleep. I was taught mainly by the graduating prisoner. Big divans and easy chairs were brought in and my job was either to re-cover them or replace the springs. Sometimes I had to build a sofa up completely from the wooden springs. I was told that some of them came from offices of the ministries in Queen's Park.

So you see, I learned a few trades while I was in jail. I haven't done much upholstering since, I've never made marmalade, and I sure haven't gone around digging holes in the ground. But I do like gardening.

I wasn't going to pay the $300 fine, so I served a full nine months in Guelph prison with some time off for good behavior. The day finally came for my release. Anne was there. She moved to every town I was in during that period and always managed to find a job. She wasn't able to hold a job for very long because the RCMP always found a way to tell the owner of the place that her husband was in jail. Although she came to the jail on the day of my release, I only got to see her from a distance. I was given back my clothes; it felt great to have my own clothes again. Then I had to wait in a kind of foyer and from there I could see Anne on the outside. Two RCMP officers were right there with me. One of them looked kind of familiar and it turned out that he had been one of the police who had originally arrested me. I never had a chance to talk to Anne. They put me in the back seat of an unmarked car, locked the door on the outside and drove off. All I could do was wave to Anne. We had only gone a short distance when the policeman turned around.

"Now look, Bill," he said, "we can either do this nice or we can do it the hard way. If you promise you're not going to get smart and try to escape we won't put handcuffs on. We also have our sidearms. So behave yourself. Don't try anything and we'll just drive on." They told me we were going to London, to the Middlesex County Gaol.

"Look," I said, "if I had wanted to escape, I could have escaped several times before I got here." They didn't put the cuffs on me.

After driving on the highway for a piece, I began to feel that there was something very familiar about the car and the one policeman. Just for curiosity I shoved my hand into the tight back of the seat, and sure enough, there was a folded paper. I wiggled it out when they had their eyes turned, and believe it or not, it was the registration form I had secreted there on the night Charlie and I were arrested. This was about nine months later. I think I shoved it in my pocket. When we got back to the London jail, they again went through the whole procedure of making me take a shower and change clothes. During the whole time that I was naked I held the form in my fist. I only finally got rid of it some time later; I think I flushed it down the jail toilet.

At the London County Gaol it felt like I was coming back to an old alma mater. I was interviewed by a commission of one. He only asked one question: why shouldn't I be interned? I told him there was no reason to intern me. I wasn't a menace to the state. I was not a menace to the royal family. I supported the war. I believed in the war against fascism and I wanted to join the army.

I don't recall all the details. He said very little; he wrote very little. All I know if that a few days later I was again picked up in the jail by the RCMP. This time I was left in civilian clothes. They put me in handcuffs and brought me to the railway station. It was a bit embarrassing on the train, but it was great to see people in civilian clothes after so long. We went to Toronto and got off at Union Station. I was handcuffed to the cop's wrist.

I remember we went into the coffee shop in the railway station and sat at the counter. The cop ordered some kind of triple decker sandwich for himself and told me to order a plain sandwich. I'll never forget the waitress. She started needling him right away. She asked if he had left his horse outside the door. Then she asked what I'd done, robbed a bank? She said, "Bet you feel like a hero, Mr. Cop."

It was all said in a manner to embarrass him. Everyone was watching us curiously. After she asked how I could eat with handcuffs on, he took them off so I could eat the sandwich. When we were finished, the cop went over to pay and handcuffed me again. Just then the waitress shouted out loudly from the back of the restaurant. "Just watch that cop," she said. "I don't know, but he may have stolen a magazine. He was looking them over. Just make sure he pays if he's got one."

The people in the restaurant were laughing and chuckling; the guy was tremendously embarrassed. I got quite a lift out of the whole thing. She had a lot of spunk, that young woman. I presume she didn't like cops.

At any rate, the policeman took me out of there and handcuffed me to himself and we got on a train headed for Ottawa. It was a long, long trip. He slept quite a bit of the way, with me on the inside seat. I noticed a sly trick of his which I thought was quite childish. He'd always keep his leg up against mine so that if I tried to get out he'd be sure to feel it. Where I could go, handcuffed to a man who weighed about 200 pounds, I don't know.

When I wanted to use the toilet I had to wake him up. He'd come with me and look inside before he'd let me use it. Then he'd disconnect the handcuffs from his wrist before I went in. I don't remember him going to the toilet at all. He certainly wouldn't have let me go free. As I say, he was a very big man. I guess he had great control over his insides; maybe that was part of his training.

At Ottawa we were met at the station by another RCMP officer with a car. He drove me across to the Quebec side of the Ottawa River and up a narrow lane through woods from the highway until we came to the jail in a clearing. As it turned out, this prison on the outskirts of Hull had not yet been used as a prison but was now serving as an internment camp for anti-fascists.

What a happy reunion! The first person I saw was Charlie Weir. He was on the welcoming committee. They sang "Hold the Fort" and other labor and welcoming songs. The welcome wasn't the only thing that was different about Hull. There were so many fellows I already knew. Also, Johnny and Charlie Weir were my brothers-in-law. We were the only family group there. The first evening I was there they gave me a welcoming party. Apparently that was the tradition whenever somebody new joined the group. We sat around in a semi-circle in the bull pen. I think it was around September or October when I got there because the weather was still fairly nice and we were able to sit outside.

At the party everyone was expected to sing a song or tell a story. When it came to my turn, I couldn't think of what song to sing. For some reason I sang "Men of Harlech." Joe Wallace was very taken with it. I had a passingly good voice and Joe asked me to sing it again. Later he had me sing the words to him alone. After that he wrote his own version called "Night is Ended," which we sang to the tune of "Men of Harlech." It was published in his *Collected Works*.

I was very often teamed with Joe on the dishwashing job. While we washed the dishes he would get me to sing various songs. One he liked very much was "When You and I Were Seventeen." It's quite a romantic piece. He'd get me to sing it many times. He said he was going to write his own words to it, but he never did.

Johnny Weir and Mitch Sago and one or two others also wrote songs. Bill Repka used to play the guitar. He would sing "The Old Apple Tree." I always associate that song with Billy. He had a good voice and played the guitar well. He was always part of the lighter side of our life there.

We did have a crystal radio set which was put together by Murphy, who had worked for the CBC. I didn't know where most of the parts came from but I know that at least one part was smuggled in by one of the guards I knew in Kitchener. He was a left-wing guy and a veteran of World War I. I remember him passing it to me. All the parts were turned over to Murphy and he built the set.

The little receiver was kept in a cell on the second floor under the pillow of a bunk bed. It was turned on only for the news. One person was assigned to listen and take notes. The first person assigned was Muni Taub. He'd take one of the earphones out from under the pillow and lie with it underneath his ear so it would not be seen by anyone passing by. It looked as if he were taking a nap. He'd write notes down as furtively as he could, trying to get the essence of the broadcast, and then the news would be passed to the rest of us when we were all together. It was never quite revealed to everybody how we got the news. We got it, never mind how.

Night is Ended

Dark your days, unknown to story,
Days of work and nights of worry,
Suddenly a shaft of glory
    Strikes you, Workingmen.

Where the battle rocks and rages
All the hopes of all the ages
Forward surge, or sink back stages,
    Save them, Workingmen!

Chorus:
Wake, the Vision splendid
Flames, for Night is ended,
Rise and March
Thro' Freedom's arch
To name and fame unended.
March in mighty millions pouring,
Forges flaring, cannon roaring,
Life and Death in final warring
    Call you, Workingmen!

At your benches planning, speeding,
In the trenches battling, bleeding,
Yours the help the world is needing,
    Answer, Workingmen!

So shall pass the battle thunder,
Poverty and pelf and plunder,
So shall rise a world of wonder,
    World of Workingmen!

The set, however, did not work well without an aerial. Our problem was: how to erect an aerial inside the building? Murphy got some very, very fine copper wire and tied one end of it to a bar of the cell window; from there it was easy enough to attach it to the set under the cot. But what to do with the other end? That's why this particular cell was selected. It was right behind and above the volleyball net in the bull pen. The other end of the aerial was tied to the pole which held up the volleyball net. It was so fine that unless you were really looking for it you would never see it.

One day the colonel came on his tour of inspection. In his usual fashion, he walked around the bull pen once. All of us who were there in the official group walking behind him were very shocked to see woollen socks and underwear hanging from the "invisible" wire. But the colonel walked right under it and paid no attention. The wire slanted upwards to the cell window and I couldn't imagine how anybody ever got up there to hang his socks up. But the colonel didn't seem to notice it, socks and all. Or if he did, he didn't pay any attention. I don't remember whose socks they were or if we ever found out.

Later on we had an official radio with a loudspeaker in the mess hall, but we only got the programs that the authorities allowed us to hear. We certainly did hear about the Dieppe landing. And at a certain point we were allowed to receive newspapers, but parts were cut out. I can't tell you what their thinking was for there was no rhyme or reason to it. Parts that they cut out had war news, but other parts that they left in had war news too. Certainly they cut out any reference to the campaign for our release.

In 1942 the fellows were gradually being released. They were called to a hearing and would not come back. We knew that they were being released straight from the hearing so there was no way they could come back and tell us about the hearings. At mine, they asked me where I was going and I said home to Windsor, which is where I had been living when I was arrested. They wanted me to sign a document stating I would never go out of the Windsor area without permission from the RCMP and that I would not speak to any meetings.

I did not want to sign any such thing. J.L. Cohen, who was there with me, said that it was all right to sign. He told me that others, including Tim Buck, had signed. I was confused. I was certainly going to go to Montreal where my family was. That was the first thing I was going to do when I got out. And I was going to talk to my friends in London. And if I was invited to speak at meetings, I was going to speak. But Cohen said I should sign, that it was just a formality. He was right; I don't think I ever reported to the RCMP and I certainly travelled about and spoke at meetings.

The worst thing was that Anne died not long after my release. That really broke me up. I joined the army soon after that, in the early spring of 1943. I got overseas and was in the Second Front in 1944. I was not in the Intelligence Corps but our own Intelligence Officer had been severely wounded earlier and I was appointed Acting Intelligence Officer.

One day I was in our cellar headquarters alone with the colonel, who was asleep in the back. There was sniping going back and forth. I was in the front manning the headquarters when a guy was escorted in wearing a Canadian army uniform, except his shoulder badge said "RCMP." He wore the insignia of a major and he was wearing brass buttons, of all things! He didn't seem to realize he was at the Front. He told me that he had left a jeep about half a mile back and had come forward on foot. He didn't know who I was, of course. He said he wanted to see the Intelligence Officer. I asked him what he wanted.

"Well," he said, "I've got to get information about Private Walsh."

"Private Walsh? What's his first name?"

"William."

"You better see the colonel," I told him. I kept him waiting there while I went into the back to see the colonel. I woke him up and told him that there was somebody from the RCMP to see him.

"What the hell is the RCMP doing here?" he said.

"He wants to know about Private Walsh," I told him.

"Who the hell is Private Walsh?"

"Me."

"Well, you go on in and talk to him," he said.

"I can't talk to him. He wants to investigate me. He wants to talk *about* Private Walsh, not *to* him."

The colonel was sure mad. Later he told me about the whole thing. They were checking up on me. They wanted to know if I was a good leader, who I associated with and whether I would lead the Canadian troops over to the Russians (by this time our allies). The colonel gave him no satisfaction whatsoever, and in fact made a monkey out of him in the bargain. After the RCMP officer left our headquarters our men started firing in the air and he had to crawl most of the half mile back to the jeep on his belly.

This came back, I presume, to the fact that I was supposed to have been reporting to the RCMP. They finally tracked me down in the front lines. With very few exceptions, those who were interned or in jail did not get to go overseas, or if they did, they got some kind of joe-job.

Dr. Howard Lowrie

Toronto, Ont.
May 1941 - March 1942

The first inkling I had of anything suspicious was one day in May 1941. As I sat in my consulting office in my house, two large, well-dressed men walked in. I asked what I could do for them.

"We are from the Royal Canadian Mounted Police, detective bureau," answered one of them, showing me his badge. "We want to talk to you about some of your patients. Do you know Jim Murphy?"

I told them I did, he was a patient of mine. They wanted to know what I knew about him and I said I had treated him for a medical problem. Then they asked if I knew that he was a radio technician for the CBC? I said of course I knew. We sometimes discussed radio when he came for a consultation.

A few days later I was asked to come down to RCMP headquarters to answer more questions along the same lines. They asked again about Jim Murphy. To double check they asked me to phone my wife to pull out Murphy's card and read the relevant material from it. This was the first inkling my wife Eva had that the police were questioning me. But she knew it was not unusual for the police to be seeking

211

information about someone, so she paid little attention to it.

I was puzzled by the incident, but busy with many things and did not let it occupy my mind. A few days later I was in my office preparing for my afternoon appointments after having delivered a baby at St. Michael's Hospital, something I'd been doing for about 25 years. I must have dozed off, because I was startled by a heavy knock on the door that reverberated through the house. I knew at once this was not a regular patient coming for an appointment. I could hear the heavy tread of two men walking to my waiting room. They had come again!

My wife came into my office to say that there were two large men—she illustrated with her hands—to see me. When they came in, I asked them to be seated, and asked again what I could do for them. They were the same men who had come before, but they were no longer the polite detectives they had been. They were officious and firm, even condescending. They showed me a paper and said it was a warrant for my arrest.

"Arrest? My arrest?" I asked them what the charge was. I couldn't believe my ears.

"There does not have to be a charge," one said. "You are to be placed in the custody of His Majesty's armed forces under the Defence of Canada Regulations."

I asked if I could call a lawyer, consult with someone...

"There are no provisions for that," said one of the officers. "We will tell your wife that you are to be interned and that you will be coming with us." He motioned to the other officer to get my wife while he remained with me.

At this point a patient of mine rang the bell and walked into my office. I told her that I could not see her that day and she'd have to go home. She looked very upset and asked if anything was wrong. The second detective returned at that moment with my wife, who looked very frightened. I repeated to my patient that I was very sorry not to see her but that she had better go home.

Looking at my wife in tears, I thought also of my two daughters who were at school and of my other patients who were relying on me. I reminded the officers that I was a doctor and that I could not just leave everything without any notice or preparation.

"The law says that you can and must," said the

policeman.

I tried to explain that people depended on me. I had to make some arrangements for them. I would have to assign patients to other doctors and tell the nurses what must be done. Otherwise my patients would be in trouble. The officers seemed nonplussed by this but called their superiors. It was agreed that I would be allowed to stay overnight and to make only the most necessary calls. Guards would be placed at the doors so that no one could come or go.

My wife was very upset by my arrest. She could not understand what I could have done. I was still trying to comprehend it myself, while at the same time trying to comfort her. I didn't feel guilty of anything, but that was of small comfort to either of us. She broke down and cried her heart out. It was the saddest, most heart-breaking night of my life.

Next day, May 24, 1941, the Toronto *Globe and Mail* carried the announcement.

RCMP Arrest James Murphy, Dr. H.A. Lowrie

Dr. Howard A. Lowrie, Toronto physician residing on Humewood Drive, and James A. Murphy, 38, veteran employee of the Toronto studios of the Canadian Broadcasting Corporation, were arrested yesterday by RCMP officers on charges of breach of the Defence of Canada Regulations. There is no connection between the arrests.

I was held one night at RCMP headquarters and then a few days in the Don Jail and the Landsdowne Barracks. I was then taken to Petawawa with James Murphy on a beautiful spring day in the last week of May. I'll never forget, we were manacled like criminals before crossing Front Street to go to Union Station.

Our treatment demonstrated to me most painfully that I was no longer the respected and useful member of society that I had thought I was; father of two daughters, doctor to many people. Instead, at one blow, I was suddenly a criminal. This was most sharply brought home to me when the officer snapped the handcuffs around my wrists. The cold steel proclaimed me an enemy of society who must be chained to an officer and then locked up. As I looked at my hands, with which I had trained for nearly a quarter of a century to handle the scalpel and other instruments, to deliver babies and to comfort human beings in pain, I could not believe what was happening to me.

Various editorials and letters appeared in the Toronto newspapers protesting my treatment. No charges were ever laid against me, and no one ever made any specific accusations. Certainly I was opposed to war between imperialist countries, but I was also opposed to fascism, particularly as it appeared in Nazi Germany. I was interested in the developments of socialized medicine in the Soviet Union. I did have a ham radio outfit, but in common with all other Canadian amateur operators, I did not operate it during the war. When the war ended, amateurs had to apply for a renewal of their license. I applied along with others and mine was renewed, as it has been every year since.

On June 26, 1941, the Toronto *Star* published the following editorial:

> Dr. Howard A. Lowrie of Toronto was arrested on May 23 by the RCMP under the Defence of Canada Regulations. A practising physician for twenty years, he was taken from his consulting office, and is still interned without opportunity of a trial or hearing, although more than a month has gone by. Meanwhile his practice is being destroyed and the family income disappears...His fellow doctors, his patients and his friends cannot understand what possible connection there can be between this man and subversive conduct. Many of them have protested to Ottawa. It is known that he was an amateur radio operator, but it is claimed that this set was, like others then in existence, dismantled at the beginning of the war, and has since been examined by government officials.
>
> The rather curious suggestion is also made that his arrest and detention may have some connection with his treating a man for carbuncles, who was subsequently picked up as belonging to an illegal organization.
>
> But the guilt or innocence of Dr. Lowrie is not a point upon which a newspaper can pronounce. If he were guilty—and his patients and colleagues do not for a moment believe it—his prominence would only add to

his offence. The real issue is that he has been interned for a month, without, so far as any one knows, a date being set for a hearing in his case.

Internees are entitled not only to an impartial hearing, but a prompt one. Yet it is said that a hearing of such cases as this is sometimes delayed three months or more.

The editorial demanded that the government do something, and concluded, "The situation is one which cries out for remedy."

My wife Eva wrote the following letter, which appeared in the Toronto *Star* on August 1 and the *Globe and Mail* on August 2.

Absolutely no provision has been made for the welfare of myself and my children. The internment of my husband has destroyed his practice and left me with no income.

My husband is not a criminal. He was and is a true democrat whose chief interest was in the welfare of his many patients and his fellow men... His many patients, especially among the blind and among the poor he so unselfishly served, will suffer by his removal, particularly those who are seriously ill...

I feel his arrest and internment is a great miscarriage of justice. It is hardly the kind of democracy our men are fighting for in Europe...

I wish to appeal to all persons interested in the maintenance of British justice to demand his open trial at which he can fairly defend himself, as is every man's unalienable right in every free country...

I and my children as well as his hundreds of patients will be more than grateful to all those who will stand by our democracy in this case...

Backing up the letter, the Toronto *Star* editorialized on August 2:

The Government is probably now aware of the extent of the growing feeling in Canada that something is seriously wrong with the handling of these cases.

It is not a question of guilt or innocence. It is a

question of fair trials and reasonably prompt trials. And
at least some explanation to relatives and friends. In
some instances there may be reasons for a certain
amount of secrecy, but it is too much like Germany
under a Nazi government, and too little like Canada
under a Liberal government, to have men like this
spirited away and held incommunicado, without a hearing and without any hint as to their supposed wrong-
doing.

The editorial then called again on the government to do
something and ended with this paragraph:

If Dr. Lowrie is guilty, the public should be told why
and of what. And he should only be considered guilty
after guilt has been proved at a fair hearing. Mrs.
Lowrie's letter will strike a responsive chord in many a
liberty-loving heart.

At Petawawa I became Number 985, a cipher in a Canadian
internment camp. After a demonstration by the internees, we
were moved to a jail outside Hull. Time passes slowly in
prison, and Jim Murphy and I rigged up a Morse code
practice set from a prison bell that was not being used. With
this homemade contraption we would practice dot-dots and
dash-dashes to help while away the time. Of course the set
was not connected to any outlet. It was simply a toy on which
one man tapped out a message while the other sat in the lower
bunk, copied it down and decoded it.

Around the same time, some kind friend on the outside
had sent in a tiny crystal radio set and earphone wrapped in
wax paper in the bottom of a pail of cottage cheese. It was
kept under a pillow so that a man could lie on his bunk and
listen to the news, which we were otherwise denied. To
improve its reception, some of our technicians strung up an
antenna. One particularly cold morning, the antenna became
highly visible as frost coated its entire length.

When this was discovered, a platoon of soldiers suddenly
burst into the cell I shared with Jim Murphy. Dramatically
they ripped out our Morse code apparatus and departed in
triumph, laughing over their small victory. Some of our men
quickly dismantled and hid the crystal set in case of a further

search. After a few days it was reassembled and again gave us news of the war at first hand. But Murphy and I were sentenced to a week in solitary confinement for daring to practice Morse code in jail.

The solitary cells in the basement had not been insulated. It was here that I got a most severe attack of gall bladder colic, so severe that the prison doctor brought me back from the dungeon to my usual cell upstairs after a couple of days. But the excruciating pain continued, and one day I collapsed on my way back to my cell from the washroom. Finally, an ambulance was brought and I was carried out on a stretcher, with a group of guards ahead and behind and sirens screaming. There was some delay before the guards at the gateway to the grounds were satisfied that it was not an escape plot. I was taken to a military hospital to recuperate for two weeks. My wife came to see me and told me that efforts were being made for my release. My sister, a missionary in China, and my brother, a doctor in New York, also came to visit me.

Some time after I returned to the jail, I was told that I was being released and to pack my bags. Just as suddenly, I was told that it was a mistake, someone else was being released. It was a friend of mine, a physicist. I was to remain. Finally on March 20, 1942, I was released, among the first of the internees.

On March 21, 1942, the Toronto *Globe and Mail* carried a news story headed:

Release is Obtained by Toronto Physician

Dr. Howard A. Lowrie, Humewood Drive physician who was arrested last May by the RCMP, arrived here yesterday from an internment camp in Quebec where he had been confined since soon after his arrest in this city...Dr. Lowrie had been charged under the Defence of Canada Regulations, but it was not revealed what his alleged offence was...

My ordeal left deep scars on my wife and family, and it was some time before my health permitted me to resume my practice. The support of friends, family and many people I had never heard of was a great comfort to me at this time. Joseph Atkinson, publisher of the Toronto *Star*, personally phoned me and my wife to express his support and congratulations on my release. The *Star* had given me extensive support during my internment, particularly in the way it had questioned the government's actions.

Recently a friend told me that late in June 1942 he was arrested and charged with violating the War Measures Act. After two weeks in jail, the case came to court. The judge asked him if he supported the war.

"Yes, 100 per cent," he replied.

"So you changed your mind?"

"Yes. The prime minister of Britain changed his mind about the Soviet Union? Why can't I change my mind?"

Case dismissed.

If my case had come to court, my answer would have been similar. If Winston Churchill can change his mind, why can't I?

Ben Swankey

On August 20, 1941, we were transferred to Hull jail just across the Ottawa River from Ottawa, a so-called "white elephant" building that had been built through political patronage and then never used. This was not unusual in Quebec under Premier Maurice Duplessis. His government was corrupt and the premier himself was an open and avowed admirer of the Italian dictator Mussolini. Duplessis tried to follow his example in establishing what he called a "corporate society" in Quebec.

We had the whole prison to ourselves. The internal administration of the jail was turned over to us. We did the cooking, cleaning and so on. We also set up a canteen where we could buy small items such as chocolate bars, soap, tobacco, toothbrushes and writing paper. We took an intense dislike to the camp commandant, not only for his dealing with us, but also because of his attitude to the wives who came to Hull in an attempt to visit their husbands.

Occasionally a work party was sent outside to do some work in public parks. I went out only once on a project like that during the year I was in Hull. But I still remember the exciting experience of riding through Hull in a truck and seeing crowds of people. But for the most part, there wasn't much to do in the camp. We suntanned, read, took part in sports and classes, and arranged our own concerts and banquets. The classes we organized covered many subjects—mathematics, German, French, music and Canadian history. One of the inmates was a highly qualified young mathematician who after his release joined Einstein in secret war work in the United States. Another, Kent Rowley, a young trade union leader, had an extensive knowledge of Canadian history from which many of us benefited.

Denied the right to buy liquor, we did our own

winemaking. It was illegal, of course, and we kept the jugs of fermenting juice hidden under our beds, hoping that the smell would not betray us when the camp commandant and his men made inspections. But they were never discovered, or if they were, they were ignored. On labor holidays such as May Day, we had special celebrations, complete with banquets and concert programs that included speeches, plays, music and readings. We also published our own camp paper.

While we were in Hull, our resident poet, Joe Wallace, continued to write. One of his poems, "Flame of the Future," expressed our feelings well. My friend Mitch Sago joined with me to compose music for this poem. Neither of us was a musician but we persevered. Our production, after our release, was recorded by a Winnipeg artist and sung in labor halls across the country.

While we were interned a widespread public campaign was being carried on outside for our release. It included a delegation of internees' wives and trade union leaders who went to Ottawa on March 31, 1941, seeking hearings with government leaders. They received a mixed response from Ottawa officials. The internees' wives especially expressed their disappointment at the attitude of M.J. Coldwell, leader of the CCF. He opposed their demand that Section 21 of the Defence of Canada Regulations be repealed and did not support their demand for the release of the internees. All he said was that instead of the present one-person advisory committee which reviewed the cases of internees he favored a three-person committee.

The campaign for our release was finally crowned with success. In 1942 the government began releasing anti-fascist detainees from Hull. However, our release was staggered over a period of many months, and came about only after hearings before a judicial commission. The hearings were a formality but were also used to try to intimidate us. We were allowed the right to be represented by a lawyer. Our lawyer was J.L. Cohen, one of the top criminal lawyers in the country. He went over our cases with each of us. In my case he did not consider it necessary to attend himself, so I went through the hearing without counsel.

The RCMP file on me that was provided to the commission was thick. One of the charges against me was that in

1932 or 1933 I had written a letter to the Edmonton *Journal* charging that the Boy Scouts were too militaristic. I had been a Boy Scout leader myself on the prairies and had given marching, saluting and other semi-military training to the young scouts. I knew what I was talking about, but in the eyes of the RCMP any such criticism was subversive.

I was released in September 1942. On my arrival back in Edmonton I was greeted by a crowd of 500 people. We paraded down Jasper Avenue to a reception which I addressed. I worked for a few weeks as a bartender and then went to the recruiting office to join the army. After they investigated me for over a month, I was admitted. Six months later I was a sergeant in the Royal Canadian Artillery in Shilo, Manitoba, and in 1945, shortly before the war ended, I was sent overseas.

Pat Lenihan

When we were moved from Petawawa we expected to go to another camp. We arrived at Hull to find a new jail, a big building, very modern. When we saw the walls around this building we refused to go in. By this time there were about a hundred of us anti-fascists from all over Canada. When we were told to go in, Norman Freed, our spokesman, said, "No man move. We're not going in there."

When the officer told us to get marching we told him that we were not going into any jail or prison. We would tolerate a camp but not this. For about an hour there was lots of excitement. The officer went in to consult his superiors, and I guess they phoned across the river to Ottawa. Finally they came back and told us that Hull was not going to be operated as a prison. We were going to run it. Before we'd move they took our committee in and showed them the whole place. A little while later Norman Freed and the committee came out and told us it was going to be all right.

On the inside, it was fine; there was a beautiful kitchen, everything shining. There were two bunks to a cell, and no locks on the doors, no soldiers in sight at all, no police, no prison staff. Any soldiers that were on guard were on the outside. There was only one lock on the whole building. That didn't stop us as we had complete freedom to go outside. There was a big compound for exercise, and there was also a door that led to the outside. We could go out to a wooded area and sit under the trees. Outside there were maybe five acres of bush. It looked like an unkempt park but it was a beautiful spot for reading and studying.

The soldiers were members of the Veterans' Guard. They were our friends. Sometimes when we were outside, there would be soldiers sitting at the corner of the fence, maybe 3 feet outside it. On a hot day, a soldier would sit down and the next thing he'd be snoozing with his rifle between his legs. If we saw a sergeant or an officer coming we'd holler or throw rocks to wake the guard.

When we received a crystal radio set in a can of cottage cheese, it was decided that it would be kept in my cell. I shared a cell with Muni Taub, right in the middle of the cell block. I was on the bottom bunk, he was on the top. The radio was put under my pillow. The cells were inspected once a day, but after a while it got pretty lax. In the afternoons, when things had quieted down after the inspections, a few of us took turns listening to all the news. So every night we had a full report on the day's news.

I'll never forget it—I was lying in the bunk one night listening and the news broke about Pearl Harbor. I sailed out of my bunk. I don't think my feet hit the ground until I got down to the end of the passage where Norman Freed was resting and reading.

"Norman!" I said. "Get up. I just got it. Pearl Harbor's wiped out."

He thought I had gone crazy. They all did for a couple of seconds. I told them to come on up and listen for themselves. And sure enough, they found out that it was true.

I imagine that set is somewhere around that building yet. We used it right until the last man was released. You couldn't take it out with because you were searched going out.

There were two attempts that we know of to plant RCMP stool pigeons among us. These fellows would come in through ordinary channels. The door would open and some fellow dressed like we were would walk in. We'd all gather around him wondering if we knew him or knew of him. Both times the guy was French Canadian. There was quite a group of French Canadians with us. We became worried right away with the first fellow. You could tell by the way he carried himself that he'd had military training. Within a couple of days the French-Canadian comrades knew that he was a plant. Our committee went immediately to the camp commandant and told him to get the plant out before he got hurt. Of course the commandant had an excuse. He said he didn't know who the guy was but that he had to keep him interned. Possibly it was true. It was up to the top brass in Ottawa.

In a way I felt sorry for the stool pigeon. He had to eat and live with us. Nobody would look at him; they would almost spit at him every time he came round. His food would be delivered to him on a plate. All the rest, say twelve men at a table, would share a big platter of meat, vegetables and potatoes. He was never allowed to touch any of the platters, only the portion that was served to him. It was often doused heavily with pepper and salt so no one in the world could eat it.

We wanted him out. A couple of times we took his kit, mattress and all his possessions and threw them outside, right next to the door that divided us from the soldiers' headquarters. When they opened the door they'd find his mattress and everything else. He'd be standing with his stuff, looking glum. After about a week they let him out. About three months later they repeated the process with someone else, but then they gave up.

All through our internment in Kananaskis, Petawawa and finally in Hull, we were treated with respect by 98 per cent of the military staff, and that included a lot of the officers too. There is one episode I'll never forget.

In Hull jail we did all the cooking ourselves; we had all the regular cooking equipment of the army, such as big seven- or eight-gallon pots for making soup. We received a lot of fruit, raisins and such, more than we could eat. We decided to make some good whisky. We had to cook the stuff in one of those kitchen pots, and make it in the kitchen. We poured the juice from the mash into this big pot and then covered it with a pan which would sink into the soup about 6 inches. Then we filled it to the top with ice. The steam from the juice would start to boil or percolate and it would hit the bottom of the ice pan. There was another pan to catch the alcohol, and that liquid was clear. Did we have a party with the first batch!

One day, the orderly officer came in to inspect the kitchen; Fred Collins, Misha Cohen and I were there. We had made maybe 10 gallons and we had it stored in vinegar jugs behind the sacks of flour. We had a supply but we were making another batch. When you came into the kitchen the smell was pretty powerful. The officer came in as we were busy chopping up meat. He looked at all the pots and when he came to the special pot he asked what it was.

"Oh, that's a new kind of French soup we're making," said Fred. I could have died laughing.

"Well now, isn't that interesting?" The officer turned to the sergeant and said, "Isn't that interesting?" We didn't hear a word more. Everything went fine.

About three days later, who should stop me but the commandant. He asked me if I worked in the kitchen. When I said yes, he asked what the stuff was we had behind the flour sacks. Obviously they had checked the kitchen at night when we were asleep. I told him it was vinegar. All he said was, "Take it easy drinking that stuff." He was the commander of the camp. That shows you what kind of consideration we got from the soldiers.

As the war went on the Communist Party told people to forget about strikes, forget about everything else except production to help win the war and smash Hitler. This speeded up our release. I was released in September 1942. I took the train and arrived in Calgary about 6:30 in the morning. About 200 people, many of them my friends, met me at the station and gave me a royal welcome.

The following Sunday I spoke at a meeting in a big hall that held 500 people. It was jammed to the roof. I said that I should never have been put in jail because we were fighting a war against fascism and if there was one thing I had hated all my life it was fascism. I also pointed out that there had been no charges brought against me and no trial.

When our people were released, most of them volunteered for active service. Some of them were killed in France and other places. I was 39, so naturally I had to look for a job. I was blacklisted everywhere in Calgary—in fact everywhere in Alberta—as a result of my years of activity with the Communist Party and as a mine union organizer throughout the province. I was forced to go to people who knew me at city hall. I talked to Mayor Andy Davison, who knew me because I had been an alderman for eighteen months before I was interned. He agreed that I'd have a struggle getting a job outside and he gave me a job the very next morning as a motor man, a streetcar driver.

Peter Krawchuk

In Hull jail we were masters of the house. We turned the jail
into a kind of university. Dr. Lowrie gave lectures on health
and Professor Sam Levine lectured on physics and
mathematics. We had concerts with Ukrainian and Jewish
dances. I remember we decided once to have a Ukrainian
Cossack dance but we couldn't find enough Ukrainians to
dance the Cossack. So Norman Freed called some of the
Jewish boys and said, "Come on, you Cossacks from
Jerusalem." Of course, this was all friendly banter, and we
danced all the dances with Norman Freed leading.

We finally were able to receive newspapers from the
previous day, papers that were new. Still we wanted to know
what was happening every hour because the Germans were
advancing into the Soviet Union and the war was of great
interest to us all. So we told the comrades outside to send us a
radio.

The People's Co-op in Winnipeg sent us a crystal set at the
bottom of a big can of cottage cheese. When the guards put a
knife into it, it would not go right to the bottom, but they let
it through anyway. Because we couldn't put up a regular
antenna, we attached one to the clothes line by the wall. One
night there was a frost, and it stuck to the wire. A soldier saw
it and when we saw him running we knew at once what was
up. We immediately hid the radio. They searched but they
couldn't find it. We had our radio to the end, and had our
news every hour on the hour.

We continued to fight and to demand to be released
because we wanted to take part in the war effort, to fight
fascism, instead of spending our days in jail. We sent a
memorandum to the government, but we never knew if the
commandant kept this memorandum or sent it on. When we
didn't get any kind of answer from the government, we sent

226

it out again and it was published in the *Canadian Tribune*.*
The *Canadian Tribune* immediately phoned the administration of the jail. The commandant responded by arresting
Gerry McManus and Norman Freed, the authors of the
memorandum. He put them in the black hole for two weeks.
We refused to write letters or go to work. People on the
outside began to worry, for the camp boys were silent. Then
they got word from the soldiers that we were on strike.
Outside pressure on the minister of justice resulted in his
giving the order to release our two comrades.

Our life was not always dull. We didn't like to let it become
too grim. We had our concerts, our jokes, we had some
arguments and we made fun of each other. I remember that
Nick Kashchak accused Myron Kostaniuk of degrading the
honor of the political prisoners because he saluted the
soldiers in the compound. Actually Myron was making fun
of the whole business. "Attention!" Myron would shout, but
Kashchak thought he was being loyal to the establishment.
He raised the point and we discussed it politically.

In Hull jail, hours were not as strict as at Kananaskis or
Petawawa. A group of us used to get together in the
washroom on the second or third floor. This was an unused
part of the jail, and it was big and clean. We would open the
parcels we got from home, and we would tell jokes and sing
until one in the morning. We didn't have to go to work so we
could have long discussions on strategy: Where are the
Germans going to go next? Which move will they make? The
most knowledgeable strategists were Tommy Chopovick and
Muni Taub. They would know all the answers. We would
say, "Well generals, what is Hitler going to do next?"

Outside, the campaign was rolling for our release. There
were petitions, and they gradually began to have their effect.
The government began releasing people. I was one of the
earlier ones, released in January 1942.

*See Appendix.

Bruce Magnuson

In Hull we set up various committees with chairmen; everybody was assigned to some committee. Some people volunteered to give lectures, others organized social activity, and some began to work on crafts and make souvenirs. Life was very different from Petawawa and the time went much faster.

The first thing that I made was a picture frame of birch bark, and then I started work on a tray, a large wooden tray made out of a big block of yellow birch. I made an oak oval inlay in it. I made the oval shape by sawing it diagonally and then I polished it up. It was a very tedious job—it took so long because I was carving it out by hand. First of all I had to cut it down with an ax, and then I had to use a hammer and chisel. I used all kinds of things, including worn-out razor blades, to scrape the thing. Last, I sanded it.

Many very nice things were made in that jail. Almost everybody showed talent of one kind or another. It was really amazing what could be done when we got together and helped one another along. But there was competition too among various people.

We organized social evenings and study sessions. We had a wide variety of books. I was able to make use of my time to study the trade union history of the United States and Canada. Pat Sullivan, who was sick in bed at the time, wanted a copy of the notes I had made. Later on, after we were released and he became secretary-treasurer of the Trades and Labor Congress of Canada, I discovered that he had used those notes to produce an outline of the history of the Canadian and American labor movement.

Joe Wallace, our esteemed labor poet, was the only man in the whole place who attended church services. Every Sunday morning the priest would come in and take Joe to the chapel and conduct mass, and then he would come back again. That was that until the next Sunday. Joe wrote some very inspiring poems and verses in Hull. We sang many of them in our singsongs.

One time my wife managed to send in a piece of lut fish. That's dried cod, a special Swedish Christmas dish. It is hard like a rock and it takes about two weeks to soften it up in water. I wasn't sure where I could do that. Since this was a great big jail and there were a lot of empty cells, I was able to get into an unused section and use a new toilet bowl that had never been used. I put the fish there and let it stay for two weeks.

I had to improvise substitutes for preparations you could get outside. For instance, in the old country we used to burn birch wood, sift out the ashes, boil it and put the fish in the resulting brown acidy water for two days. In this case I used a lye mixture. The fish then had to stay in the water for another two or three days before being cooked. It swells up to three or four times its size. By the time I got the fish all prepared nobody would eat it with me, except for Charlie Weir. It was really some delicacy!

During the time we were in Hull, there was a growing movement outside for our release. I remember how people collected names for ads that were published all over the country. These were full-page ads that called for our freedom and an end to the Defence of Canada Regulations. People from all walks of life were involved—professionals, trade unionists, leaders of the legal profession, some from the academic community, teachers, and Members of Parliament and of the various legislatures.

The campaign finally led up to huge meetings in Toronto, Winnipeg, Montreal, Vancouver and Edmonton. Some meetings were even attended by representatives of the Soviet Union, our staunchest wartime ally. The public called for increased support for the war effort, particularly for the Soviet Union, which had suffered the most from the war. This was combined with a big campaign for the opening of the second front in Europe.

Eventually they had to release us. We got out one by one. I got out on August 12, 1942. Others were released as late as the early winter of '42, but eventually everyone got out.

A number of the people who had been interned with us

were prominent leaders of trade unions, people like Muni Erlich and Dick Steele, who had been participating in organizing the Steel Workers Union. Both of them took part in the invasion of Normandy in 1944. As soon as they were freed from internment they joined the army. Muni and Dick—and there were others—were killed in Europe and lie buried in French soil.

That shows how the situation changed. People who had been considered enemies of their country at the beginning of the war were among its greatest champions and gave their lives to help win the war.

William Repka

The night journey from Petawawa brought us to Hull, where we were taken to a huge jail out in the woods. I remember being lined up in the prison yard in the bull pen, with our duffle bags in front of us, and being told by the officer that we would find the conditions here entirely different and much better than Petawawa.

To a large extent they were better. We had a kitchen in the basement, a very large modern kitchen, with good double sinks. The young fellows were the pot wallopers or dishwashers, as we could swish through all the stuff quite quickly. Louis Binder, Ben Swankey, Kent Rowley and I would do the dishes and some of the menial tasks. Others were on the cooking crew, the sweeping crew, the floor washing crew, and so on. The camp council would meet regularly and decide on the maintenance of the camp.

The jobs were not particularly onerous and in an hour, or at the most two, you could complete all your work for the day. Then in a very real sense the time was your own. There were volleyball teams and fierce games out in the jail yard. There were walks around the compound and in the winter there was a skating rink.

We had classes in French, led I think by a man named Villeneuve, who conducted the class completely in French. I actually did pick up a smattering of French by the time they were over. Jake Penner led a class in German so I also learned a bit of *sprechen Sie deutsch*.

I enjoyed one thing very much. The whole national committee of the Ukrainian Labor Temple was interned, and I was asked to be their English teacher. Not only did I get a very good education in Ukrainian, but it also did a great deal for my English grammar. One of the difficulties of the English language for Ukrainians is pronunciation. There was great hilarity when people tried to differentiate between such words as *hog*, *hug* and *hock*. The sounds were not easy to distinguish. We had a lot of fun exchanging two-language puns or comparing the way English people spoke with new Canadian Ukrainians. One of them tried to translate the English saying, "The spirit was willing but the flesh was weak." It came out, "The vodka was good but the meat was terrible."

The gerund, a verb form that has the effect of a noun, also gave us a lot of trouble. For instance, "swimming is considered healthy"; the verb "swimming" in that context becomes a noun. The late Matvey Shatulsky, whom we called Diadia, always used to say, with mock indignation, that the gerund was a *yurinda*, which in Ukrainian means "a bunch of foolishness."

Sometimes we were sent out into the woods on a work gang. One day I went out with a gang to do some loading of gravel onto a truck. While we were loading the gravel and the rocks and sand, who should arrive in a car but Mackenzie King. I think his curiosity must have got the better of him. He wanted to see the human beings that his government had locked up for such a long period. He stayed for quite a while, watching from a respectable distance, as we loaded the truck. Before we finished, he got into his car and drove off.

One day a scruffy looking, self-effacing man, perhaps 35 or 40 years old, was brought into the jail. We were very curious about him, especially as he brought with him a stack of elevating literature—a bundle of girlie books, wild west stories, *True Confessions*, and other stories of adventure and love. One of the men from Montreal recognized him for a Liberal ward-heeler and stool pigeon that the RCMP had used against the labor movement in Montreal. Our leaders at once recognized the danger of this situation, for there was no way to control what he reported. The informer could spin outrageous tales about what happened in the camp and we would be defenceless.

On the other hand, he too was in a very dangerous position. What might happen if the establishment decided to provoke a situation in an attempt to harm our leaders or perhaps harm all of us? If this man was murdered in the jail by some tool of the establishment, we would be held responsible. It created a very difficult situation. In any case, the boys labelled him a stool pigeon and immediately asked for his removal. The commandant replied that the man had been placed in his charge and that was the end of the matter.

When Fred Collins and Pat Lenihan got wind of that they marched into the cell, lifted up his mattress and his books and heaved them down two flights of stairs. All hell broke loose in the jail. The guards came rushing in and demanded to know what was going on. Pat and Fred very quickly told them that they weren't going to have any stool pigeon in their midst. Immediately a platoon of guards came in, picked up the mattress and the magazines and took the man back to his cell. No sooner were his effects back in the cell when back down the stairs they came again. This went on a few times.

Finally the camp spokesman Norman Freed was called in by the commandant and told that we couldn't carry on that way.

"This man is interned along with the rest of you," the commandant said. "I have no other jurisdiction over him. If you keep throwing down the mattress, we will keep taking it back up there."

"So," said Norman. "If you play games, we will play games. This man could be murdered in this camp and everyone here could be accused. The man's own life is in danger, but primarily he endangers the life and well-being of every prisoner in the camp. He is a paid stool pigeon and we will not have him here."

Finally a compromise was struck. A soldier was assigned to sit next to his cell all the time so that he would not interfere with us, and so that we could not be accused of harming him. It really seemed funny to have this guard sitting there by the stoolie, twiddling his thumbs. Finally Kent Rowley, who spoke French fluently, went into his cell and explained to the man the very serious danger he was in.

When the man recognized that he could be used as a political bomb to create a great uproar and that his own life was in danger, he finally confessed to Kent. He had been recruited by the RCMP to go into the camp as an informer. He named names, and explained exactly how it happened that he was asked to do this job—for a great monetary inducement. As he spoke, Kent wrote down his words, and the man agreed to sign the statement. We then kept a copy for ourselves and gave one to the commandant. The commandant was able to use the confession to prove to the authorities that the man was absolutely useless for their purposes and was a danger to himself, the camp and the government. He was then completely segregated from us and kept under constant guard until he was removed entirely. Our success in this action was a great boost to the morale of the whole camp.

I recall another incident of a different kind. One wintry night, it must have been in December of 1941, there was a heavy snowfall. A few of the fellows had gathered in Ben Swankey's cell, a popular meeting place. Ben had moved into the death cell. It had several advantages, most notably that it was away from the rest of the cells. The lights of most of the jail were controlled by one central switch, and were all turned off at the same time. But the light in the death cell had its own switch and Ben could keep it on as late as he chose. Also, the cell was soundproof, so a late night party could be held with no risk of interference.

On that night, I was awakened by a ruckus out in the hall. I looked out through the bars and saw the clean, fresh snow sparkling in the moonlight. After the snowfall had stopped, the moon had come out bright and clear. There must have been two feet of snow, and it was bitterly cold. I went out into the hall. Several fellows were clustered together looking out the window. It seemed that someone, on his way from Ben's cell to his own, had seen a man staggering up the road and fall in the snow. There he was, out like a light in a drunken stupor. It was two o'clock in the morning and the guy was just far enough away to be hard to distinguish. Periodically someone would shout down the hallway, "Did you see him move? There, he moved again." Then there would be silence.

And again someone would holler down the corridor. "Are you going to let a man freeze to death?" Finally somebody, perhaps Archie Gunn, went and woke up one of the guards.

"There is a man out there in the snow who is going to freeze to death if you don't do something," he said. With much grumbling the guard pulled on a pair of big boots and went out into the cold, moonlit night. The entire population of the jail, now completely awake, watched the drama, the rescue of an errant human from freezing to death. We cheered the guard on, giving him directions.

When he reached the man, Archie shouted from his open, barred window, "Aren't you going to pick him up?" There was complete silence. The guard just stood there with hands on his hips. Finally he shouted back, "It's not a man; it's only a stump."

What a hee haw went up through the camp! The next morning, on the dining room blackboard used for announcements, there was a big sign in very large letters: "Aren't you going to pick him up?" That incident entertained us for a long time. When anyone started pushing some fancy theory someone would be sure to say, "It's only a stump."

Medical services in the jail were rough and ready. The only way you were considered sick was if you were out cold. If you applied for sick leave you were given an aspirin. Some of the men who were ill must have gone through a great deal of physical pain and torture. Sawiak, editor of the Ukrainian farm paper, and Bill Kolisnyk, who had been a Winnipeg alderman, were very sick in the camp. Sawiak had dropped from 140 pounds to about 85 pounds before he was no longer considered a menace to Canada's security. Reluctantly, they released him; he died very soon after. Bill Kolisnyk, the first Communist alderman in Winnipeg, broke out in a rash and had many difficulties, gastronomic and urinary problems. He too was released to die. Of course it couldn't be said that these men died in the internment camp.

As prisoners were released, one or two at a time, there was a great deal of excitement in Hull. I wrote a parody on the song, "For the Great Big Saw Came Nearer and Nearer." We began to sing, "For our release comes nearer and nearer and nearer and nearer." That song swept the camp and was very popular.

Later on, as some of our people were released there was an influx of anti-fascist Germans who had been used as cannon fodder by the Nazis. Communist, labor and social democratic people in Germany were arrested or murdered. Their children were then conscripted into the Hitler Jugend and transported to Africa where Rommel used them as suicide squads. These units were placed wherever the German generals wanted to draw Montgomery's fire.

However, as soon as these young men, who were against

CANADIAN PACIFIC
TELEGRAPHS
World Wide Communications

W.D.NEIL, GENERAL MANAGER OF COMMUNICATION, MANITOBA

RECEIVED AT CORNER ST W - DIAL 7-2023

D42 SEP 17 PM 6 40

RNA215 23 DL

OTTAWA ONT 17 607P

MRS M P BOYCHUK

58 GAGE AVE N HAMILTON ONT

THE MINISTER OF JUSTICE HAS ORDERED THE CONDITIONAL

RELEASE OF WILLIAM REBKA WHO WAS RELEASED TO LETHBRIDGE ALBERTA

SEVENTEENTH SEPTEMBER NINETEEN FORTY TWO

COMMANDANT HULL CAMP

the war in the first place and hated their fascist government, got an opportunity, they deserted to General Montgomery's forces. Thus some of them found their way into the Hull jail. The stories that they told about their parents and members of their families were hardly believable. People were systematically dragged out of their homes, taken out on the front doorstep and, in full view of the whole community, shot down without trial. There was no legal process. These were simple, coldblooded Nazi executions.

Louis Binder, Kent Rowley and I were the three youngest internees. Lou Binder and I were released at the same time and went almost directly to the CCL convention, just two years after I had originally planned to attend a CCL convention as a representative of the beet workers. We both felt a bit stir-bushed, a little bit in shock. We were given a tremendous welcome by the delegates, including people from the Auto Workers, the United Electrical Workers and other unions.

How does a person feel after being in an internment camp for two years? The most moving thing was to hear the voices of children, their joyous cries and their laughter. It was such a treat to hear the birds singing again, to walk out through the grass. To walk down a city street was such a release, such a feeling of freedom. Louis and I went into a beer parlor in Ottawa and had a few beers. There was a beautiful dark-eyed young lady sitting with another young lady there. We could not keep our eyes off them. The lack of female company for so long was clearly expressing itself.

When we arrived in Winnipeg we went to a party where Jake Penner was speaking. I was asked to say a few words, and in the middle of the speech my voice broke. I suddenly realized that my nervous system had taken quite a beating and was going to need to rest.

When I came back to Lethbridge I found that the union that we had so carefully built had been smashed. The leading people in our union had been moved out of the area. A mass of Japanese had been moved from the British Columbia coast into the Lethbridge area to do the work in the sugar beet fields. Since I was quite ill, there was nothing much for me to do in Lethbridge. I went to see my family, who had moved to Ontario.

Soon afterwards I enlisted in the army but was discharged on account of ill health before I made it overseas. The stay in the camp took its toll on everyone in one way or another. I got a job in a factory in the east end of Toronto. I had not been there very long when an RCMP came to check up on me. He told my employer I had been interned under the Defence of Canada Regulations, and I was promptly fired. This kind of harassment went on for some time for a number of the internees, but gradually they started to leave us alone to begin normal lives again.

Tony Bilecki

The soldiers assigned to guard us in Hull jail were very friendly. They knew we were Canadians and anti-fascists. They told us the news. They begged us not to make it hard for them, as there were rules we had to obey and they knew we would be released soon.

In Hull I was pressed into the position of cook. I had never had anything to do with a kitchen and knew nothing about cooking. But Peter Kerewaga, John Dubno and I were assigned to the job. Kerewaga instructed us and after a while we became expert cooks, making the best of the secondary cuts of meats we received. There were many cut fingers, and sometimes we worried if the soup would turn out well, but we always did the best we could and the things I learned there have been useful to me.

After a while some of us were released. As each one was let out, we said farewell by singing "Hold the Fort for We are Coming." Strangely, when the time came to bid farewell to the comrades who remained behind, the departing ones were sad to leave. Not that anyone did not want to go free, but it was sad to go when the friends with whom you had shared this harsh experience remained behind.

As we were released, each of us had to sign a declaration that we would not do anything to help the internees and that we would not divulge any camp secrets. What secrets could you have in a jail? We had to report to the RCMP twice a month. John Navizivsky, Peter Kerewaga, John Dubno and I were actually the last ones to be allowed out of the camp. There was no one to sing the farewell song for us. Nevertheless, we were glad that this dark episode in the history of Canada had ended, an episode of which the Canadian authorities can never be proud.

Upon my release I went to live in Montreal where my wife

239

and my son had moved from Winnipeg. For some time I worked in a factory to build up the family finances. My wife had been working all this time while her parents looked after our one child. Later I volunteered for the army and went to serve the country on the battlefields of Europe. The world's future was at stake; it was no time to hold a grudge. But the hurt remained, a hurt against the capitalist class, for it had never shown any interest or loyalty outside of the desire to make profits anyway it could, even at the expense of the welfare of their country and people. Nearly two and a half years of my life were taken away from me.

Peter Prokop

The jail building outside of Hull, across the river from Ottawa, was condemned as unsuitable to house criminals, but it seemed the authorities thought it was good enough for us. Many of us came out of it with chronic arthritis.

In the winter of 1941-42, the country-wide movement for our release gained great momentum. By January the political climate had changed enough that the justice department began releasing us, one by one, two to three weeks apart. Also at this time an advisory commission of three judges was set up to conduct hearings at the Hull internment jail. Most of us were called before this commission. Here, unlike in Kananaskis, we had a brilliant labor lawyer, J.L. Cohen. He was wise to their tricks and wasn't intimidated by the court.

During these hearings they still wanted to establish some reason for having interned us. The RCMP officer who accompanied the commission supplied the judges with so-called evidence from the dossiers they had kept on each of us. They kept grilling us. They wanted to know all about the Ukrainian-language schools for children and about the children's other activities in our halls. They really grilled Philip Lysets on this subject. Lysets had prepared some Ukrainian readers for the schools, and the commission tried to establish that the children were taught communist doctrines.

As recording secretary of the central executive committee of the ULFTA, there was a great deal of evidence against me. I had conducted educational courses in our organization and they wanted to know what textbooks I had used. They showed me a book—*Politichna Hramota*—which was a general introduction on social and political questions. The police had been informed that the book was prepared by A. Mankovsky under my guidance and that I had edited it and

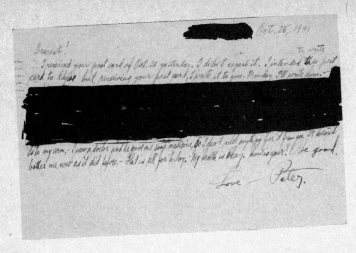

written the introduction. This was true, although the introduction was unsigned. The police said that whoever wrote the introduction knew very well what he was writing about, and they tried to get an admission to that effect from me.

They had a lot of written material—documents, circulars, newspaper articles—which no doubt the stool pigeons had supplied. The commission wanted me to admit that I had written the documents and to explain them. I did write most of them but they were issued under the names of various committees and were without personal signatures.

They tried to prove that at the beginning of the war we issued propaganda against the Canadian armed forces. I denied this accusation; neither in our press nor in any documents did we ever attack or write against the Canadian army. We never advised people not to join the army. We reported the news from our point of view. We exposed German fascism for what it was, with its plans to subjugate all European countries and its determination to conquer the Soviet Union as a prelude to world domination. It is unfortunate that I haven't got any record of our discussions and documents which contained our policy statements. They were all lost during the time of our internment. I had given one man two suitcases containing important documents to hide, but when I asked for them after I was released he informed me that he had taken them out to a farm to hide them, but they had disappeared.

As the hearing went on they continued to refer to and quote from newspaper reports and articles in our press that had supported the labor movement. They claimed the labor movement was Communist. We were accused of all the same crimes that labor leaders had been charged with and imprisoned for under Section 98 of the Criminal Code (which was later repealed) and other anti-labor laws. These were the same attacks that working people faced as they struggled during the hungry thirties for jobs, unemployment insurance, trade union rights, against oppression and so on. They read me a list of things, one by one, asking what I was for and what I was against—mostly, they wanted to confirm that we supported strikes and demonstrations and that we circulated various petitions, including one against the Padlock Law. I answered that the Padlock Law as well as Section 98 were anti-democratic laws. And yes, I said, we support the struggle of the Canadian people for democratic rights and for a better life.

I remember that they spent a lot of time accusing our organization, and me as a leader of it, of advocating the use of force and violence. I argued with them that we were not for force and violence for the sake of violence, but that we stood for democratic change. However, I asked them what possibility there was for democratic change in Nazi Germany. In that situation there could not be any change without force. The hearing spent a whole day on this subject. But with the help of our lawyer, their arguments failed. They could not establish that I advocated the overthrow of the Canadian government by force and violence.

But they did not give up easily. The next day they found something else to accuse me of. It had nothing to do with our Ukrainian mass organizations. But they implied that since we supported Soviet Russia, and the Soviet power was established by force and a loss of blood, then we must endorse the same. I told them that the October Revolution in Russia was the most bloodless revolution that ever took place. Compared with the terrible blood-letting that took place in the French Revolution, the Russian October Revolution was almost a peaceful takeover of power. I pointed out to them that it was the Second All-Russia Congress of Soviets of Workers and Soldiers Deputies on November 7 and 8, 1917, that had voted power to the

Bolsheviks. There were very few people killed. The blood-letting took place only after the October Revolution when reactionary elements, with the help of the military intervention of Britain, France, the USA and even Canada, tried to take the power away from the Soviets.

At this point J.L. Cohen requested that I be released as I had been interned for almost two years on charges based on matters about which the court had a great deal to learn. In actual fact, they did not know history, and if I had known English better I would have told them a lot more, for I know the history of the Soviet Union very well.

When J.L. Cohen took the judges to task, they resented his comments and asked him to withdraw them or be held in contempt of court. Cohen didn't withdraw them right away, but after a while he said, "Oh well, if you feel that I've overstepped propriety, then I am sorry that I have hurt your feelings."

Actually, by then the judges were looking for a way out of this embarrassing situation. It was clear that despite their informers and stool pigeons, they were uninformed on the subject upon which they based their accusations against us. In withdrawing his remarks, Cohen suggested that they study history.

After the hearings it was still several months before everyone was released. I was released and arrived in Toronto on September 5, 1942, and Mary arrived from Winnipeg two days later. I understand that by the end of the month the Hull internment jail was closed. The shadow continued to haunt me and many of my brother internees for many more months. I had to report twice a month to the RCMP and was not allowed to leave Toronto.

After my release I joined the editorial staff of our paper *Ukrainske Zhyttia*. Through our new organization, the Association of Ukrainian Canadians, its newspapers and public meetings, we began to mobilize the Ukrainian community for an all-out war effort and to campaign for the opening of the Second Front. At the same time we immediately plunged into an ongoing campaign for the lifting of the ban on the ULFTA and our publishing company, and for the return of the confiscated property of the ULFTA.

John Weir

In July 1942, at a time when our release was already near, my father died. We were informed that one of us, my brother Charlie or I, could attend the funeral. I was the eldest son so I was chosen. We then learned of the conditions under which the visit was to be made: I would be brought, handcuffed, to the coffin for a couple of minutes and then whisked back. I felt my mother had enough grief already and I turned the offer down. As much as I wanted to look on my father's face one last time, I think it was the proper decision.

The releases began and each man, as he was freed, left to the strains of "Hold the Fort." My turn came at last. There was a brief, perfunctory hearing with J.L. Cohen there to pilot me through, and I walked out. I walked around Ottawa for some time before my train left for Toronto. After two long years it was wonderful to hear children's voices again, and to be able to return to my work.

At the beginning I said that two years of incarceration were two years too much. I didn't intend that as a complaint. After all, many millions have fared far worse, and I knew that repression against opponents of the powers that be was natural under capitalism. The imprisonment was not too onerous. But it was the isolation and the injustice of it that was galling. People like me expect such treatment, but there is no reason in the world why we should accept it. Anger and struggle against it are part of the whole fight to which we are devoting our lives.

The fight of the people outside deserves full praise and credit—not only our relatives and comrades, but the progressively larger sections of the Canadian people who fought to have the draconic law withdrawn and its victims freed. The victory was theirs. But we should never forget that the power to repeat such arbitrary action remains, and there is no reason to doubt that the ruling group will use it if and when they see fit. The sending of the army into Quebec and the arbitrary arrests of 1970 are surely proof of that. The struggle against such violations of democracy continues.

I think of the people who were in camp. Many have already passed away. Some are still working hard for peace and progress. I hope and expect that this book will bring justice to those good warriors who fought for such a grand future for our country and our people, a grand future that will inevitably be won.

Appendix
An Open Letter to
Prime Minister King

Internment Camp "H,"
c-o Base Post Office,
Ottawa, Ontario.
Sept. 10, 1941

The Right Honorable W.L. Mackenzie King,
Prime Minister of Canada,
Ottawa, Ontario.

Dear Mr. Prime Minister:

At Hull Jail, within sight of the parliament buildings across the Ottawa River, eighty anti-fascist Canadians are being held in a concentration camp.

We have been denied our liberty, separated from our loved ones, and prevented from carrying out our duties as Canadian citizens, some of us for as long as fifteen months, under the arbitrary powers granted the minister of justice, the Right Honorable Ernest Lapointe, by the Defence of Canada Regulations.

Our appeals against this injustice have gone unheeded. At the "hearings" no charges were presented that we were in any way guilty or even suspected of sabotage, spying or subversive activity. The only excuses for our incarceration that have been presented to us have been that "representations have been made" that we had been members of the Communist Party of Canada, or some other labor organization, or that we had "associated with" Communists.

The "particulars" supplied consisted of references to trade union and anti-fascist activities in the past, as far back as twenty years ago. The "hearings" constitute a recounting of "crimes" on our part, such as trying to improve the living standards of our fellow Canadians, defending civil liberties, or urging the Canadian people to fight against fascism!

Not one of our number has been charged with a single overt act; in not a single case has reason been shown why any should be imprisoned in the interests of the security of the state.

We have presented several petitions to the minister of justice, declaring our loyalty to Canada, our support of the maximum war effort against the fascist states, our support of your government in all measures to carry the just war against fascism to victory, and our views in favor of democratic unity of the whole Canadian people to these ends. We do not know whether these petitions actually reached the minister, only that no action has so far been taken to effect our release.

Therefore, although we are aware of the multitudinous responsibilities that claim every minute of your time, we, nevertheless, take the liberty of addressing this appeal to you as the head of the state, feeling that your personal intervention will serve to right these injustices.

This past week the eyes of all Canada have been rivetted on you and your visit to embattled Britain, your conversation with Prime Minister Churchill and others with first-hand information on the progress of the war, and your visits with our Canadian troops over there, among whom many of us have sons, brothers and friends. Your journey, spanning the ocean overnight by airplane, brought home forcibly to many people on this continent once more the fact that we are not far removed, but actually near to the front lines of the conflict.

And together with the whole Canadian people we hope that the success of your undertaking will bloom forth in welding Canada's war effort the more closely with the states and peoples battling against fascist barbarism, in profoundly influencing our powerful neighbor, the United States, to throw its full weight into the titanic struggle and in encouraging and rallying the people of Canada to the victory over Hitler and his satellites; and hasten the end of the slaughter.

Despite our physical isolation, we have never allowed our personal plight to spiritually separate us from the desires and aspirations of our fellow Canadians and the worldwide struggle against fascism. We share with them all their trials and tribulations, and all their hopes and determination for victory.

We are aware that the turning point in the war is upon us, that the future is being decided on the battlefronts of Eastern Europe, that the glorious struggle waged by the U.S.S.R., its army and peoples, together with the peoples and armies of the British Commonwealth, in which Canada is participating, will determine the whole course and duration of the war, the security and freedom of all humanity, and of Canada herself.

We know that it is exactly now, and in the momentous months to come, that our country is called upon to exert its utmost to bring victory.

We are convinced that the answer to Hitler's and Mussolini's totalitarian war is a democratic people's war, uniting the anti-fascist forces both internationally and within each country against Nazi barbarism. Stern suppression of fascist groups and intrigues within the country, the greatest extension of democratic rights to the common people, determined struggle against war profiteering and exploitation on the part of selfish interests, the boldest rallying of the common people for fullest participation in both the production and military branches of the war effort—these are the guarantees of Canada's full contribution to the epochal struggle which has engulfed the entire world.

We, who are flesh and blood of the Canadian laboring and farming people, are sure that these things can and will be done. The working people of Canada are loyally and heroically fulfilling their duties in the factories, mines and mills, on the farms, and on the battlefields. The difficulties and interruptions of production experienced in the past period arose from the provocative practices of a small group of selfish employers who placed their greed for profits above the interests of the nation, and we are sure that when labor's rightful place and role are recognized, Canadian labor will demonstrate still greater marvels of production and self-sacrifice.

Sir, we know the heavy responsibilities which rest upon your shoulders as the head of state at this hour. It is with the full realization of this responsibility which you bear before the nation and before history that we venture to address this appeal to you this day. As your immortal grandfather, William Lyon Mackenzie, a century ago, turned to the "yeomen and mechanicks" in the struggle for democratic self-government for our country, so again today, when the security and survival of our nation, the democratic rights won by many generations of struggle, and the very future of generations to come are at stake, the workers and farmers, the common people of Canada, the democratic forces of our nation will be victorious over all enemies.

We urge you, in the interests of the democratic war program, to use your office to order our release from the concentration camp, so that we can do our best in helping to rally the Canadian people to contribute, together with ourselves, our all to the democratic war effort, to provide guns, tanks, planes and munitions to the armies of Britain, the U.S.S.R. and their allies for all-out economic and military participation in the war to defeat Hitler Germany.

We hope that you will heed our appeal and assist our return to freedom, to our families, to our citizen duties as loyal Canadians.

On behalf of the imprisoned anti-fascist Canadians,

Respectfully yours,
T.G. McManus,
Camp Spokesman.

Reprinted from the Canadian Tribune

Printed in Canada

g